JOHN GRIERSON

edited by Forsyth Hardy

—

GRIERSON ON DOCUMENTARY

JOHN GRIERSON

A Documentary Biography
by
Forsyth Hardy

FABER AND FABER
London & Boston

First published in 1979
by Faber and Faber Limited
3 Queen Square London WC1
Printed in Great Britain by
Latimer Trend & Company Ltd Plymouth
All rights reserved

The publisher acknowledges with thanks
the financial assistance of the
Scottish Arts Council
in the publication of this book

British Library Cataloguing in Publication Data

Hardy, Forsyth
    John Grierson.
1. Grierson, John   2. Moving-pictures
    Documentary—Production and direction
    Biography
    791.43.0232.0924   PN1998.A3G/

    ISBN 0–571–10331–6

Contents

Contents

Illustrations

Illustrations

Illustrations

43. John Grierson addresses staff of the National Film Board of Canada during the Board's 25th Anniversary in 1964.
44. After speaking, John Grierson is applauded by Guy Roberge, Film Commissioner.
45. John Grierson, Claude Jutra, Pauline Kael and Eric Gee at the 1962 Vancouver Film Festival.
46. John Grierson's visit to the India Films Division, 1971. Shri G. P. Asthana, John Grierson, Mushir Ahmad, Ian Chatwin, Pramod Pati.
47. Reta Kilpatrick, Secretary to the National Film Board of Canada; Sydney Newman, Film Commissioner 1970–5; John Grierson; André Lamy, Film Commissioner.
48. Edgar Anstey handing Sir Charles Chaplin his Honorary Membership of the Association of Cine and Television Technicians at Shepperton Studios in 1956.
49. Basil Wright.
50. Alberto Cavalcanti.
51. John Grierson, Hyderabad, 1971.

Acknowledgements for permission to reproduce pictures to:
Central Office of Information (nos. 6, 7, 8, 9, 11, 12, 13, 14, 15)
Charles Oakley (no. 16)
National Film Board of Canada (nos. 18, 24, 25, 26, 34, 35, 44, 45)
Axel Poignant (no. 17)
The Gas Council (no. 10)
The *Scottish Daily Record* (no. 42)
John Maddison (no. 38)
Harold C. Huggins (no. 45)
Scottish Television (no. 39)
PA-Reuter (no. 48)
Len Chatwin (no. 51)
Other photographs are from the private collections of the author
and Mrs. Margaret Grierson

1 Growing Up by the Gillies Hill

Deanston, the village in which John Grierson was born on 26 April 1898, lies on the River Teith, in the parish of Kilmadock, on the borders of the counties of Perth and Stirling, Scotland. The swift-flowing river was the source of power for the extensive cotton mills which, since 1785, were the main means of livelihood for the villagers. The mills were in decline by the end of the century when Grierson's father was headmaster in the local school but the solid red sandstone buildings have now been handsomely restored and have been given another lease of life as a distillery. The village, with its well-ordered relationship between the mills and the double row of stone-built houses above the mill lade, held a fascination for Grierson to the end of his life—not because of any intimate knowledge he could have had of the place as a boy but perhaps because of the impact of industrial change on a small community. Whatever the reason, he often returned to Deanston and was recognised by the villagers after he had become a familiar figure on television.

Grierson was born in the old schoolhouse attached to the original school building, past which flowed the mill lade, so that the infant Grierson would hear from birth the sound of running water. His father, Robert Morrison Grierson, had been brought up among fishermen in the village of Boddam, near Peterhead, on the north-east coast. 'He didn't know it', Grierson said later, 'but his eyes lit up very specially whenever he saw the sea.'[1] He had begun his schoolmastering in the Atholl territory under Schiehallion in Perthshire and had moved as headmaster to the small school at Deanston where he quickly came to be respected as a dominie in the old tradition of Scottish education. One of his pupils remembered him as having 'the keenest eye I have ever seen in any man'. It was the same pupil who made the fatal error of reporting to his father that he had had 'a few with the tawse' from the headmaster. 'What I got that night from my father was the licking of my life.'[2] In these days the influence of a dominie's unchallenged discipline could be felt throughout a community.

By becoming a teacher Robert Grierson had broken a long family

11

link with the sea. He had been born, the son of a lightkeeper, at Rhu Vaal, on the tip of Islay in the Inner Hebrides. All his immediate forebears had been lighthouse men, 'perched on the wilder rocks and promontories of the Highland seas'. A John Grierson appears in the earliest records kept in Edinburgh by the Commissioners of Northern Lighthouses. Grierson himself claimed that he went back in a constant line of lightkeepers to the Bell Rock light and its builder, Robert Stevenson, who 'speaks a trifle violently of my progenitor on the Bell, for he seems to have been an independent fellow like Robert himself, and one might say the first and original of Stevensonian critics; but none the less, as I was taught it in my family, *Treasure Island* and *Kidnapped* were just what you could expect when the lighthouses were in your blood and what chiefest end could a man or woman find than in the middle of an ocean?'[3]

On his mother's side Grierson came out of an Ayrshire radical family. Jane Anthony's father was a shoemaker in Stewarton and his reforming zeal made a lasting impression on the young Grierson. Some forty years later he was to begin writing a book on the thesis of 'the old Scots radicalism of grandfather Anthony, brought up to date. I've long intended to do the old boy proud and this is it.'[4] Grierson, who clearly held his maternal grandfather in especial esteem, said that 'one of the manifestations of his persuasion was to be eloquent on the Clearances and sorry for all the poor devils who came out of the North. In fact he married one of them and so got me into the blood of the wild McCraws of Auchnashiel. The McCraws or McCraas or Macraes had reason to be an especial object of radical compassion. They were Lord Seaforth's people and it was after looking at them that Dr. Johnson observed that "he would not have men treated as brutes." '[5]

In Grierson's mother her family's radical tradition flourished. She was a suffragette, a woman before her time. A teacher like her husband, she loved argument and debate; but whereas Robert Grierson tended to be reserved in manner, she had all the confidence of an extrovert. At a time when it was unusual for a woman to be involved publicly in politics, she often took the chair at election meetings for Tom Johnston, who stood in 1918 against the firmly established Conservative Member of Parliament for West Stirlingshire, Sir Harry Hope, and was elected by a narrow majority in 1922. She found in Tom Johnston, that bonny fighter and leader of the Scottish Socialist movement, later to become Scotland's best loved Secretary of State, a man whose dedicated involvement in radical reform she could whole-heartedly support.

12

Growing Up by the Gillies Hill

When the time came to leave Deanston in the summer of 1900, John had three elder sisters, Janet, Agnes and Margaret, and a baby brother, Anthony. Their new home was the schoolhouse immediately adjoining the school at Cambusbarron, a village in the parish of St. Ninian's, a mile and a half south-west of Stirling. Robert Grierson took up duties as headmaster on 14 August 1900, in a school which had accommodation for some 270 children. Here John and his brother were enrolled in November 1903. Later they were to be joined by his younger sisters, Dorothy, Ruby and Marion. Margaret died in 1906, the school record-book noting that the headmaster was absent during the forenoon of 25 September, 'attending daughter's funeral'.

Given the liberal outlook of both parents and the encouragement to read which came naturally from teachers, the family atmosphere was endlessly stimulating. There were the stirrings of what was to become the Socialist movement and the beginnings of the assertion of more freedom and independence for women. The members of the growing family were drawn into the debates in the sitting-room and were encouraged to hold forth, gaining experience and confidence in self-expression which served them well at school and university. The family divided itself naturally into three groups, the elder sisters, the two boys, and the younger sisters who occupied the large room called the nursery. The boys were in the back room upstairs overlooking the school playground and with a cherry-tree invitingly within reach of the window.

Cambusbarron stands on the slope of a hill. To the north the town of Stirling rises from the plain to its castle solidly set on the rock. To the north-west the nearer Grampians are massed like a bulwark against the unknown. 'Where I grew up', wrote Grierson, 'you did not need to read it in the Bible: you just couldn't avoid lifting up your eyes to the hills. But what did I really have in my own bailliwick to match their distant splendour? Yes, I did have something: in its own special way the very mightiest of Scottish landmarks. I had the Gillies Hill, that one blessed knob of earth which settled the Battle of Bannockburn. Whenever Ben Cruachan tried to diminish me, as it so often did, I would shout back: "And the Gillies Hill to you my friend." '[6]

Grierson had Ben Cruachan in his eye when, having been enrolled at the High School of Stirling in September 1908, he walked every day from Cambusbarron by the edge of the park into the town and eventually up the steep Back Walk to the school. Built in 1888, the High School stands on the site of the Franciscan or Greyfriars' yard in the street named for Robert Spittal, the King's 'tailleyour' in the early 1500s. The entrance with its arch of stone carvings is directly from the street and immediately suggests the earnest acquisition of knowledge in Spartan conditions. With examples around him, Grierson was dimly aware of the Scottish Renaissance in architecture. 'I don't complain of the local masters', he wrote later, 'for they taught us at least about the battles and bridges of the Forth, but it seemed a pity to have to take the long journey to Amboise to be proud of the lodging of Argyll, and to Blois to know the privilege of having grown up, not unsubstantially, in the long shadow of François Ier.'[7]

His teacher of English and history was John Amess with whom he maintained a friendly association throughout his life: the teacher was to outlive the pupil. In class he appeared to learn without apparent effort. He would not make a parade of his knowledge but when asked would have an answer. His own estimate of what his schooling meant to him he gave many years later in a letter to John Amess, written after they had met when he opened the new Cambusbarron primary school on 10 October 1967: 'As I remember it wasn't what any of you taught that made the impact but what incidentally and perhaps without knowing it you conveyed or let fall. Take Menzies. Was he an intellectual ball of fire? I don't know but certainly he said something that finished up in Haushofer and geo-politics—and his "man in many lands" in anthropology. You mention Thomson. He wasn't there long enough but got across somehow or other the difference between writing essays and writing anyway, which is an exercise in revelation which a fellow called Roland Barthes is making a lot of in Paris right now. Yourself, what did you do but create a sort of snobbery round constitutional history which was bound to drive your innocents to Machiavelli and the consideration of power and the nature of propaganda and thereby myth making itself. I am your witness.'[8]

By his fellow students Grierson was considered something of a daredevil. He was now making the journey to and from school by bicycle and would challenge his class-mates to ride with him on the cycle's back-step down the steep, bumpy, rutted track known as the Back Walk. By his skill, rider and precariously perched passenger survived. On his bicycle he made excursions into the surrounding countryside, to Loch Lomond and Loch Katrine, and 'was over Glencoe many and many a time on the old road that is now disappearing into the heather it came from'. When he walked to school with his brother there was invariably a ball to kick along and across the road. He played soccer (right half) for the school and, later, Rugby

14

for the former pupils. If he did not have the build for a forward he had all the nippiness and opportunism of the born fly-half.

Back at Cambusbarron he did his evening study in one of the classrooms of his father's school, away from the commotion of the schoolhouse. It was warm and quiet, although he would readily lay aside his books to talk to the cleaners. One of them was Margaret Allan, known to the pupils as the Duchess. To Grierson she was the Queen of Letters. She had read every book in the old village institute library and was stuffing him with Carlyle and Byron, Don Juan and all, before he was ten. There were always things to talk about and his father was at the heart of many of them. Robert Grierson pioneered school gardens and domestic science for girls. He supported the village institute, with literary papers on Carlyle and Ruskin for the enlightenment of the villagers. To bring a wider horizon into the class-room he gave the first film show ever seen in educational circles in Scotland. He was devoted to his pupils, especially the lads o' pairts, and he thought nothing of trudging into the country to prevail on some stubborn ploughman, who needed the extra money for his family, to give his son a chance and not put him to work at fourteen. Familiarly known in the village as Baldy Grierson, the headmaster's somewhat forbidding appearance was misleading. He was infinitely kind.

Grierson was later to express reservations about his father's teaching: 'The basis of his educational philosophy was deeply rooted in Carlyle and Ruskin and the natural rights of man. The wind of the French Revolution still blew behind it. But it was strictly individualist. Education gave man a chance in the world. It put them in good competitive standing in a grim competitive world. It fitted them to open the doors of spiritual satisfaction in literature and philosophy. But it was in the name of a highly personal satisfaction. Behind it all was the dream of the nineteenth century—the false dream—that if only everyone had the individualist ideals that education taught, free men in a free society, each in independent and educated judgment, would create a civilisation such as the world had never seen before. . . . The smashing of that idyllic viewpoint has been probably the greatest educational fact of our time. I saw it smashed right there in my village. I saw the deep doubt creep into the mind of that schoolmaster that everything he stood for and strove for was somewhere wrong. What were the delights of literature when a distant judgment by a distant corporation could throw a man into six months of economic misery? What were the pleasures of Shakespeare and *A Midsummer Night's Dream* in the evening schools, when industrial conditions were tiring the boys to death? What was the use of saying that a man was a man for a' that, when you were dealing day in and day out with a war of economic forces in which only armies counted and where the motivating powers were abstract and unseen? Before my father finished teaching the true leadership in education passed to other shoulders, passed to the miners themselves and the economists among them. They read their Blatchford and Keir Hardie and Bob Smillie; they attended their trade union meetings; and the day came when they elected their first Labour Member of Parliament.'⁹

This experience and the capacity to analyse it and bring it into focus still lay ahead of John Grierson, in the last years of his education at the High School of Stirling. And there was no slackening of the dedication of his parents to their work as teachers. As early as 1908, when her youngest daughter Marion was under a year old, Mrs. Grierson had been teaching as an interim at the school in Cambusbarron and she was to do this on many occasions in the next ten years. She taught mathematics to pupils in their last year and, a strict disciplinarian, was regarded by some as a better teacher than the headmaster. She had been a lecturer at the teachers' training college (later Jordanhill) in Glasgow. It was under her influence that a soup kitchen was instituted in the village when there were hard times for the miners and an entry in the school record book for 4 December 1909 notes, 'Much good to the children experienced by the distribution of hot soup in the middle of the day.'

The war came early to Cambusbarron. In August 1914, part of the school was occupied by the Army. Temporary accommodation was found for the senior pupils in the parish church hall and the headmaster was able to record that all the classes had begun on 17 August.

On the day war broke out Grierson was on holiday at Ardgour. He spent the whole day watching the trawlers and the drifters breasting the tide, puffing their way back in hundreds to become minesweepers and anti-submarine patrols. 'We all sensed, like a cloud on the mind, that here was the end of one epoch, the beginning of another, and all our personal worlds might never be the same again.'¹⁰

However hard it was to concentrate on schooling, with a fluctuating flow of disturbing news from France and the Atlantic, there was a last year in the class-room for Grierson. Application was difficult but the higher leaving certificate examinations, giving entrance to the university, had to be sat. His parents had the University of Glasgow in mind: his elder sisters, Janet and Agnes, were already there. In June he went to Gilmorehill to sit the bursary examination which in Scottish universities is both a measure of intellectual capacity and a source of subvention. The results would not be known until October. In July 1915, he left the High School (with an overall subject mark of eighty-two per cent. John Amess recalled that two pupils in the class had higher marks but observed that there was 'an effortless superiority' about Grierson's examination papers).

In a country at war, Grierson was too restless to await the outcome of the university bursary examination. He applied for munitions work at Alexandria, in the Vale of Leven, south of Loch Lomond, and spent the next few months in the long, low, red sandstone building, the original home of the Argyll Motor Company which early in the century had produced the first complete motor car in Scotland. Among other things the experience left him with no love of motor cars. He always preferred to be driven and would often sit reading his newspapers while the driver struggled through traffic.

When the bursary list was published, the second name was that of John Grierson. He was awarded the John Clark bursary, for which 'the sons and daughters of Protestant parents, entering their first session in the Faculty of Arts', were eligible. It was tenable for four years.

Minesweepers at work. A pen-and-ink sketch by John Grierson in a letter to Frances Strauss, 7 September 1927.
Transcribed by Jack Firth

2 Able Seaman to Clydeside Radical

But the next four years were not after all to be spent at the university. Munitions work at Alexandria gave him no satisfying involvement in the war effort. He wanted to be an active part of it and he was not content to wait until, through call-up, he would have been in the armed forces. He wanted to decide for himself, by volunteering, which form of service he would give.

For him the Navy was the natural choice. The Grierson family's long link with the sea was a living influence with him. It had been fed by visits to many of the lighthouses in Scotland and by holidays he had spent with the family at his father's house at the Corran light-house, Ardgour. While there he came to know well Donald Buchanan, the ferryman at Ardgour, and later liked to recall an occasion when the ferryman was being invited to take part in a B.B.C. programme. 'The poor devil of a B.B.C. man didn't know that you called him *Mister* Buchanan, and had better. "Buchanan", says he, hoity toity, speaking of course with pianos in his mouth, "Buchanan", says he, "it will be a great privilege for you: all Scotland will be hearing you". Donald moved slowly down the slope to where the waters of Loch Linnhe were rushing, as ever splendidly between Lochaber and the Light, and never a word. "Buchanan", says the B.B.C. man, pressing, "why England itself will be hearing you". Never a word, and Donald still walking. "Buchanan", says the B.B.C. man pressing still harder, "it may be that the whole world will be hearing you". At this point Donald spits into the great tide of the western sea. "I have decided", says he: "The world will not hear my voice." '[1]

To prepare for the approach he was to make to the Royal Naval Volunteer Reserve, Grierson went for training to the Crystal Palace in London. It was a great empty shell of a place, with thousands of young yokels like himself tramping around on the old wooden boards. He never heard a place echo with so many commands. 'When they shouted you to attention you were still clicking your heels five minutes after. With all the glass around it was the coldest barracks in the world. One day Clara Butt came down and filled the whole place with

18

that billowy voice of hers which was a miracle in itself. And another day there was Jack Johnson to show us what the champion of the world looked like.'² In his recruitment application Grierson gave his date of birth as 26 April 1897, and with the help of this fictitious extra year entered the R.N.V.R. on 7 January 1916, as an ordinary telegraphist (Official No. CZ/6359). He was posted to the wireless telegraphy station at Aultbea, on Loch Ewe, Ross and Cromarty. The loch was used extensively as an anchorage by ships of the Home Fleet and during the year Grierson spent at Aultbea there was constant movement. Midway through the year, on 2 June 1916, he was promoted telegraphist.

On 23 January 1917, he joined the minesweeper H.M.S. *Surf* and served as telegraphist on that vessel until 13 October 1917. His commanding officer was Commander Henry W. A. Clark, R.D., R.N.R. (Retired). On the following day he joined H.M.S. *Rightwhale*, with Lieutenant-Commander Lawrence S. Boggs (Acting), R.N.R., as commanding officer. He was to remain on this ship until he was demobilised on 17 February 1919. During this time he had three other commanding officers, Lieutenant-Commander Gilbert H. Flavell, R.N.R., Lieutenant Gilbert Thompson, R.N.R., and Lieutenant Percy Hawkins, R.N.R. He was promoted leading telegraphist on 2 June 1918, and when demobilised was awarded the British War Medal and the Victory Medal.³

As a telegraphist he lived in a world of sound—a mysterious, far-away and totally unseen world of its own. He could tell from the sound whether it was a destroyer or a battleship. He even got to be able to tell a particular ship from the style of the di-di-di-da's before it gave its call sign: a telegraphist put his personal character into the transmission key. Later they gave him another gadget—an instrument pushed down into the sea by which he was supposed to hear submarines. But all he ever heard was the chug, chug, chug of his own engines, so they had to stop, which was dangerous and against orders.⁴

Minesweeping gave Grierson more drama and excitement than he had known in his nineteen years. For some three years he sailed the North Sea with sudden death a constant possibility. There was no telling when a mine would blow up. The weirdest incident could come, as it once did to him, on a wonderful calm day. 'We were all lounging about the ship, holding faces up to the sun and saying everything was swell, when "Blop", a ship in front, where everybody was lazing around the same as we were and saying everything was swell, went up in a column of black smoke. Our ship just jolted and wobbled. We picked up three survivors out of twenty-five and two guys that were so mutilated they died.'

The minesweepers never hunted alone but in twos at the very least. Grierson himself never saw less than half a dozen. It was when a minesweeper became isolated that the German submarines attacked and gunned them. 'I remember one such incident on the west coast when a trawler called the *Robert D. Smith* got isolated and a sub. attacked. It played hell with her, shot her away in bits, until it got the bridge and swept captain and mate into nothing.' It was at times like this that minesweeping was transformed from adventure at sea into the harsh reality of lives at risk. With ships going up around him or surfaced submarine blasting away, Grierson was at times, in the earlier period of his service, in a dead funk. An older hand would help a boy to pull himself together, induce him to puff out his chest and feel a man. 'I did it myself all of a sudden, after weeks of fear, and felt like I had got religion.'[5]

When the night comes down there is for the minesweepers the terror of sailing without lights. There are the look-outs, the dark figures on the bridge, the only light on—the poop light for the compass—reflected in the glass front of the bridge-house, up and down with the swing of the ship. With daybreak, a misty blue morning in the North Sea, the signal is given from the bridge that the ship is in position. All hands are around the rails looking for mines. Suddenly a cry: mines are all around. The ship stops practically dead. Nervousness everywhere in hands and faces. Gradually the ship picks her way out of the minefield, the men not daring to hope that they will get away with it.

Grierson knew that situation because he once sweated blood over it. As part of the drama of the ceaseless warfare against the mine and the submarine, he was becoming familiar with the Scottish coastline. 'I have been in and out of every sea loch from Cape Wrath to the Mull of Kintyre and in every sheltering harbour east and west from the Butt of Lewis to Barra Head. Nor can there be many islands in the great Highland galaxies that I haven't been to, and that includes St. Kilda and the Flannans, North Rona and the Monachs. I knew the old *Sheila* and the old *Plover* on their run from the Kyle of Lochalsh to Stornoway, like any native. What's more I knew them in the winter as well as the summer, when you had to sleep on the fiddley to keep warm and nearly suffocated. I have been on ships the world over but there have never been ships again for me like the Highland and island ships.'[6]

One of the ports used by the minesweepers was Stornoway. On one of the short spells in harbour there he happened to see the beginning of the effort made by Lord Leverhulme to influence the economy of Lewis and improve the life of the islanders. 'I saw the beginning of that strange adventure in Stornoway during the war when the festive arches were raised by the miserable shop-keepers of Stornoway town to welcome "the new Laird to his Highland home". I saw the grim reaction of the men of Back and Carloway with whom I sailed, though I could not comprehend it at the time. I have now seen the end of that adventure, as honest men in pilgrimage should, in the desolate ruins of Leverburgh. It is symbolic, however, not of the death of Leverhulme, who was in his own way a great man, but of the death of all the exploiters who passed before him.'[7]

The war had been over for some three months by the time Grierson was demobilised: three more months of necessary minesweeping. For days he did not leave Harwich, his port of demobilisation. He wandered disconsolately along the waterfront, taking a last look at the ship which had been his home for years. He had become accustomed to shipboard life and knew his neighbours. 'I was scared to leave the disciplined, co-ordinated, harmonious life of the navy, where you knew exactly where you stood and what you had to do, and for your well-ordered duty received in return a well-ordered security.' 'Clumsy and unhappy' were how Grierson thought of his attempts 'to exchange this systematic and disciplined life for the individual and unprotected free-for-all which civilian life suddenly appeared.' He thought he had lost four years of his life and that he had a great deal of leeway to make up. 'I came back, as I thought, to an alien world of dreary people who were still doing the same old things, teaching the same old things in the same old way, as though this war of ours had made no essential difference to the world.'[8]

There had been many spells of inactivity in the little telegraph-room on board the *Rightwhale* and these he had used for study, with books sent by his parents from Cambusbarron. 'During my navy days I spent four hours a day learning Italian, philosophy, French literature. I had got through most of the university first year work by the time I got in.'[9]

The students he joined when he matriculated at the University of Glasgow in 1919 were not a normal intake. There were older men who had joined up in 1914 and others from later stages of the war. There were men who had been in industry or elsewhere on the home front. They were an angry generation, 'discourteous and arrogant and impatient with our masters', according to Grierson.

'We had learned skills; we had acquired experience of people and events beyond our years; but none was wise enough to confirm us in this thought and strengthen our sense of confidence. We had learned at an early age, some of us, to organise and to lead and to hold our own in the tough company of men; but people were stupid enough to hold us at arm's length and say, more or less, these attainments may have been all very well in the war, but are less than useless in the civilian world which you now enter; it is the certificates of merit we want and the paper qualifications and the smooth ways and, first and last, your accommodation to the old patterns. To tell the truth, these were the very things for a long time that we were not very good at. We could not concentrate; we could not learn; and the boys who had not left for the war were skating rings around us for a while, and we knew it. It was not perhaps for a couple of years or more that we quietened our anxieties and cooled our heads and began to fit in.'[10]

Grierson, then and later, criticised the professors who, with only a rare exception, 'gave no indication of any understanding whatever of the psychological gulf a life on active service can create between a service and civilian life'. He was given to quiet mutterings of dissent during lectures. One morning at the moral philosophy class, he attracted the attention of Professor Sir Henry Jones. There was a moment's silence, then the question addressed to Grierson: 'I don't see you taking any notes, boy. Don't you think you ought to?' Grierson took no lecture notes in that class during that year.[11] Perhaps he resented what he regarded as the political bias apparent in some of the professor's lectures. Sir Henry Jones was a staunch Liberal and, irritated when Keir Hardie was nominated as the Labour candidate at a Rectorial election, 'would interlard his lectures with what he considered conclusive swipes at Socialist doctrine' and 'orated with great eloquence upon how Socialism had failed in ancient Greece and Peru'. It was not surprising that he disturbed both Grierson and Tom Johnston when he took Sir Henry's class.[12]

Grierson fervently believed that those who thought like him were right and that the professors were wrong. 'The war had, just as we imagined, made a profound difference to the world and to ourselves. We were a new kind of generation with a new and directly personal concern in the problems which nearly killed us. The world was quite certainly . . . entering into a new phase of development of a crucial sort in which it would be decided whether or not war between people could be prevented. It was wrong to treat us as school boys, to try to accommodate us to the old ways, as though nothing had happened.'[13]

22

Able Seaman to Clydeside Radical

The rebelliousness which had been generating in Grierson's mind since his return from war service began to take deliberate and articulate form. There were significant influences both within and outside the university. Grierson was a member of the University Fabian Society—not so much a member as its star performer. The society held its meetings in a small room in the women students' union where the business of the evening would be delayed until the appearance of Grierson, wearing a bowler hat and an overlong military trench coat, his small moustache and the rolling gait completing the Charlie Chaplin impression. There was nothing humorous about his contribution when he made it. Some of his ideas originated in the writings of A. R. Orage in the *New Age* but they were presented with 'racy speech, analytical penetration, thrusting logic and visionary enthusiasm'.[14]

The Fabian Society was dissolved in 1921 on Grierson's suggestion. He had become dissatisfied with intellectual discussion and wanted a body which would be more closely allied with the politically conscious Labour movement beginning to make its presence felt along the Clyde. And so the New University Labour Club was formed. Strong Conservative and Liberal Clubs were already in existence. Their main opportunities to show their comparative strengths were the elections for the Lord Rector (who traditionally represents the students on the university governing body). On 13 November 1919, Grierson had heard the Rectorial address given by Raymond Poincaré who, unable to speak English, was yet able to deliver it with the aid of a phonetically written script. Poincaré had been elected unopposed in 1914 but his inauguration had been delayed by the war.

At the 1922 election the Conservative candidate was Lord Birkenhead and the Liberals put forward Sir John Simon. H. G. Wells accepted the invitation of the Labour Club. In the subsequent riotous campaign Grierson played a leading part, both by speaking at the Labour meetings and by heckling at the others. The battle was waged physically, with rotten fruit and eggs, flour and soot as ammunition, and pugnaciously in print and pamphlet. The result was: Birkenhead 1,165 votes, Simon 530, Wells 353. But Grierson felt that a gesture of support for the working class had been made from the intellectual heights of Gilmorehill.

In Glasgow and Clydeside it was a time of social upheaval and it would have been strange if Grierson, with the influence of his parents' concern added to his own humanist inclination, had not responded. During the war Clydeside, with its great concentration of engineering

23

shops and shipbuilding, had made a major contribution to Britain's war effort. The workers were well aware of their power and began to organise to use it, the result being the formation of a number of groups, the most militant being the Independent Labour Party. After the end of the war and a brief burst of activity in the shipyards while the merchant fleet was being repaired and replaced, depression hit the heavy industries. Unemployment accentuated the social deprivation already present and increased during the four and a half years of war when housing was inevitably neglected. The mood of protest found expression in the return of ten members of the Independent Labour Party at the 1922 general election when the surge of the Red Clyde reached Westminster. Grierson was stirred by the Clydesiders. He was impressed especially by James Maxton's rhetoric, his power to convey visually the plight of the poor.

One of Scotland's most heroic revolutionary fighters was John Maclean who had a large following on the Clyde. He was in prison in Peterhead when Grierson was demobilised and was later also in Barlinnie prison. Maclean had been on hunger strike and had been forcibly fed. Visitors said of him that he had the look of a man who was going through torture. When he last came out of prison Grierson was among the group who organised a reception for him. 'Here was this great man who had been in jail. We didn't know he had been broken. We had organised a mass meeting and we brought him up on the stage to speak. What did we bring up? He was just a hulk. He got up and spoke and I burst into tears.' Recalling the experience some twenty-five years later Grierson described it as 'one of the most tragic moments of my life'.[15]

Grierson was acutely aware of the ferment around him. Later he was to acknowledge what the Clydeside had taught him. 'The Clydeside cult was the most humanist in the early Socialist movement. This was its deep political weakness, as Lenin himself pointed out, and men like James Maxton came practically to demonstrate. But while recognising this, as one must, the over-riding humanist factor did not lose its ultimate validity as the harder forces of political organisation have taken control of the thoughts we had and the sympathies we urged. For myself, I shall only say that what I may have given to documentary—with the working man on the screen and all that—was simply what I owed to my masters, Keir Hardie, Bob Smillie and John Wheatley.'[16]

These leaders of the Independent Labour Party were among the men who influenced him outside the university. His Professor of Moral

Able Seaman to Clydeside Radical

Philosophy was latterly A. D. Lindsay and his Professor of English Language and Literature was William Macneile Dixon. Enough of his undergraduate writings on philosophy have survived to show that he was a gifted, very widely read student. Kant, Dostoevsky, Bentham, Byron and Plato were often quoted in his essays, written with a mixture of incisive knowledge and fervent belief. He was an intellectually aggressive scholar, never afraid to criticise others and unequivocally firm in his own opinions. His political philosophy was influenced by the works of Bertrand Russell, notably *Roads to Freedom* and *Social Reconstruction*.

His stance as revealed in the essays could be described as an enthusiastic utilitarianism founded on an almost mystical faith in and regard for life. He constantly stressed man's ability, through reason, to cope with a universe basically inimical: 'Life is in the beginning and in the end cruel, a struggle for existence at all costs.' Philosophy he argued should be purposive. (Much later he was to write: 'There is a way the Scots use the word "purposive", with the accent on the second syllable, which rushes out of my diabolic infancy to frighten me everywhere I go.')[17] He used philosophic inquiry to write about a world as it should be organised, rather than seeking an arid objective truth, and to enunciate policies—and pragmatic ones at that. The desire for life—'We desire life for the hope that is in it'—and for what Grierson called 'the ultimate fullness of life' was seen in his essays as basic to man, and man's progress had been towards a more conscious awareness of, and more deliberate working towards, these ends.

Generally in his essays he was developing and strengthening his concepts of man and society which were to be so important to him in his later work. Often he used a forceful preaching style, with extended metaphors and inverted sentence structure. In the words of a tutor, he showed 'a tendency to sacrifice precision to the Graces'.

Grierson's intellectual achievement earned the respect of his fellow students although this did not necessarily make him popular. Charles Oakley, whose life was to be almost as closely linked to films as Grierson's, recalls that fellow students were disinclined to get into an argument with him: 'He would leave them with wounds which didn't heal easily.'[18] J. C. M. Conn, beside whom Grierson sat at the moral philosophy class, said: 'There was never any doubt about Grierson's high intelligence: near to genius I have always maintained.'[19] According to Charles Dand (their lives were to touch at many points in the next forty years), 'It was the variety of his poses—and genuine performances—that made him *persona grata* with so many of his fellow students, the athletes, the medicals, the divinity crowd, as well as the would-be intellectuals, to whom he was, of course, something of a god.'[20]

Then as throughout his life Grierson loved argument. James A. Smellie, later to become literary editor of *The Scotsman*, recalls that 'he was always holding forth'. There were some among his friends who were prepared to take him on: William Barclay, for example, later to become a notable parliamentary correspondent of the *Daily Express* in London. Many of his friends were writers. He was often to be found in the Union smoke-room with William Jeffrey who was to send him his slim volumes of verse published after he had joined the *Glasgow Herald*. To this newspaper also went another friend, Bill Law, to whom Grierson was the 'sonsie wee Lenin', always popping into Law's digs, making speeches, and popping out.[21] Other fellow students included Daniel Jack who became Professor of Economics at the University of Durham and served on many advisory commissions on African affairs and John Maule Lothian who went to the University of Saskatchewan in 1927 as Professor of English.

Perhaps the most colourful of Grierson's friends was Alexander Werth, the Russian *émigré* who came to Glasgow from Paris and brought with him the feeling of another world, introducing Grierson to the avant-garde movement. Together they made what Grierson later claimed to be the first translations in English of Beyli, Blok, Ehrenburg and Mayakovsky.[22] Together they also paid visits to France where Grierson tutored in French families and returned with much patter about wine and food to provoke his less adventurous fellow students.

Early in his university career Grierson began to contribute to the *Glasgow University Magazine*, his first poem appearing there, over the pseudonym 'Tel', in November 1920. He continued to write, mainly verse, for the magazine until February 1923. The verses were in the main light and frivolous, all neatly turned and one or two touching a deeper note. One contemporary reviewer commended the 'rollicking rhythm' of Grierson's 'apparently lugubrious verse' and advised readers to get into the spirit of his work and they would enjoy themselves. He wrote one about Pygmalion which ended with the lines:

> And Pygmalion, in his Sunday suit,
> Committed adultery with his Absolute.[23]

When the magazine was attacked by Professor W. L. Renwick, Grierson wrote with the utmost vigour defending the editor and his literary discrimination. His barbed comments did not affect the friendship between teacher and student. He often visited Professor Renwick in his home and found there paintings which stimulated his interest in art.

It was in one of his prose contributions to the magazine, 'Pay-Day', that there was the first hint of his interest in films. Chaplin indirectly became the subject of a kind of philosophical disquisition: 'He is a builder's labourer now, but you know all about him. "Who builds stronger than a mason—or weaker—tell me that"; *c'est toujours le même système*. He was a rich man once, and a shopwalker; perhaps he was always a tramp—for you left him on the road, you remember, and always going away somewhere else. . . . And you know that the foreman will be great and terrible—and the little man will be late, and peep furtively through the doorway and offer an impossible lily, for a peace offering. But you will laugh. . . .' The film was *A Dog's Life*.[24]

Two Glasgow graduates of an older generation, O. H. Mavor (James Bridie) and Walter Elliot, both continued to take an active interest in the magazine they had helped to foster. Grierson met them at the university and they became friends. He was to write a brilliant analysis of Bridie's work—not an easy subject—and their paths were to cross at various times. Elliot was to be involved again with Grierson at a key moment in his life.

When the University Fabian Society was dissolved, Grierson initiated not only the Labour Club but also the Critics' Club where the members considered developments in literature and the arts. Charles Dand confessed that he remembered 'little about the Critics except John's enthusiasm for Benedetto Croce on art and Trotsky on everything else'.[25] Carl Sandburg was another of his enthusiasms, one he was to retain throughout his life. He read widely. As an admirer of Lenin and Trotsky, he was interested in the social experiment being launched in Russia, less in the methods of organisation than in the possibilities it held forth for the release and orientation of human energies.

An audience anywhere acted like a magnet for Grierson—and would go on doing so for most of his life. With his Presbyterian upbringing he had heard many a sermon in the church the family attended in St. Ninian's and in other churches while on holiday. He knew his Bible well, as was the habit of his generation in Scotland. It was not surprising therefore to find him preaching sermons, in churches around Glasgow and in little Highland churches at Acharacle and Glenborrodale in the Ardnamurchan peninsula. The texts of several of the sermons have survived and they give proof of both careful preparation and a disinclination to talk down to congregations who surely must have been stretched to follow the revolutionary thinking of the young student preacher.

In one sermon he took, characteristically, as his text: 'Whosoever will come after me let him take up his cross and follow me' (Matthew XVI: 24). Three things, he said, were essential if we were to bear our responsibility well and truly for the world. 'The first is faith in one-self, the second is hard thinking. There is yet another, however, and that is the secret of activity. It is what those who take no part in the fight never realise and the whole secret of it is that each one of us must take our part in the establishing of good things, before good things can come to pass. Leaving the matter to a few people, as we leave our politics to the politicians, is no use in the wide world. It is for each of us to take our active part in the organisation of our world, it is for each of us to live and to live strongly for the community of men, and to act according to the light that is in us. For a world of earnest men, and hopeful men, and thoughtful men, is the world of God indeed. It is a world doing great things, and wise things, and there is nothing better we can hope for. The harmony of blessedness is there, and it is ours for the striving—ours if we can take up the cross of our responsibility, and bear it with the might and main of our own individual effort.'

Grierson's life was to be a fulfilment of what he preached in that little Highland church.

He and his brother Anthony, studying medicine, had lodgings together in the western suburb of Scotstoun, where from their windows they could see the 'glade of cranes' on the Clyde to the south. Charles Dand, who thought of Grierson at this time as something of a poseur, remembers Grierson putting on an act as 'the man who did so well in his examinations because he had the courage to stimulate himself with drugs and posing in front of the mantelpiece with a bottle of Nux Vomica, to Anthony's derision or disgust—I forget which.'[26] Whatever last minute stimulus there may have been there was a basis of hard work and solid study. Grierson received the Buchanan Prize in the Ordinary Class of English Language and Literature in the session 1919–20: the Buchanan Prize was awarded annually to the most distinguished students in the classes of logic, moral philosophy and English literature. He received a prize and first-class certificate of merit in the Ordinary Class of Moral Philosophy in the session 1920–1. He studied a four-year course and graduated Master of Arts at the end of the session 1922–3.

Grierson later claimed that, before he left Glasgow University, he was offered a couple of constituencies, by two different parties. I have found no one who can identify the constituencies, or the parties; but his interest in politics, his concern for the underprivileged, his skills as a speaker, and his youthful eagerness would all combine to make him an attractive prospective candidate. With general elections in 1922, 1923 and 1924 and with the Socialists winning ten of Glasgow's fifteen constituencies in 1923, Grierson must have been tempted to stand in the hope of joining John Wheatley, James Maxton, Tom Johnston and the other members of the Clydeside Group in Parliament. When he said later that the soap-boxes of Glasgow Green weren't good enough for him and that he felt he could do a better political job by putting the working class on the screen, he was, of course, rationalising from hindsight. Involvement in a possible social use of films was still, in 1923, a long way off. In Grierson's decision there must also have been a disinclination to make an explicit party commitment—a disinclination which was to be present throughout his life.

The adviser on studies at Glasgow University at that time was Dr. J. R. Peddie. Another Glasgow graduate, Dr. J. Y. T. Greig, was registrar at Armstrong College, Newcastle-upon-Tyne, part of Durham University. Dr. Peddie sent Grierson with a recommendation to Dr. Greig and the result was his appointment as assistant registrar, a post which included some lecturing in philosophy. Professor Renwick had gone to Armstrong College in 1921 and the friendship of professor and former student was resumed.

Kant and Plato dominated the subject matter of the lectures Grierson gave at Armstrong College. 'Four Points of Kantian Doctrine' was one and another was based on Harald Hoffding's chapters on Kant in his *History of Modern Philosophy*. Others were derived from A. D. Lindsay's lectures in Glasgow. The lectures gave Grierson little satisfaction. He thought 'the old clerks and spinsters' to whom he lectured 'would have been better occupied raising hell about the slums of the city, the malnutrition of its children and its horrible schools.'

Grierson showed his concern about social conditions in other ways. He was often in the Byker, the city's worst slum area, and came to know the people there. He shared this social concern with a fellow Scot, James Dickinson, a lecturer at Armstrong College who thought of himself as a worker priest. Grierson was often in his home where he read poetry he had written about the people of the Byker. They were friends for only a short period but Dickinson remembers him well as a man determined to alleviate the hard working conditions he found.[27]

Grierson suggested to the Literary and Philosophical Society of Newcastle-upon-Tyne that they should invite John Skeaping to give a lecture on sculpture. While waiting for the result of the *Prix de Rome* examination (he was later to win the scholarship) Skeaping had taken a teaching post at Armstrong College and he and Grierson became very friendly. 'An intellectual and an advanced thinker, he opened my eyes to the real meaning of art.' Grierson coached him for his first public lecture and Skeaping gained much from his 'kindly and experienced advice'. They were to meet again.[28]

The principal of Armstrong College was Sir Theodore Morison who served on the selection board advising the Laura Spellman Rockefeller Memorial on fellowship appointments in the social sciences. The chairman was Sir Geoffrey Young at Cambridge University. The chain of recommendation was clear. At the end of June 1924 Grierson learned that he had been awarded a fellowship.

3 Chicago, Hollywood, New York

According to John Marshall of the Rockefeller Foundation, a fellow-ship of the kind awarded to Grierson was 'a pretty privileged thing at that time'. He had his fare paid, his tuition paid and a stipend of 1,800 dollars, regarded as adequate to live on. His original subject of study was 'Immigration and its effects on the social problems of the United States' which was later modified to include 'Public opinion—social psychology' and 'Newspaper psychology'.[1]

Grierson sailed from the Clyde and landed at Halifax, Nova Scotia, in October 1924. He moved south, first to Boston and later to New York. He was often to claim—it became part of a picturesque story—that he arrived as a bootlegger, on a vessel carrying 30,000 cases of whisky. He travelled west to Chicago where, in November, at the university School of Political Science, his studies came under the supervision of Professor Charles E. Merriam, whose writings were already known to him, and Professor Robert E. Park, a sociologist. This was but one of the influences which drew Grierson to the

> Stormy, husky brawling
> City of the Big Shoulders.

In Glasgow he had become familiar with Sandburg's poetry and in America was often to say 'I came for Carl Sandburg.' In Chicago he met Sandburg who claimed that Grierson recited his poetry better than anyone else he knew. A sentiment in a verse from 'The Sins of Kalamazoo' was to remain in his mind for years (at least until *Night Mail*):

> Sweethearts there in Kalamazoo
> Go to the general window of the post office
> And speak their names and ask for letters
> And ask again, 'Are you sure there is nothing for me?
> I wish you'd look again—there must be a letter for me.'

Sandburg, Vachel Lindsay, Sherwood Anderson—they were among the attractions. He was aware, too, that it was Chicago which had

31

alerted the reforming zeal of Upton Sinclair. In the Midwestern background was the giant figure of Frank Lloyd Wright. Grierson had learned while in Glasgow of some of these influences and innovations from the pages of the American journal *Dial* in which he said he had first read T. S. Eliot's *The Waste Land*. 'It was from America that we there in Glasgow, Scotland, got our first sight of most things new in the arts.'[2]

Among the earliest contacts Grierson made in Chicago was that with the painter Rudolph Weisenborn. Some time before they met there had been a fire in Weisenborn's studio in North State Street and all his paintings and charcoal drawings had been destroyed. In a frenzied spell of activity over six months, Weisenborn reproduced the drawings he had made over the previous twenty years. In his studio Grierson looked at the twenty-five undated drawings and placed them in exact chronological order. According to his son, Gordon Weisenborn, 'From that time on Grierson was the person.'[3]

Grierson spent a lot of time with Weisenborn 'and much of that time we spent just wandering round the city and looking at its sprawling growth, sprawling outward and sprawling upward, building and boiling. I never knew a man so dedicated to his home town, but not as William Allen White was in the case of Emporia, Kansas, because of the worthiness of its citizens and their devotion to the ultimate cultural decencies. Weisenborn was excited by the thing in itself: the images of action everywhere, the visual dynamics that went with this city on the build; images many of them that had never been seen or seeable before: the vast volumes of the buildings and the overhead railroads and the swinging curves that connected them. And above all there were the extraordinary effects of light on the new materials the builders and engineers disposed of. An asphalt surface could look brighter than the bright sky above. The concrete and the glass and the aluminium and the steel and the synthetic materials the architects were now using were catching the light in a new way as, indeed, by all the laws of science they had to. You were a world away from the light on satins and silks and velvets and all the substances of ancient interiors. You were a world away from the natural surfaces of nature itself.'[4]

Grierson learned much from Weisenborn. (Years later, when he could afford to do so, he bought a dozen of his paintings.) Weisenborn responded to Grierson's friendship. They went together, or with Weisenborn's wife Fritzie, to the cinema and there were sometimes violent arguments about the films they saw. They went together to Negro cafés and heard the first of the American jazz. They made an

1. (*left*) Outside the schoolhouse at Cambusbarron, Mr. and Mrs. Grierson and their family. Left to right: Nancy, John, Mrs. Grierson, Ruby (baby), Janet, Anthony, Margaret, Dorothy, Mr. Grierson, the headmaster of Cambusbarron school

2. (*right*) John Grierson in his R.N.V.R. uniform

3. Left to right: Walter Elliot, Baroness Elliot of Harwood, O. H. Mavor (James Bridie) and John Grierson. Grierson knew Elliot and Mavor at Glasgow University and they remained close friends

4. **Drifters** (1929)

5. John Grierson directing **Drifters**

(*facing page*)

6. (*above*) **Night Mail** (1936) Produced by John Grierson. Directed by Harry Watt and Basil Wright.

7. (*below*) **Granton Trawler** (1934) Produced by the E.M.B. Film Unit. Directed by John Grierson with Edgar Anstey

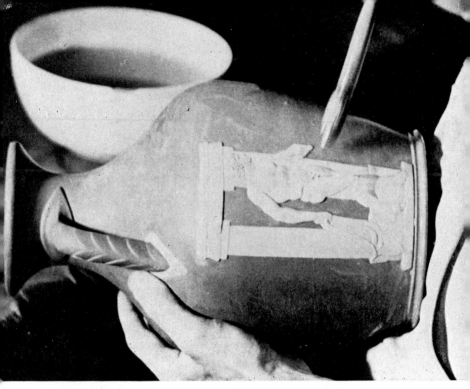

8. **Industrial Britain** (1933) Produced by the E.M.B. Film Unit.
Directed by Robert Flaherty and John Grierson
9. **The Song of Ceylon** (1934–5) Produced by John Grierson with the Ceylon
Tea Propaganda Board. Directed by Basil Wright

10. **Housing Problems** (1935) Produced for the British Commercial Gas Association. Directed by Edgar Anstey with Arthur Elton, John Taylor and Ruby Grierson
11. **North Sea** (1938) Produced by the G.P.O. Film Unit. Directed by Harry Watt

12. **Weather Forecast** (1934) Produced by the G.P.O. Film Unit. Directed by Evelyn Spice
13. **Children at School** (1936) Produced by the Realist Film Unit. Directed by Basil Wright

14. **Aero Engine** (1933–4) Produced by the E.M.B. Film Unit. Directed by Arthur Elton
15. **Pett and Pott** (1934) Produced by the G.P.O. Film Unit. Directed by Alberto Cavalcanti

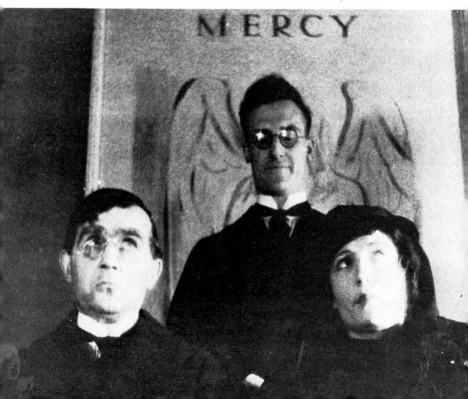

16. Welwyn, 1932: the first attempt to found a British Federation of Film Societies: John Grierson (back row), with Charles Oakley, J. S. Fairfax-Jones, Stanley Hawes, Norman Wilson and Forsyth Hardy

17. Harry Watt

expedition to a tavern in Cicero, Illinois, to hear a young man called Louis Armstrong blow his horn. These were the pioneer days of Chicago jazz. 'I was quite sure then that it would inevitably contribute from its fresh and different springs of inspiration to the mainstream of music, just as the folk songs of Europe had contributed to the classical music of Beethoven and Brahms and Bartók and Sibelius.'[5]

When he arrived in Chicago Grierson lived on Ontario Street, next door, he said, to a gangster, Dion O'Banion, boss of the North Side Mob, who was shot down one day in his flower shop. His funeral—there was a ten thousand dollar silver casket—made a considerable impression on Grierson. The gang warfare he considered as only one aspect of the growing pains of a fast-growing immigrant town, the sort of thing to be expected in a city where foreign origins and loyalties had not yet been resolved. The first generation of immigrants had been caught up in foreign-speaking households with their own European loyalties, and the new community had its very different loyalties. As a result the new generation, Grierson found, often grew up in streets without real benefit of either.

Immigration was Grierson's chosen subject for research and it soon became all-absorbing, leading naturally to related fields and arriving at the power of the mass media to influence public opinion. He quickly came to the conclusion that the yellow press, for all its sensationalism, was the most important factor in making over the immigrants from the European way of life to the American way of life. He found that the yellow press was the only English press the immigrants read, with its simple headline stories and its pictures. As a European he was fascinated by the way the Hearst press and its imitators could turn into a story what in European newspapers was called a report. A dramatic form was the basis of a means of communication.

This seemed to Grierson a highly logical way of approaching the problem of mass communication. What he found significant was that the story-line was a peculiarly American story-line. The contemplative headline was as dead as the dodo. The active verb had become the hallmark of every worthwhile story. Something had to do something to something else. Someone had to do something to someone else. The world the newspapers reflected was a world on the move, a world going places. It was from this period and this experience that Grierson derived the greeting which later was to become familiar to all his friends: 'What's new?'

Grierson had not yet come to relate his analysis of the impact of the yellow press to the world of the film. He had learned from Charles

Merriman (and kept a copy of his *American Political Ideas* handy on his bookshelf until the end of his life). He did not, however, spend much time at the University of Chicago. Describing his American experience to Professor Renwick, he wrote: 'There were the universities and the begoggled academics. I expected them and survived them and left them as gracefully as I could a long time ago. They completed my education in filing systems and called it sociology and the empirical method. I sat quiet for perhaps a couple of months. Gave birth even to a little filing system of my own to show how humble I was. . . .'[6] University lectures and filing systems were not for Grierson. He had to find a more active involvement.

Grierson moved to New York in July 1925. It was about this time that he met Walter Lippmann, then editor of the *New York World* and already well known for his book *Public Opinion* (1922). Lippmann was saying at that time that the older expectations of democratic education were impossible, since they appeared to require that the ordinary citizen should know every detail of public affairs as they developed from moment to moment. The view of education which assumed that stuffing the citizen with facts would enable him to act intelligently according to his interest was untenable in a modern society. Therefore dramatisation of the facts in terms of their human consequences was necessary to make an impact on the public.

Grierson gave credit to Walter Lippmann for turning this educational research in the direction of film. 'I talked to him one day of the labour involved in following the development of the yellow press through the evanescent drama of local politics. He mentioned that we would do better to follow the dramatic patterns of the film through the changing character of our time, and that the box-office records of success and failure were on file.'[7]

This shift of emphasis from newspapers to films did not happen suddenly or completely. The Rockefeller fellows were encouraged to travel and Grierson needed little urging to be up and away. In the space of two months at the end of 1925 he visited Albany, Buffalo, Toronto, Cleveland, Toledo and Detroit. In the following year, between March and June, he visited St. Louis, Kansas City, Lawrence, Denver, Salt Lake City, Spokane, Seattle, Portland, San Francisco, Los Angeles, Houston, New Orleans, Birmingham, Atlanta, Washington, Baltimore and Philadelphia.[8] He must have been moving fast.

Invariably, in these cities, he called on the editor of the leading daily newspaper. This was, among other things, the best way of learning what was new. One such editor was William Allen White of the *Emporia Gazette*. White took him through a local department store to tell him where everything came from. The editor said it was a part of the civic pride of Emporia, Kansas, to be getting things from all over the world and keeping upsides with whatever was new anywhere. White said that a department store could be a powerful influence on the imagination and a powerful spur to the future, because it talked a language everyone understood, and was talking it each day and every day all the time.[9]

With some other editors he would say, if the circumstances were encouraging, 'I'll be around here for a week. Why don't you let me be a volunteer in writing editorials?' In this way he gained admittance to editorial conferences and could observe opinion-forming methods at first hand.

His journalism began in Chicago, where he contributed a column on painting to the *Evening Post*. (The caption under a reproduction of Weisenborn's portrait of him read: 'A Vorticistic portrait of the young Scotch newspaper man and art critic who, within less than a year, has made a place for himself in bohemian circles of Chicago.') There were many references in his column to Picasso, Cézanne, Impressionism, Post-Impressionism, Vorticism and the like. In a critical column on Whistler ('the root of the matter was not in him') he wrote characteristically: 'There are, as I understand it, two paths of imagination and beauty. There is the path which enters bravely into the affairs of men and of nature, and separates the golden rhythms of life from the slip-shod of mere events. And there is the path of fantasy which begins where one's insight has failed. It winds its way in the moonlight and the half-light and presents a vision to its wanderers only when things are already fantastic and obscure. It is the path in the end to sentimentality, for while it pleases our nostalgia for a different world, it reveals nothing about this one. And one's real longing, as an artist, which is to live deeply and express greatly, is not satisfied at all.'[10]

In its approach to painting Grierson found America 'generations ahead. A weekly supplement to one of the popular papers in Chicago runs hardly anything but Post-Impressionists. Picassos, Cézannes, Matisses and Derains everywhere. Survage the Cubist sells every picture he shows. Even the advertisements in the *Saturday Evening Post* show the influence.'[11]

In Denver Grierson met Ben Lindsey, a veteran judge of the juvenile court, who had been expressing concern in public about the relationship between films and juvenile delinquency. Reacting to this he wrote an article on 'Flaming Youth of North America' for the *American Journal of Sociology*. It was read by Jesse Lasky in New York and by Walter Wanger in Hollywood. When Grierson reached Hollywood in the early summer of 1926 it was Wanger who opened doors for him. In particular Wanger opened up the files for him at Famous Players–Lasky so that, in fulfilment of Walter Lippmann's advice, he could make an analysis of box-office success and failure.[12]

Later Grierson drew on this research for a series of seven articles published in the *Motion Picture News*. In general the articles accepted that film was a popular art: 'It belongs to the strange and primitive animal with lusts in its body and dreams in its eyes which we call the mob'; but he argued strongly that the producers should not despise their audience. The cinema, he urged, 'belongs to the people as no other social institution in the world before. It is the only genuinely democratic institution that has ever appeared on a world wide scale.' He criticised Hollywood for taking life too easily. 'I imagined that I would find there a set of adventurers, men young and eager in a young and eager popular art, working by day and planning and plotting by night, seizing like young eagles on every new method, analyzing, developing, asking themselves questions at all times, why this was good, why this was bad, and how the good might be better. But not on your life! ... I missed the fever that goes with creative work. I missed the appetite for criticism that goes with ambition. I suspected that instead of craving discussion and asking always for more, they discouraged it, were frightened for it. I suspected, in the end, that they were often not so much concerned with making the cinema great as with serving their own private interests.'[13]

In this criticism Grierson made exceptions: Chaplin, Fairbanks, Von Stroheim, Von Sternberg, King Vidor, Harry Langdon, Raymond Griffith. In Walter Wanger especially Grierson found a ready response to the ideas he was beginning to formulate about the deliberate use of the film for social change. Grierson credited him with the development of a policy for the creation of stars to meet the challenge of the revolt of youth at that time. He also said he had much to do with the initiation of the early documentary films like *Grass, Chang* and *Moana* and that it was from him that the first analysis of the montage of Eisenstein's *Potemkin* had come.

When, in 1942, Grierson spoke in Hollywood at the awards ceremony of the Academy of Motion Picture Arts and Sciences, he recalled that it was with Walter Wanger (Academy president for 1942) that he first discussed the theories and purposes of the documentary film movement. 'At that time some of us thought the Hollywood film of play and story and romance was unnecessarily out of touch with the social realities. Some of us had come in from the other arts; some of us were frankly social scientists and educators. We saw the growing complexity of modern affairs; and we thought that if our half-bewildered, half-frivolous generation did not master events, it was not unlikely that events would master us. We saw the enormous power of the film medium and believed it had the very special public duty to interpret the contemporary scene. I am not surprised that we were at first called a bunch of intellectuals and propagandists and told that the documentary idea had nothing to do with entertainment.'[14]

In Hollywood in the mid-1920s Grierson's interest had not yet wholly focused on the film as a moulder of public opinion. It was broad enough to embrace a variety of contacts and to give him a range of experience on which he was to draw most rewardingly when he was reviewing films regularly in the early thirties. He was staying at the Mark Twain Hotel, a small three-storey wooden building with twenty-eight rooms. The other guests included several writers—company which Grierson must have enjoyed—who were to become known internationally, among them Marc Connelly, Robert Benchley and Donald Ogden Stewart, whom Grierson came to know well. According to Stewart, Hollywood at that time 'was still the wild untamed territory of Before Sound, and before the cultural pretentiousness and social snobbery which were to come. There were still living vestiges of the days of Mabel Normand and the Keystone cops, of Francis X. Bushman and Pearl White, of John Bunny and Theda Bara.'[15]

It was Stewart who introduced Grierson to Chaplin and 'shared several interesting discussions between the two and also with Charlie's circle of assistants and ex-assistants. These included Jim Tully, the hobo-novelist; Harry d'Arrast, who had directed *A Woman of Paris*; Harry Crocker, who was acting in Charlie's current production of *The Circus*; and Joe von Sternberg, who showed me *The Salvation Hunters*, an experiment which Charlie had encouraged him to produce and direct. Most of our discussions took place in a delicatessen restaurant on Hollywood Boulevard which Charlie had financed for old Henry Bergman, his beloved "heavy" from Mack Sennett days.'[16]

At one of these discussions Raymond Griffith and Harry Langdon were present, with Grierson, Stewart and Chaplin. According to Grierson, Chaplin 'upheld the Christian clown very brightly against the clown of the Anti-Christ. The comedy which was rooted in failure was set against the comedy rooted in superiority. Stewart mentioned the moment in *Hands Up*, when Griffith in the course of being hanged by the neck loosed an unforgettable grin on his executioners. Chaplin stood by the Testament, partly in consideration of the fun to be got by inflicting Christian innocents on the world, but more particularly for the tragedy latent in the idea. He was not quite so sure as Langdon that innocence proved its own reward. It could also be inadequacy, and failure, and futility.'

Grierson was also in Hollywood when *The Woman of the Sea*, successor to Chaplin's *A Woman of Paris*, was made (it was never to be shown in public and Grierson was one of the few who saw it). Chaplin gave it to von Sternberg to direct but the two men had very different views of how to treat the story of the contrast between the woman who went from the fishing village to the big city and the woman who stayed at home. 'It was a strangely beautiful and empty affair—possibly the most beautiful I have ever seen—of net patterns, sea patterns and hair in the wind. When a director dies, he becomes a photographer.'[17] This was to become one of the most quoted of Grierson's aphorisms. He had a great liking for Sternberg and saw a lot of him in Hollywood.

There were memorable meetings with other directors. He saw great slices of Eric von Stroheim's *The Wedding March* shot 'and great hunks of financiers' hair torn from the roots in the process'. Stewart introduced Grierson to King Vidor whom he liked for his seriousness and who was later to make *The Crowd* and *Our Daily Bread*, films which had an affinity with the documentary idea. Grierson sensed the promise of the early William Wyler and found Cecil B. de Mille so good a craftsman that he was always worth watching. F. W. Murnau he dismissed as 'an artist who never smelt an honest wind in his life'. From his vantage point of the filing-room at Famous Players he could bring a sharp eye to bear on pretension and achievement.

By the time Grierson moved to New York, cinema had become his dominant interest and although films did not appear in the originally listed subject-matter for research, he prepared a report on the cinema for the Rockefeller Foundation (as well as a general report and a list of the newspaper men he had met). He was being paid a retainer by Famous Players–Lasky for analyses of film technique and production methods.

On 15 September 1925—the day Greta Garbo and Mauritz Stiller arrived in Hollywood—Grierson was in New York, lecturing at the Paramount Theatre Managers Training School on 'The Conditions of Popular Appeal'. Understandably he drew on his newspaper research and spoke more about William Randolph Hearst than about any film producer. If there is any lesson to be learned from the history of the newspaper, he said, it is this, that he who attempts to uplift will soon be in a position to be uplifted himself, and uplifted dead. Unless a newspaper story had the texture of life in it, the flicker and appeal of common sentiments, it failed.

When he spoke about films he said that *The Last Laugh*, which had come out of the pain and pessimism of post-war Germany, was not keyed to the state of the American imagination. America had suffered little as a nation, he said. It had begun for the majority as the land of promise and its people had still every reason in the world to be optimistic. They believed in success and hated sadness more than anything. 'They are all either making their fortune or going to make it and they are much too busy doing things to get into that state of super-criticism and super-consciousness that comes from leisure and sometimes from loss.'[18]

Grierson had some reservations about being described in the film trade-press as a 'celebrated English showman' instructing managers on 'how to haul the coin to the bank'; but he was becoming known both to film-makers and to film commentators. He was invited to contribute to the New York *Sun* by the newspaper's film critic, Jack Cohen. His first article appeared on 22 September 1925, when it was introduced somewhat quaintly: 'To-day these columns are turned over to an essay, written at my request by John Grierson of Scotland, who is in this country on a mission that need not be described. He has studied the screen and knows whereof he speaks. In this essay he gives illuminating ideas on the possibilities of the cinema as an art medium, starting with the recent development of the phonofilm.'

Grierson asserted that 'The screen has a value of its own as art, and that value would disappear if its silence were violated'—a not uncommon reaction in the early days of sound. He went on to argue that all art has been built on the unnatural. 'When the drama was really dramatic it was made up of poetry. In Shakespeare, Corneille and the rest, the action went through in blank verse or rhyme, as the case might be. The declaration of a lover and the protests of a mistress were in faultless feet. It was unnatural, perhaps, from a superficial point of view, but it gave a rhythm, a tempo, a power of expression to the drama which caught reality itself. Silence means the same thing to the screen. It, too, is unnatural, but it ensures that psychical distance, that magical and mysterious quality, which all art places between itself and the actual.'

Chicago, Hollywood, New York

In another early article for the *Sun*, clearly derived from his Hollywood experience, Grierson wrote about Chaplin's preparations for *The Circus*. 'Chaplin has a hut on his Hollywood lot where he retires of an afternoon to remember that he is an Englishman. The Californian sun filters through yellow shades into a cool interior and there are white tablecloths and rocking chairs and tea to remind one of that primeval and not unwise laziness which Americans have forgotten. But Chaplin is as vital in his lazy moments as in his occupied ones, and to sit with him for the first time is to sit and watch an amazing body, which is its own ceaseless commentary on everything its strange occupant happens to think of. As he told the story of *The Circus* one looked, rather than listened, and to all intents and purposes Chaplin's mind was not engaged for a moment. The face and eyes articulated and here if anything was the lost example of the Behaviorists, one whose body was his entire process of thought. Syllogisms rippled over his face and logic was a subtle affair of arms and legs that sought and found their conclusions of themselves.'[19]

With writing of this quality his work was in demand and soon it appeared also in the *Herald Tribune* and the *Motion Picture News*.

His closest critical affiliation, however, was with Jack Cohen and the *Sun*. The first of the Russian films were arriving in the United States and Grierson, who was 'the sort of odd body who looked after the lost causes, including, as I remember, most of the people who happened to be good', wrote about them for the newspaper. They were the first proletarian movies the Americans had seen. *The Peasant Women of Ryosan* had a great impact in New York. The great joyful harvest scene with the wind blowing spectacularly over the wheat fields was a fresh experience. Surprisingly the film was presented with sound. The theatre hired a group of Russian *émigrés* who stood behind the screen and sang and played and shouted in chorus according to the action.

Of more lasting significance for Grierson was the work he did on *Potemkin* about which Douglas Fairbanks had brought back an excited report from Moscow. With Jack Cohen he prepared the English titles for the film and before he was finished he knew it foot by foot and cut by cut. He realised how much it contributed technically to their notions of the cinema: in its use of vast movements, in its building of tempo, in its violent use of montage for smash effects and symbolic counterpoint. His close working familiarity with the film placed him in a unique position to analyse its techniques. Grierson did most of the critical writing associated with the presentation of the film

40

off Broadway and perhaps set the fashion for its reception by the English-speaking critics. But he did *not* re-edit the film. A chance use of the expression, taking *Potemkin* apart and putting it together again for the American market, was mistakenly read in a physical rather than a critical sense.[20]

Grierson was later to recognise the special place Eisenstein held among those who influenced his generation of film-makers. 'He was the first to make it plain that the film could be an adult and positive force in the world. He was the first to demonstrate what the deliberate exercise of the power of the cinema might be. He was the first to prove that the art of the cinema might be as great as any other, with an inspiration as deep, a range as wide and a creative ambition as intense as any other.'[21]

Much was to follow from *Potemkin*. Much, too, was to follow from another New York experience. Grierson first met Robert Flaherty in New York in 1925, no doubt in his favourite haunt, the Coffee House Club. He had already seen *Nanook of the North* 'on its first outing', before leaving Scotland. He also said he had seen a good part of an earlier version of the film, the negative of which was lost in Toronto when Flaherty dropped a lighted cigarette into it and it went up in flames. A partial assembly had been made, known as the Harvard print, and it was this Grierson must have seen in the United States. If he did not think much of it neither did Flaherty: 'It was a bad film; it was dull—it was little more than a travelogue. I had learned to explore, I had not learned to reveal.'[22] According to Grierson, 'In the first version Flaherty was still with the old travelogue of Hale's Tours, and planning learning from the ground up, not to mention the backs and fronts of sledges. The second *Nanook* marked the point at which, after long labour, the flame shot up and the light kindled and the art form had been added to observation. I say that, after all, there was only one *Nanook*.'

Grierson was therefore familiar with Flaherty's work. *Nanook* had been shown first to Paramount (the theatrical distribution side of Famous Players–Lasky) and had been declined, and its subsequent relative success in the United States and greater success overseas was known to Grierson. Flaherty was engaged by Jesse Lasky to make a film in the South Seas and when he returned with *Moana* it was shown (at twelve reels) to Lasky, Adolphe Zukor, Walter Wanger and other executives. Although the initial response was enthusiastic, the enthusiasm had evaporated by the time the film was re-edited. When Grierson met Flaherty he was having difficulties with Paramount.

41

Later he was to write: 'I took Flaherty's case like a sort of critical attorney. Off and on, and not without the stresses and strains that go with such a relationship, I have been his critical attorney ever since.'[23]

When Grierson met him Flaherty was in open conflict with Paramount. Under pressure from one or two critics, including William Allen White, Paramount had agreed to show the film in six tough locations, ranging from Poughkeepsie in New York State to Jacksonville in Florida. To help promote these showings, Flaherty arranged for the film to be seen and reviewed by the National Board of Review and leaflets incorporating the favourable review were mailed to individuals and organisations likely to be interested in the six test locations. The comparative success of these showings led eventually to its presentation in New York. But if the lesson of specialised promotion was not lost on Grierson, it was on Paramount. When *Moana* opened at the Rialto on Broadway on 7 February 1926, it was blazoned as 'The Love-life of a South Sea Siren'.

Grierson's review appeared the following day in the *Sun* (an article based on the National Board of Review leaflet had already appeared). He wrote:

'The film is unquestionably a great one, a poetic record of Polynesian tribal life, its ease and beauty and its salvation through a painful rite. *Moana* deserves to rank with those few works of the screen that have the right to last, to live. It could only have been produced by a man with an artistic conscience and an intense poetic feeling which, in this case, finds an outlet through nature worship.

'Of course *Moana*, being a visual account of events in the daily life of a Polynesian youth, has documentary value. But that, I believe, is secondary to its value as a soft breath from a sunlit island, washed by a marvellous sea, as warm as the balmy air. *Moana* is first of all beautiful as nature is beautiful. It is beautiful for the reason that the movements of the youth Moana and the other Polynesians are beautiful, and for the reason that trees and spraying surf and soft billowly clouds and distant horizons are beautiful.

'And therefore I think *Moana* achieves greatness primarily through its poetic feeling for natural elements. It should be placed on the idyllic shelf that includes all those poems which sing of the loveliness of sea and land and air . . . and of man when he is a part of beautiful surroundings, a figment of nature, an innocent primitive rather than a so-called intelligent being, cooped up in the mire of so-called intelligent civilisation. . . .

'. . . *Moana* is lovely beyond compare.'[24]

42

And so the word documentary was born. Grierson may have been aware at the back of his mind of the use the French made of *documentaire* to describe serious travel or exploration films. In any case it had not yet the burden of significance it was to carry. Grierson was later to have doubts about its value to the movement which was to attach itself to it. 'Documentary is a clumsy description but let it stand.'[25]

The movement, and the misgivings, still lay ahead. The term of his fellowship was nearing its end. He intensified his travelling, prepared his reports and continued to write for the New York journals. He even made a tentative inquiry about a post in Britain ('for a man with a taste in art and a Scots–Oxford complex'). The two and a half years he had spent in the United States had been lived at a hectic pace. The energy which had left his fellow students at Glasgow gasping seemed inexhaustible. He had not missed an opportunity, either in the formal educational setting of Chicago University or in the newspaper world where he was increasingly at home. Films were claiming him more and more: 'Even the skyscrapers, the nigger songs and Krazy Kat, I find, can't survive the movies.'[26]

4 'Drifters'

Grierson sailed from New York on the last day of January 1927. Impatience was boiling up inside him. In a year he would be thirty and, by his reckoning, he had done nothing. His war service, Glasgow University, his years in the United States had all been preparation. But for what? He was still torn between journalism and the cinema. The indecision was to continue, even after it appeared that he was on a chosen course.

While in the United States Grierson had kept in touch with public opinion in Britain by reading *The Times* whenever he could lay his hands on a copy. In August and September 1925, he had read in *The Times* a remarkable series of articles on the theme 'Why don't we get better pictures?' by the poet Robert Nichols, based on research he had carried out in Hollywood and New York. It may be that he met Grierson then. Certainly there was a marked similarity in their ideas. In one article on the gullibility of Hollywood Nichols wrote: 'With one possible exception, there are no critics of the screen on this entire coast who, were they by profession critics of the drama, music or painting, could gain five minutes' hearing in a circle of dramàtic, music or art critics in any big capital in Europe. Nor are the critics of the screen in New York (again with one exception) much better.'[1] Was Grierson the exception in New York? If they did not meet and compare notes in the United States they undoubtedly did in London.

In *The Times* Grierson had also read something of the work of the Empire Marketing Board, established in May 1926, to promote the marketing of the products of the British Empire and to encourage research and development. With a letter of introduction from Nichols, Grierson called on Stephen Tallents who, after having served Lloyd George, Winston Churchill, William Beveridge and others in a variety of ministries over a long period, had been appointed Secretary of the E.M.B. As Tallents was to write later, 'I took to Grierson at first sight. He put his ideas, as he has always done, with persuasive conviction. I did not fully grasp their purport at that moment; but, looking back, I can give a clearer account of them than I could have

44

done at the end of that first meeting. Grierson had been steeped but never dyed in the colours of orthodox education, which he had never seen as rising above the informational level to that at which apprehension enlists the imaginative faculties. The meagreness which he found in modern community life seemed to him due to a lack of essential understanding of the stuff on which that life was made up. If life itself was to yield its riches, then the raw material of life must be worked by processes which would elicit not merely its bare facts but its essentially dramatic qualities.'[2]

Tallents found that Grierson's approach fitted with his own. The call had gone forth at the Board to bring the Empire alive in the minds of those who belonged to it and to use every medium of communication to reach the people in the quarter of the world still coloured red on the map. Film seemed the most obvious medium but its value was unrecognised: film came at the foot of the list of forty-five departments and sub-departments at the E.M.B. There was a film officer, Walter Creighton, who had experience of pageantry in the staging of the Aldershot Tattoo and who, shortly after his appointment, was sent in August 1927 to Canada (the Toronto Exhibition) and the United States; but of film activity at the E.M.B. there was virtually none, nor was there conviction in the Government and at the Treasury that there should be.

To Grierson, who 'looked on cinema as a pulpit and used it as a propagandist',[3] such reluctance must have seemed baffling. In his conversation with Tallents he put forward the arguments in favour of the film he was later to express precisely: 'It gives generous access to the public. It is capable of direct description, simple analysis and commanding conclusion, and may, by its tempo'd and imagistic powers, be made easily persuasive. It lends itself to rhetoric, for no form of description can add nobility to a simple observation as readily as a camera set low, or a sequence cut to a time-beat. But principally there is this thought that a single say-so can be repeated a thousand times a night to a million eyes, and, over the years, if it is good enough to live, to millions of eyes. That seven-leagued fact opens a new perspective, a new hope, to public persuasion.'[4]

By the end of the conversation Tallents was determined that he must enlist Grierson in the service of the E.M.B. He could not, however, immediately add him to the staff. His device was to commission Grierson to prepare a series of memoranda on the film position in various countries. Grierson drew on the knowledge he had acquired while in North America. He paid visits to Berlin in July and Paris in

October for his reports on the uses of the film in Germany and France. His research was thorough and his arguments were persuasive. Interests which did not and could not find their ends satisfied in the commercial cinema, with its mass appeal, were beginning to look elsewhere, as he felt they must do. There was a case, he argued, for the organisation of supplementary production units and supplementary exhibition arrangements. New efforts being made, he found, were haphazard and isolated. Alongside the little theatres in the larger cities (he knew well the Fifth Avenue Playhouse, the Cameo on Broadway and the Vieux Colombier in Paris) there was a movement towards special showings by public authorities—what was to be known later as the non-theatrical audience.

Out of this investigation came a suggestion by Grierson that he should arrange a series of screenings at the newly opened Imperial Institute cinema, so that members of the Board and its committees could study the best examples of films relevant to their work being made in Britain and overseas. In the absence of Walter Creighton in North America, Grierson could give these demonstrations the stamp of his forceful personality, especially as the films were introduced either by himself or by Tallents with previous guidance from him. A typical programme might include *Solid Sunshine*, on butter production in New Zealand, *Electricity on the Farm* by Jean Benoit-Lévy, *Influenza*, a German health propaganda film, and a film on cancer research by Dr. R. J. Canti of St. Bartholomew's Hospital. The *Secrets of Nature* films, produced for Bruce Woolfe by Percy Smith and Mary Field, appeared frequently in the programmes.

Grierson's enthusiasm emerged more clearly in his choice of the longer films. He showed the early American Westerns, *The Covered Wagon* and *The Iron Horse*, and *Grass*, the record by Merian C. Cooper and Ernest B. Shoedsack of the trek of the Baktyari tribes in Persia in search of grass for their flocks. Flaherty's *Nanook* and *Moana* were in other programmes. Daringly, in this setting, Grierson showed the early Russian films, still unseen by the public in Britain. *Potemkin* was followed by *Turksib*, with its director Victor Turin, in the audience. Later came Pudovkin's *Storm Over Asia* and Dovjenko's *Earth*. The programme notes were written by Grierson who, of the Soviet filmmakers, noted that their 'massing of detail, the distribution of detail and sequences, of rising and falling tempo, the enthusiasm for dramatising working types and working gestures, combine to make their films of work as exciting as any in the world'.

In one mood Grierson found it 'a great responsibility taking the

46

world through the movie wilderness'.[5] In another he felt frustrated by
the failure to respond to what he was doing. He was furious when the
Board's officers sent to his shows 'their wives (damn them) and their
brats and their brats' nurse maids'; when they didn't send many of
these; and when, at 7.30 p.m., they thought 'of their stomachs and
dinner (damn dinner) and quit, quit, quit. In the middle of *Moana*.
In the middle of anything. I'll do anything sooner than compete with
an Englishman's dinner.'[6] In another mood he could look beyond the
temporary exasperation to what he believed could be the larger outcome. 'The job sets to look bigger'n hell with every passing day.
Should I drop it now solid or wait till the job's created and pick up
what's going for having done it? It's a case of fighting and staying put
and hanging on with your teeth.'[7]

Many of these misgivings Grierson was expressing in letters to an
American girl, Frances Strauss. He had met her in New York where
she wrote for *New Masses*: according to Lewis Jacobs, she was 'a
strong, opinionated, aggressive person and worked very conscientiously
for liberal and progressive causes'.[8] In London Frances was a guest
at Grierson's flat, 27 Hogarth Road, Earl's Court, before going to
Berlin. Over a period of some nine months he wrote to her almost
every day, addressing her as 'baby' (she was ten years younger) and
ending with 'love. J.' Frances was an aspiring writer and in many of
the letters Grierson was commenting on her stories, analysing their
weaknesses and expressing delight when they were successful. Grierson
saw her at the Hotel Excelsior in Berlin during his visit to Germany
in July 1927. Something appeared to go amiss during their meeting
and shortly after Grierson's return to London he was writing: 'I'll get
some work done—you'll get some work done. Then we'll bask around
in the sun somewhere. . . . Don't cry too much—because there's less
to cry about between you and me than you'd ever believe.'[9] Frances
returned to New York directly and not through London as Grierson
had suggested and the correspondence continued into 1928.

Frances Strauss was one of Grierson's links with the United States—
one of several links which he was anxious to retain while his future
remained uncertain. He continued to write for the New York *Sun* and
Herald Tribune, commenting on the London film scene and the new
films from France, Germany and Russia. He took this writing with
some seriousness: 'A critic's always got to think how his stuff will
sound in years ahead.'[10] His salary from Paramount was still running.
He wrote to Jesse Lasky suggesting that Paramount should produce
three films for the British Empire—one on Canada on the lines of

The Covered Wagon, one on the Hudson's Bay Company and one on Mackenzie's exploration of the West. His restlessness found expression in almost every letter to Frances Strauss. 'I gotta pack again, sister, because the nightmare is on me so it doesn't stop. I'd go a whaler, or a trawler, or a anything, so it took the memory of London out of me. No ma'am, they don't get me after six months' waiting because I'm not one of these youths plodding from Log Cabin to Park Avenue. I thank no gods for lifting an eyelid on me. I'll go where I can take, without any body in particular's permission.'[11]

Much if not all of this restlessness was concealed from Stephen Tallents whose belief in Grierson was unshaken and who, whenever possible, tried to find outlets for his energies. He sent Grierson to Edinburgh (his parents had moved with his younger sisters to Malleny Grove, Balerno) where he arranged with the Department of Agriculture to stage film demonstrations for farmers on market days in Scottish towns. At Victoria Station in London an automatic daylight projector was installed and attracted crowds so large that the showings had to be spaced out. When the Imperial Agricultural Research Conference was held in Edinburgh, Grierson showed films in a guard's van to the delegates on their rail journey back to London. Special film performances for children were given in Newcastle and Gateshead and a small cinema was included in the E.M.B. pavilion at the North East Coast Exhibition.

Tallents did not need to be told by Grierson that these efforts were not enough and that the E.M.B. must have its own films. The first hint that he might make a film was given to Grierson in the middle of November 1927—the film on the Scottish herring fleets which would become known as *Drifters*. Before a decision could be taken there was one further demonstration to be given, this time to Lord Balfour, Stanley Baldwin, William Joynson-Hicks and other ministers. On 24 November Grierson, uncomfortable in formal clothes, spoke at dinner and later again when introducing the film programme. He had no doubt about its success. He knew the effort he had put into organising and propagandising. 'I've crashed the Cabinet and, in essence, the whole shooting match, so far as getting the officials to take an interest in films. . . . It means that the scheme I figured out will go forward—forward, however, just as far as the English mentality can reach.'[12]

There was movement but the way forward was by no means clear nor was Grierson yet free of the agony of personal indecision. Tallents had several good reasons for the choice of the herring as the subject of the film he wanted Grierson to make. The E.M.B. wanted to do something for the home fishing industry. Grierson had served in minesweepers and knew well the world of the steam drifter. The third reason was tactical. Tallents expected strong opposition from the Treasury (and was not to be disappointed). Arthur Michael Samuel (later the first Lord Mancroft), Financial Secretary to the Treasury, had studied the history of the herring fisheries and had written a book: *The Herring: Its Effect on the History of Britain.*

In addition to the film on the herring, the E.M.B.'s production programme included a film fantasy on the Empire plum pudding, *One Family*, written by Walter Creighton in consultation with Rudyard Kipling. The programme was resisted by the Treasury (Samuel was not present) and the issue had to be put before ministers. This was done at a meeting at the Dominions Office in Whitehall on 27 April 1928 (the day after Grierson's thirtieth birthday). Opposing the programme, Samuel said it would be folly to think of increasing the sale of Empire products by means of the Cinema. Walter Elliot, who as chairman of the E.M.B.'s Film Committee knew and sympathised with Grierson's arguments, countered by explaining that the proposal was not for advertising films but for background films on Empire products which could be widely shown and which would indirectly foster a demand for products. He was supported by L. S. Amery, the Dominions Secretary, who reminded the others of the American domination of the British cinema, recently underlined in the House of Commons. The Treasury representative said there were commercial companies which could make the films as effectively.

Towards the end of the meeting, with the issue unresolved, Samuel responded to a skilful compliment by saying that he could probably give some help with advice on the herring film.[13] Approval was given for the expenditure of £7,500 on both films. Grierson's employment as assistant film officer was confirmed: his letter of appointment was dated 15 May 1928.

It was just in time. Grierson had been ill with blood poisoning for seven weeks—a pin in a finger while editing film—and was bitter about the action of the E.M.B. in laying him off as soon as he was sick. He had moved first to 7 Taviton Street and later to 109 St. George's Square and had been since 19 February 1928 in a basement flat at 3 Upper Park Road, Haverstock Hill, Hampstead. Initially the furnishing was spare: 'I got a table and a chair and a carpet and forgot about a mattress, so it's been cool on the hips, and will be until I get cash again.'[14] He drove himself hard: when he did get a bed, the first thing he saw in the morning when wakening was a poster of his own design on the opposite wall bearing the words, 'Eventually— Why Not Now?' And so he would get up.[15]

He could slip easily into a mood of disillusionment: 'The E.M.B.'s been impossible these two months and I sinned grievously kidding myself about it. . . . It's too slow, and worse, the whole place is set to a tune that's Dutch or Chinese or something. I make it out less and less. The kind of a tune you couldn't like even if it was good. Schedule this, schedule that, to a penny, to a minute. Say it in triplicate. Say over the say so and quote your authority. Flag me a ref. Register and Return. Put away and bring up for action in six days . . . or three. Christ, and I thought to make movies.'[16]

At long last the making of movies seemed to be within sight. First there was a film on Liverpool to research, a symphony of a city in the style of Walter Ruttmann's *Berlin*. But before that could be taken very far he was visiting the harbours and had begun to write the scenario for the fishing film. He spent some time at the marine laboratories in Aberdeen and Plymouth, discussing how the undersea effects could be obtained. He visited Lerwick which he regarded as the main base for the film, saw where the bird scenes for the film would be shot, and on the west coast of Shetland found at Hamna Voe a fishing village whose natural beauty satisfied him. The preparations, on paper and with people, were intense and demanding enough to absorb all his restless energy.

Grierson began with the conviction that it was not necessary to go to the ends of the earth for a drama of reality and that there were stories on the doorstep of struggles for existence which were as vivid and romantic as stories of the primitive. The herring fishing he regarded as one of the great dramas of the world: 'Two miles of nets to every ship, hand over hand agonies of eight hours on end, a dash for harbour in heavy seas, the long labour of unshipping the catch at whatever hour of day or darkness the boat arrives, putting out again, shooting hauling, shooting hauling, seven days out of seven, with no mercy to muscle and the only mercy to mind the participation in one of the most beautiful spectacles on earth. This is the herring fishing. It is its own story—an adventure story in a ready-made sequence of dramatics. Adventuring forth under the heavens, achieving with toil and danger under the heavens, bringing home what one has got to the quiet of harbour. Is there any tale in life so plainly significant as this?'[17]

So it seemed to Grierson as he prepared for the film. His only difficulty was to give the story 'that atmosphere of higher meaning without which no drama is any drama at all. In my scenario I accordingly entered a long list of what I called hopefully "poetics". I proposed like a stage producer to give my fishermen a setting—a setting of cloudy skies, wind on water and seagulls in thousands. And to add that hint of mystery which is inseparable from the life of the sea, I introduced a night scene of dark sinister monsters of the deep, and frenzied shoals rushing through the water in their silvery myriads.'[18]

Filming began in July when Grierson and his cameraman, Basil Emmott, set out for Lerwick. The bird scenes—gannets, puffins, kittiwakes and cormorants—were shot at Noss Head. The fishery cruiser's siren was used to drive the birds into the air and rise they did in clouds that darkened the sky, but from a cinematic point of view they flew so high they might have been a smoke cloud. A drifter was used and a catch of herring thrown into the sea but still the birds were suspicious. They could get within camera range of only the young ones. However, at other times and places there was much shooting of gulls (enough to satisfy anyone in British films who wanted sea-bird shots for years to come).

For the interiors of the ship's cabin Grierson took over part of the fish market at Lerwick and here John Skeaping supervised the building of a set he had designed. Asked to reproduce their everyday life under these artificial conditions, the fishermen responded magnificently. They twitched never an eyelid. They turned in for the night, got up to haul, cooked, conversed, ate their meals and swore at the cook as though they were on the high seas fifty miles away.

When they were on the high seas, in the commissioned *Maid of Thule*, the herring could not be found. Grierson became desperate and, failing a real catch, tried to stage one. He bought a few crans from a more successful ship, the fish were put by hand into the nets, and the fishermen hauled them to the camera. But life was out of more than the fish and the scenes had to be scrapped. In the cinema of reality, Grierson found, you cannot lie with impunity. The life of the thing which is everything has to be captured at the source: absolutely so in the scenes that matter.

John Skeaping accompanied Grierson and Emmott when the *Maid of Thule* put to sea. He was a good sailor—Emmott was not—and he discussed camera angles with Grierson who shot much of the film himself. From the unproductive sea round Shetland they were forced to go south to Lowestoft where another drifter, the *Renovelle*, was commissioned. For the big scene of the film Grierson wanted a full-

'Drifters'

dress gale and a full-size haul. They waited for weeks and went to sea only when the gale signal had been run up and most of the ships had taken to harbour.

It was a dreadful night. 'We lashed the camera and ourselves on top of the bridge and let the drifter buck its worst and then in the early hours of the morning with the ship riding to a nor'east gale the fish came up to us, hand over hand, in silvery blankets of light. With the heavy seas dragging desperately at the nets, every foot had to be fought for. The heroic labour of the men went on for eight hours at a stretch, with never a let up. . . . We took the hand camera and stood to the roll of the ship that we catch the men as they rose and fell against the horizon. We leant far over the rail to catch every detail of the sag and pull of the nets. . . . By a crazy piece of luck a whale—the living symbol of laboured energy and heavy seas—came alongside in the middle of it and took its share of the catch. It ran along the incoming nets and shook the herring free with its tail, lumbering through the storm like ourselves.'[19]

Grierson sensed that the shots from the bridge would have been useless without the intimate details of energy and effect. There was similar reasoning behind some of the other added detail. The night scene of the deep-sea monsters was shot in a tank at the Plymouth Marine Biological Research Station. Because herring will not live in tanks and cannot be brought in alive anyhow, they used roach from a local pond, made to swim, and swim hard, by a strong jet of water at one end of the tank. The dogfish and congers and sharks were similarly filmed in tanks. For the scenes in which congers and dogfish plough through the shoals they used baby congers and baby dogs so as not to give the show away among the shoals of roach hardly a finger long.

Shooting was completed towards the end of November and Grierson was back in London, facing the task of editing some twenty thousand feet of film. A contract for technical services, including the developing of the negative and printing of rushes, had been made with New Era Productions whose chairman, Gordon Craig, had expressed to Stephen Tallents his view that the production was in a mess and should be abandoned. Grierson asked if he could speak personally to Craig and presumably reassured him as the production went forward. He had now moved to a basement flat in Belsize Park and it was here that the editing began.

Grierson had only a theoretical experience of film editing. He was to live for months with the strips of film hung round his room on clothes

52

pegs. He was to learn that, with a film so loosely scripted as *Drifters* had inevitably been, editing was a case of choosing, trying, discarding and choosing again, creating effects of speed, effects of energy, or the quiet moments when the poetry of man against the sky would be felt. He had deliberately kept off story, hoping that he would get sufficient variety and sufficient point in the actual life of the herring fleet to make it grow into a living thing. Charles Dand, now also in London with his wife Mona (a fellow student of Grierson's at Glasgow University), visited him regularly and was invited to comment on the sequences as they were assembled and run through the projector.[20] Grierson had a lot to learn, and learn he did, driven by desperation to make a success of the film.

He had the help of a film editor he had met by chance in 1927 while searching for film material for the E.M.B. Margaret Taylor, who was to become his wife, was working as a secretary in the office of Blunt and McCormack at 12 Charing Cross Road. The company had made films, including a series on Cabinet Ministers, for the Conservative Party and—of more interest to Grierson—had also worked for the Express Dairy Company: the E.M.B. was contemplating a film on pedigree cattle and the marketing of milk products. J. R. Watson, a partner in the company, had known Grierson at Glasgow University. He noted the increasingly frequent visits and alerted Margaret: 'I think he's falling for you.'[21] When Blunt and McCormack moved out, Grierson took over the basement at 12 Charing Cross Road as a cutting room (rental: 7s a week). Margaret left the company and, after managing a cinema in Wood Green for some months, joined him as his assistant.

While the editing was in progress Grierson became involved in a curious diversion, the direction of puppet films, which seemed an unlikely pursuit for a man seeking realism in the cinema. A collection of marionettes built up over some two hundred years by the Italian Gorno family had been destroyed in a fire at Wembley Studios. Grierson's advice was sought by the general manager of Associated Sound Film Industries, the company owning the studios, and he suggested that instead of re-making the old puppets, new marionettes of popular film stars should be made and used in short burlesques about Hollywood. And so the Gornos made dolls of Tom Mix, Buster Keaton, John Barrymore, Gloria Swanson and the Marx Brothers (there were about a hundred) and the films were directed by Grierson and Sergei Nolbandov.[22] At least one of them, *Don Dougio Farabanca*, appeared in film society programmes. Marionettes were to become an enthusiasm of Grierson's which he would stoutly defend against all criticism.

When the editing of *Drifters* was completed in the summer of 1929 it was shown to the E.M.B.'s Film Committee. The members were startled. This was not the smooth conventional film some of them had expected. Montage was still a new conception. They found the sequences which Grierson had so painstakingly edited revolutionary and upsetting. They must come out. The committee would not be moved by Grierson's persuasive eloquence. And so the director and his assistant were forced to make the changes. At Belsize Park the offending sequences—according to Grierson the best bits of the film—were removed and carefully kept in order on the pegs. The film was shown again to the committee and approved. Back in the cutting-room Grierson replaced the sections and sent Margaret off with the cutting copy to the Olympic Kine Laboratories at Acton where she cut the negative.[23] The first print was made.

It was a moment of immense significance for Grierson. Here was the product, not only of eighteen months of hard demanding work but of all he had absorbed in the first thirty years of his life. Behind it were the family's lighthouse tradition, his own service at sea, his study in America of the social use of film, his conviction that the drama on the doorstep could be as exciting as any studio confection. Failure was unthinkable.

The prestigious platform for the launching of new work in London was the Film Society, founded in 1925 with Ivor Montagu, Sidney Bernstein, Lord David Cecil, Julian Huxley, Maynard Keynes, George Bernard Shaw and H. G. Wells among its founder members. E. McKnight Kauffer, the artist who designed many of the E.M.B.'s most striking posters, was a member of the Society's Council. Ruttmann's *Berlin*, Alberto Cavalcanti's *Rien que les Heures* and Pudovkin's *Mother* and *The End of St. Petersburg* had been among the films shown at the Sunday afternoon performances, held originally at the New Gallery, Regent Street, and later at the Tivoli in the Strand. These were exciting occasions when new films challenged conventional conceptions of what might be achieved in the still young medium of the cinema.

When it was suggested to Grierson that *Drifters* might be shown by the Film Society he said cheerfully 'Yes, as long as I come first.' 'Why, of course,' they said, '*Potemkin* is the big picture.' Grierson knew what he was doing—and so did Eisenstein, who was present for the performance, held on 10 November 1929, and who could sense how much his film had influenced Grierson's creative editing. 'Why,' said Eisenstein to Grierson, 'you must know all about *Potemkin*.' 'Foot by foot and cut by cut', said Grierson, with his New York experience in mind.[24] The newspapers had been built up to expect from *Potemkin* a new revelation of film techniques: although the film was known by reputation this was its first public performance in Britain. But the edge was taken off the revelation by the discovery of *Drifters*.

According to the *Birmingham Post* the film was 'rapturously received by the sophisticated audience' while the *Daily News* considered it had 'more real art than the much-belauded Russian picture'. The praise of the daily newspaper critics was echoed in the weeklies. 'I am far more pleased with this night in the North Sea than by all the Nights in the Underworld of a thousand narrative films', said the *Saturday Review* while the *Spectator* considered that *Drifters* 'is unquestionably the best British film which has been made. . . . The construction is admirable and the photography is not only an artistic achievement but at times it must have been a *physical* achievement.' Grierson knew how true this was.

There were many more reviews welcoming the film and its director. Grierson's faith in his film and in the stand he had taken were justified. One analysis in particular was important for him. It was by Robert Herring in *Life and Letters Today*. He wrote that *Drifters* 'does more than tell a story; it gets through to the impulses behind a story, revealing them in image and rhythm, limited neither to things as they are nor to things as we see them, but to things as they make themselves felt in the mind. Since all this exists in life, there is no need for a story. Mr. Grierson has followed a fishing fleet; he has entered into the life and outlook of the men by being there, not as a cameraman so much as a man using a camera to express what it means when men go out in drifters. The film lays before us, it makes us feel, all the conflicting elements that go to make up their work. The very source of cinema is conflict; light interrupted by an object. Without this primary conflict there could be no film, and without a film built on a sense of conflict there can be no good cinema.'[25]

Drifters had scored a *succès d'estime* and discerning critics like Herring were conscious of the approach which Grierson was now to build into a movement. Almost immediately, helped by the enthusiastic reception given to it by the film trade reviewers, notably Aubrey Flanagan in *Today's Cinema*, the film went into a public cinema—the huge Stoll in Kingsway—on 9 December and was later widely shown throughout Britain.

'Drifters'

Stephen Tallents sat beside Grierson at the Film Society showing and was delighted and relieved by the reception. To find a comparable relief from official anxiety, he said, he had to go back to a day in February 1918, when, having helped Lloyd George and Beveridge to frame the country's food-rationing scheme, he saw the ending of the food queues.[26] The public triumph was Grierson's. The quiet man who had made it possible was content.

John Grierson and Sir Stephen Tallents.
A cartoon by Emmwood in the *Radio Times*

5 The Documentary Movement

How to build on success? Stephen Tallents thought that the obvious thing would have been for Grierson to start another film of his own. Grierson thought otherwise. He advised that the right line was to build up a small school of film-makers to work in the field he had begun to explore. In the pursuit of his objective Grierson set aside personal ambition. He believed it was more important to create opportunities for others to make films—and therefore to have many more films—than to concentrate his energy and effort on directing them himself. It was a deliberate choice, to be later as often misrepresented as it was misunderstood. When ignorant critics referred to him as a 'one film man' he shrugged it off. There was much bigger achievement ahead of him: achievement which would involve thousands of film-makers.

He did not have long to wait before he was approached by the first of what was to be a long procession of eager young tyros. Among those who saw *Drifters* at its first performance were Basil Wright, Arthur Elton, Paul Rotha and Edgar Anstey. They were all greatly excited by what they had seen. Wright, just down from Cambridge where he had made some amateur films, spent the next two days trying to reach Grierson, unaware that there was a letter in the post from Grierson asking him to have a talk. He had seen a film by Wright at an amateur festival and was sharply critical of it.

When they met and Grierson had invited him to join the E.M.B. Wright asked 'What's the E.M.B.?' Grierson: 'Young man, if you want to work with me you should be better briefed.' He offered him £2 a week. Wright joined just before Christmas 1929, and was set the task of making, from some old instructional footage about cocoa, a four-minute film which would sell the idea that cocoa came from one of the great British colonies, the Gold Coast. It was not to cost more than £7! Wright's prentice production was the pioneer of a series of poster films which were shown on continuous projectors in railway stations.[1]

The success of *Drifters*, now beginning to earn revenue from cinema

57

The Documentary Movement

showing, had not brought an overnight transformation at the E.M.B. There was very little money for paying wages, hiring premises, purchasing equipment. For a time editing—and everything else—was done in two small rooms, and a lavatory/projection booth. The films were shown on a square of blotting paper. It was in this primitive setting, in Dansey Yard off Wardour Street, that Grierson and Wright worked with Victor Turin, preparing the English version of *Turksib* with its revolutionary use of exploding titles to heighten the drama of the uncompleted Turkestan–Siberian railway. It was here too that another of Grierson's ideas, a film on the pioneering development of Canada, began to take shape. For it Grierson persuaded Hollywood companies, particularly Paramount, to give him the use of material from such films as *The Covered Wagon*, *The Iron Horse* and *Pony Express* from which he and Wright made *Conquest*. The material was North American but the editing style was wholly Russian.

From Dansey Yard, where Wright was joined by J. D. Davidson, the cameraman from New Era, and John Taylor, Margaret's brother, who had left school in his sixteenth year, the little unit moved to two rooms, not much larger, on the top floor at 179 Wardour Street. I cannot recall ever again seeing so many people working in so small a space. They appeared to be on layers, those on the top having their heads out of the skylight windows. By now the unit had grown. Arthur Elton, who had read English literature and psychology at Cambridge and written film criticism for *Granta*, had joined after some experience in the script department at Gainsborough and in Germany on a series of Anglo-German films. Also from Cambridge came the Irishman, J. N. G. Davidson, who had been editing *Granta*. Edgar Anstey, working as a junior scientific assistant in the Building Research Station at the Department of Scientific and Industrial Research, was looking for something more creative to do and thought that the E.M.B. would give him the opportunity he sought.

Paul Rotha, meeting Grierson in a coffee shop in Gerrard Street, told him he was the author of *The Film Till Now* and that he would like to work with him. There were others: Marion Grierson, his youngest sister, who did work for the Travel Association, Evelyn Spice whom she had met when they had been together on newspapers in Regina, Donald Taylor whom she was later to marry, Adrian Jeakins, the cameraman, and the boys, Jonah Jones, Chick Fowle and Fred Gamage. Stuart Legg was to come later and add his individual gifts to the movement. So also was Harry Watt.

But it was hardly yet a movement. Grierson himself had a clear

58

conception of the social use of film and where he wanted to go. For him documentary was never an adventure in film-making at all but an adventure in public observation. 'The basic force behind it', as he wrote later, 'was social and not aesthetic. It was a desire to make a drama from the ordinary to set against the prevailing drama of the extraordinary: a desire to bring the citizen's eye in from the ends of the earth to the story, his own story, of what was happening under his nose. . . . I liked the idea of an art where the dramatic factors depended exactly on the depth with which information was interpreted. I liked the notion that, in making films of man in his modern environment, one would be articulating the corporate character of that environment and finding again, after a long period of sloppy romanticism and the person in private, an aesthetic of the person in public.'[2]

Grierson gave full credit to Tallents who 'marked out the habitation and the place for our new teaching of citizenship and gave it a chance to expand'. Tallents in turn said of Grierson that he 'fused and welded the eager and miscellaneous concourse—internally often an argumentative crew but in their outward front united—into an enthusiastic, hard-working and single-minded company'.[3]

During 1930, as Tallents and Grierson won approval for a larger expenditure on production, something like a programme of films began to emerge. For some members of the unit at least the days of endlessly editing material from other films was over and they could go out with a camera. Basil Wright, who had made a compilation film about Canadian timber, *Lumber*, with a score by Dennis Arundel, directed *The Country Comes to Town*, on the virtues of home-grown food, and later, on Walter Elliot's sheep farm in the Borders, *O'er Hill and Dale* (he preferred the title *Shepherd's Spring*). Arthur Elton went to Sutherland to make his film about salmon fishing and, while waiting to catch on film the salmon leaping the Falls of Shin, created consternation in Whitehall by sending back reel after reel of salmon-less negative. For *Shadow on the Mountain* he went to Wales to film Professor George Stapledon's experiments in producing a new strain of grass to improve sheep farming. Edgar Anstey joined an Admiralty expedition to Labrador and made *Uncharted Waters* and *Eskimo Village*. Paul Rotha was a member of the unit for some four months in 1931 during which he made a number of striking poster films before leaving to pursue an independent and highly productive path in documentary.

If Grierson expected the members of the unit to work early and late (and to be content with only the E.M.B.'s 'dog biscuits' as reward) he did not spare himself. At 2 Queen Anne's Gate Buildings, head-quarters of the E.M.B., he maintained a constant pressure to get money for films, equipment and people. In the autumn of 1929 he had rented 17 Merrick Square in Southwark, an early Victorian house on two floors with a basement. In January 1930 he married Margaret Taylor. There was no public announcement and for a year or more the members of the unit, who had been urged by Grierson to lead a monastic life, were unaware that Miss Taylor, who gave so many of them their first lessons in film editing, was indeed Mrs. Grierson. They were devoted to her and often found her gentle, understanding sympathy a balm for the wounds Grierson would inflict in his urgent, driving demands. They came to know the house in Merrick Square well. Editing was often done in the basement. If Grierson were ill in bed a projector would be placed in his room and he would comment with his customary forthrightness on the shortcomings of rushes or rough-cuts.

Grierson had begun to write film criticism regularly in June 1929, when his first article, 'They Now Converse', appeared in the Socialist monthly, the *Clarion*. He was in good company: Bernard Shaw, Bertrand Russell, G. D. H. Cole, Humbert Wolfe, Mary Agnes Hamilton and Storm Jameson were frequent contributors. The Labour politicians he met in a restaurant in Craig's Court at the top of White-hall. Among them was John Scanlon, private secretary to John Wheatley, who kept him in touch with the activities of the Independent Labour Party. He was to continue to write for the *Clarion* and the *New Clarion* until the summer of 1932. In October 1931 he added to his regular writing a weekly article for *Everyman* and later contributed weekly to *New Britain*.

Any critic who had produced this flow of witty, stimulating, in-formed writing might have felt that in this alone he had justified himself. Caroline Lejeune was to write in the *Observer*: 'There was never any nonsense about Grierson; no one could fool him; neither the small, undeveloped talent, nor the big meretricious bluff escaped him. Apart from his work as a film producer, he has written some of the most sensible and penetrating comments on films ever committed to British journalism.'[4] The American critic, Warren Nolan, wrote in the *New York Telegram*: 'I believe Jean Nathan, Aldous Huxley, Carl Van Vechten, and such consistently brilliant gentlemen, should write less about the cinema, for they know nothing of it. John Grierson knows more about motion pictures as a medium and as a force than any writer I have read. He is a Scotchman. He is profound.'[5]

The Documentary Movement

For Grierson it was a by-product of his other work but it never read as such. His analysis of the clowns of the screen, and of Chaplin in particular, was brilliant. When he discussed how Hollywood looked at life he was writing of what he knew. He gave Hollywood credit for getting into its however limited picture of reality more details of ordinary life than appeared in the films of any other country. He relished Ernst Lubitsch and René Clair, detected the hitch in the early Hitchcock, wrote of Anthony Asquith's *Dance Pretty Lady* 'a more cynical and shameful waste of time I cannot imagine', and failed to respond to Greta Garbo (in *The Rise of Helga*): 'I say she is surely a frigid lady, this: making love with the enthusiasm of a codfish in the Arctic.' In these few years of regular film criticism his writing sparkled. It was compulsive reading for any film critic seeking a demonstration of how to come to terms aesthetically with a popular art. I was not the only critic at the time who never willingly missed one of his articles.

My first meeting with Grierson was early in 1930. I had written a review of *Drifters*, supplemented with some personal information about the director, given to me by his mother at Malleny Grove, Balerno, while his sister Ruby sought to restrain her: 'You were told not to say that.' On his next visit to Edinburgh he stormed into the office of the *Scotsman* and demanded in a voice which still retained its Chicago cutting-edge: 'Where's Hardy?' The voice seemed even louder in the cathedral calm of the reporters' room, especially when it came from someone talking to the youngest member of the staff. He was impatient when I suggested we should continue the conversation in the comparative privacy of a coffee shop. It was the beginning of a long friendship. As each new film was completed he would arrange for me to see it, either in London or in Edinburgh. Whenever there was an advance, or a reverse in fortunes, at the E.M.B. I would learn of it and comment accordingly.

This was part of a country-wide pattern, part of Grierson's policy. In London Caroline Lejeune was writing about Grierson and the E.M.B. film unit almost every week in the *Observer*, pointing out that 'there is no other practical workshop than the Empire Marketing Board in which a film apprentice can learn his job with a mixture of imagination and hard common-sense.'[6] W. A. J. Lawrence in *The Times*, Cedric Belfrage in the *Sunday Express* and Aubrey Flanagan in *Today's Cinema* were other London-based writers to whom Grierson could turn with confidence. William Jeffrey, Grierson's fellow student at the university, was on the *Glasgow Herald*. Ernest Dyer wrote for the *Newcastle Chronicle*, Charles Davy for the *Yorkshire Post* and Robert Herring for the *Manchester Guardian*. Grierson was a skilful propagandist; but there would have been little response to his methods had we not respected the man and what he was doing.

Grierson was moving constantly about the country, talking to audiences everywhere about the work of the Empire Marketing Board. Some lectures were to the film societies being organised in the larger cities on the model of the Film Society in London, on whose council Grierson was now serving. He spoke to the Film Society of Glasgow on 14 December 1930, when *Conquest* was shown with *Potemkin*. Earlier that year he had been at an Easter conference of the National Union of Students in Cambridge. The subject of the conference was 'Modern Tendencies'. Bertrand Russell was speaking about education and Grierson about the cinema. He was met at the station by Trevor Lloyd (he was to know him later as a scientist in Canada). Grierson asked him 'Can you get me a projector somewhere?' Lloyd said he probably could and asked why. Grierson replied 'I've brought a couple of films with me and I'd like to run them after my talk. I don't think we should announce the titles because I've just smuggled them into the country from France in my suitcase. They've never been shown in Britain and the less said about them the better.'[7] They were *Storm Over Asia* and *Turksib*. These were only two of scores of such missionary occasions all over Britain.

Grierson's yearning to return to North America was satisfied in February 1931, when the E.M.B. sent him to Canada. He sailed on a Cunarder and was in action immediately, making critical observations in the kitchens. The eggs came from France; the vegetables, fruits and canned goods from the United States. The cooks told him that other countries put their vegetables aboard washed and properly prepared. Was there not a lesson in marketing for us here, he asked Stephen Tallents in a note from New York.

Grierson had with him a bundle of introductory letters to ministers and newspaper editors from William G. Noxon, Agent-General in the British Isles for the Ontario Government. He was described in them as 'a Scotchman and a Cambridge [*sic*] man and now Chief Film Officer of the Empire Marketing Board, who is visiting Canada with a view to seeing in what way they could use some of our film work for the advantage and benefit of trade between the two countries'. His main purpose was to see Frank Badgley, head of the Canadian Government Motion Picture Bureau who had seen something of the working of the E.M.B. when he visited Britain in 1928. This pioneer among government film organisations had been established in 1917 as a branch of the Canadian Department of Trade and Commerce. It had developed a highly effective network of outlets, reaching an audience of twenty-five million in North America each year. Grierson wrote to Tallents that the Bureau's equipment 'made our Unit seem a very poor relation indeed. . . . In cinema qualities we have not so much to learn on this side, but on the equipment side and in the creation and management of circulation we have almost everything.'[8] The connection with Badgley was to extend over the next decade.

For the E.M.B. the visit was highly productive. Grierson discussed with the president of the National Research Council the possibility of various scientific films. He noted Canadian subjects he thought would make good films, especially exploration and development in the Arctic and sub-Arctic territories—subjects he was not to forget ten years later. He met some of the newspaper editors (it would have been out of character if he hadn't) and reported to Tallents their plea for the transmission of less sentimental old-country matter and more concrete stuff about Britain's modern scientific and industrial achievements. He had been asked to report on the strength of the nationalistic spirit in Canada and especially the strength of the English spirit in Toronto. Against the background of his Chicago experience he noted that the melting-pot process in the United States had not been repeated in Canada, largely because the French-Canadian initiative in maintaining an ethnic cultural identity had encouraged the other groups—Ukranians, Italians, Greeks, Scots—to retain theirs also.

Grierson returned with seventeen new films for the growing non-theatrical library at the E.M.B. and 15,000 feet of positive film as editing material for the unit. Tallents had no doubt that the visit had been worth while.[9] Immediately it gave Grierson fresh enthusiasm. For his future it was a significant pointer.

Not long after his return in the early summer Grierson received a telephone call from Frances Flaherty in Berlin. Robert Flaherty had hoped to make a film about the Russian woman but had failed to get entry into Russia or to raise finance for the project. Grierson invited him to come to London as an instructor in photography for the unit, with the understanding that he would also make a film about the English countryside.

And so Flaherty, the Flaherty of *Nanook* and *Moana*, joined the E.M.B. Unit, 'the ugly ducklings of Wardour Street' in Cedric Belfrage's phrase who, Grierson apart, had still to complete a film. It was a situation rich and strange and held a potential danger, as

63

Grierson well knew. He was familiar with Flaherty and his work, was aware of the gulf between his romantic approach and the documentary of social realism, and knew that his shooting methods absorbed miles of film and small mountains of money. The risks for a modestly financed government organisation like the E.M.B. were considerable; but if the arrangement worked, how great the rewards might be!

Basil Wright, at work on *The Country Comes to Town*, his first film, was sent off with Flaherty to Devon for ten days. They were diverted *en route* as Flaherty discovered cricket and wanted the game explained to him. The explanation was leisurely, as fitted a leisurely game as well as Flaherty's temperament. On location Flaherty never told Wright what to do but he would look at what Wright was shooting and would say things about the trees, the landscape, and the animals and almost unconsciously he began to convey to Wright the way to look at things through the camera, to make the camera the extension of the eye. Such teaching, indirect though it was, Wright was never to forget.[10]

When Flaherty went off to the English Midlands to begin his search for craftsmanship he was accompanied by John Taylor as his assistant and J. P. R. Golightly who had been engaged by Grierson as a production manager and who was to become much more, both to Grierson and to the documentary film movement. To be on an expedition with Flaherty was an experience to remember. He was a large man, a host in the grand manner, and one of the best story-tellers of his time. He imposed his own leisurely tempo on everything he did. His method was to make what he called tests, leaves from a cameraman's sketch-book. Grierson found them superb to look at; but as they grew, pile upon pile, with no apparent theme emerging, he began to feel that Flaherty did not wish to bring the film to completion but was sketch-book crazy.

In the commercial film world, with an indulgent producer and limitless finance, there might have been time to wait. In the tightly controlled little world of the E.M.B., operating under the immediate eye of the Treasury, there wasn't. Grierson, alerted about what was happening by Golightly and alarmed over Flaherty's location expenses, was forced to act.

The moment of confrontation has become part of documentary mythology. Certainly it was later to be exaggerated and elaborated. In the favoured version it occurred in the Grand Hotel, Birmingham, where Grierson was having dinner with Flaherty, Golightly and John Taylor. The evening went well, as it would do in the company of two brilliant raconteurs. Eventually Grierson announced: 'By the way,

Bob, by the time we pay for this darned dinner we'll have spent the budget for the film. Your number's up.' Flaherty said he would not go on unless he got the promise of more money. Grierson: 'I accept your resignation Bob, as there's no more money.' Flaherty protested: 'Go down Whitehall, John, and tell them who I am.' Grierson: 'Bob, do you know what they think you are down in Whitehall?' Flaherty: 'No.' Grierson: 'They think you're a photographer, one of those chaps you see working on holiday beaches.' Flaherty stood up, raising both fists to the skies, speechless with rage, until merciful release came with 'Oh fuck them, fuck them.'

According to John Taylor, the crisis over expenditure occurred later, in Derby, where, at the end of a day's shooting, Golightly phoned London to be told that the E.M.B.'s budget had been cut.[11] The work was not abandoned. Grierson himself went out and shot at steelworks. Other shooting was done by Basil Wright and Arthur Elton. Grierson was well aware of the quality of Flaherty's shooting. One of his tests was of a man making a pot. Grierson considered it 'the quintessance of Flaherty' and it became a separate film, *The English Potter*. Five other short films were made from Flaherty's tests and Grierson later claimed that 'we . . . in fact got more from our turn with Flaherty than anyone else ever did.'[12]

Industrial Britain was eventually completed, edited by Edgar Anstey under Grierson's supervision. They worked at Merrick Square while Grierson was ill, using a hand-wound projector in the basement and occasionally in his bedroom. It was the key film in a group known as the Imperial Six which were sold for distribution to Gaumont–British. The E.M.B. equipment did not include sound recording and Grierson had to accept what the distributors offered—Donald Calthrop as commentator, his thin, high-pitched, West End actory voice out of the spirit of Flaherty's splendid shooting in *Industrial Britain* and inappropriate also for the style of the other films in the series: *The Country Comes to Town, O'er Hill and Dale, Upstream, The Shadow on the Mountain* and *King Log*, a version of *Lumber*, re-edited by Marion Grierson. The films were, however, widely shown. Coupled with Grierson's ceaseless propagandising, in Whitehall, in the public prints and in lectures all over the country, they demonstrated that documentary was something more than a theory.

As for the theory, Grierson had begun to give formal expression of the 'First Principles in Documentary' in articles he wrote for *Cinema Quarterly*, the journal which Norman Wilson and I founded in Edinburgh and in which Basil Wright and Paul Rotha also wrote regularly. He analysed the uses being made of natural material in the cinema, moving from the speedy snip-snap of the newsreel, through the interest films with their frequent beauty and skill in exposition, to arrangement, re-arrangement and creative shaping of natural material, i.e., the documentary. To him the choice of the documentary medium was as gravely distinct a choice as the choice of poetry instead of fiction. Documentary, he said, must master the material on the spot and come in intimacy to ordering it; and, rejecting the surface description of a subject, it must explosively reveal the reality of it. He drew a distinction between romantic documentary and realist documentary which had given itself the job of making poetry where no poet had gone before it and which required not only taste but also inspiration.[13]

In his first contribution to *Cinema Quarterly* (Autumn 1932) Grierson described a visit he had paid to the Aran Islands to see Flaherty. 'The pre-Christian fort of Dun-Aengus hung above his cottage, opening its great concentric half-circles over a high cliff to the Atlantic. The rock flats above him, the fields built over the rock with patient hand-gatherings of soil, the white smoke clouds from the iodine fires, the natives in home-spun, tam o'shanters and oxhide pampooties, and the curraghs upturned on the shore, indicated for any one who knew Flaherty's work the essentials of his latest scenario. He introduced me to his boatman, who was also his hero, and to his kitchen-maid, who was also his heroine. Brighide, the fine, dark-eyed old lady who whirled the large Irish spinning wheel by his door, suggested a curse in the last reel but one—the curse implied in everything Flaherty makes—on things new-fangled and unnecessary, on everything destructive of the ancient dignities she represented. The overhanging fort of Dun-Aengus, with its twenty centuries or so of primitive power, was clearly a chosen presence: integral to the set.'[14]

Grierson spent a few weeks with Flaherty. They went on a shark-hunting expedition on a Brixham trawler. They didn't succeed in finding any sharks but in various small hotels up the west coast Grierson and Flaherty sat up late talking and drinking, so the expedition was not unproductive. They were great talkers.[15]

Grierson was to write often about Flaherty and always in appreciation of his great and remarkable virtues as a film-maker. He thought of him as one of the five great innovators in the history of film—with Meliès, Griffith, Sennett and Eisenstein. He gave him credit for being the first to seize on the enormous powers of the motion-picture camera to observe nature and the natural.

With these and many other tributes on record over many years, it was disturbing to find later references to antagonism between the two men. Grierson tended to ignore them but on one occasion, when reviewing Arthur Calder-Marshall's biography of Flaherty, *The Innocent Eye*, was prompted to comment on the reported differences.

'The differences were, of course, all rooted in our difference of economic approach', he wrote. 'Much as I loved him, I was totally unsympathetic with his quixotic hope that he would get from the industry what I knew it could not and would not give him. I hated waiting for the inevitable disturbances and the inevitable crash. The trouble was that for all his good taste he liked being in the big time and was therefore vulnerable. Other troubles too. One was that the story-telling talent of the great raconteur failed him as soon as he became exposed to the discursive pleasures of the camera-in-itself. Worst trouble of all, his approach to a budget was haphazard to say the least. He had an apparently innocent belief—I didn't think it was innocent—that there was always more money where that first lot came from.'[16] Grierson had had first-hand experience of this with *Industrial Britain*.

Grierson's writing gave *Cinema Quarterly* critical authority. He was uncompromising in his criticism of the publication when he thought it was lowering its standards. In a letter to me he dismissed an article on montage as 'Baby stuff. A statement of the obvious, a beating of dead dogs.' The reviews he thought were 'much too enthusiastic for a tough world. I ask you to look over some of the phrases in cold blood. The number of "brilliants" and "delights" are a pain in the neck.' He was coldly furious on the telephone when we allowed a heading, 'Let's Be Perverts', to appear on an article. He thought we should have recourse to the professors to build up the body of the magazine. 'There aren't half-a-dozen names in actual film criticism to play with. I suggest the academes for lack of anything better but also for the authority they would give you.'[17]

That suggestion we did act on and Herbert Read, then Professor of Fine Art at Edinburgh University, wrote with elegant authority on 'Poet and the Film' and 'Experiments in Counterpoint'. Grierson himself took his ideas to the universities. There was a series of weekly lectures, for example, at University College, Leicester, on 'The Art of the Cinema and its Social Relationships'.

Grierson was keeping in close touch with the film society movement. He played a leading part in the first attempt to found a British Federation of Film Societies at Welwyn in August 1932. Among those attending were Charles Oakley and Norman Wilson from Scotland and, from Birmingham, Stanley Hawes who was later to work in documentary with him. On the Sunday of the weekend conference Grierson said to me: 'We'd better get *The Observer*.' Caroline Lejeune had headed her column 'The Documentary Fetish' and had attacked Grierson as 'a dangerous influence'.[18] He told me the reason for this extraordinary *volte face*. Her article was written out of loyalty to her husband who had just been sacked from the unit.

By now the E.M.B. Film Unit had moved to larger premises, with a viewing theatre, at 37–39 Oxford Street, round the corner from Wardour Street. As the activity expanded so did the number of hours worked grow, with Grierson sitting on the back of his chair (to give him extra height?) in his corner room, cracking a long whip like a devilish ring-master. Golightly, whom he once described as 'the quiet eye at the storm centre', would organise the daily showing of rushes. A director would inform Golightly that the rushes were spooled and ready to be seen and the word would be passed to Grierson.

Suddenly his door would be thrown open and he would come hurtling along the passageway and into the theatre, followed by Golightly. He would sit down and say 'Right. Shoot.' His comments could be blistering and were not in any way restrained if a stranger were present. I heard them once, with some embarrassment. His authority was accepted without question. As unquestioningly the members of the unit would work every hour there was, sometimes sleeping on the cutting-room floor, to cope with a rush job. When the working day did end it continued in talk at the unit's favourite pub, latterly the Highlander in Dean Street.

The senior members of the unit were now all directing their own films, some of them for outside bodies, in itself an indication of a growing development. Stuart Legg made a film for the Chesterfield Education Authority, *The New Generation*, and started editing the material which would become *Coal Face*. Arthur Elton, with a flair for technical and scientific subjects, completed a five-reel account of aeroplane engines, *Aero-Engine*, and undertook *The Voice of the World* for the H.M.V. company. Donald Taylor made *Spring Comes to England* for the Ministry of Agriculture and, for the Travel Association, a film on the changing landscape of Lancashire, *Lancashire at Work and Play*. Marion Grierson, also for the Travel Association, made a memorable film on Edinburgh, *The Key to Scotland*. Harry Watt completed *Six Thirty Collection* and *B.B.C.–Droitwich* which Anstey had largely directed before he left to form the Shell Film Unit in accordance with a brief commissioned by Shell from Grierson.

Basil Wright went to the West Indies to shoot material for the

E.M.B. and the Orient Line. Two fine films resulted, *Cargo for Jamaica* and *Windmill in Barbados*. Some material which Grierson had shot for a film, never completed, on the Port of London was used by Wright in *Cargo for Jamaica*.

In addition to controlling this steadily growing volume of film-making Grierson took time to direct another film himself. He went off on the *Isabella Greig* out of Granton, to make *Granton Trawler*. The weather on the Viking Bank between the Shetlands and the Norwegian coast was more than usually rough and Grierson, for the first and perhaps the only time in his life was, if not seasick, at any rate sick of the sea. But he did not give up: he couldn't as he was shooting the film himself. He was using a tripod, as he insisted all E.M.B. camera-men should, and, with the tripod falling over in the stormy weather, the camera was gyrating all over the place. When he returned to London and looked at the material he was gloomy: he had had a plan but hadn't been able to work to it. 'See what you can do with it', he said to Edgar Anstey.

Anstey, himself somewhat despondent about the material, looked at it again and began to make some interesting discoveries. When the camera had fallen over it had been left running and there were re-markable shots of the sky giving place to the deck of the boat and the horizon rising and disappearing overhead. He found that with this material he could create a storm in film terms irrespective of what the reality had been. It was a classic illustration of two of Grierson's theories: you make the film from the material and not the words in which you first expressed the idea; and you let the film grow in the way it wants to go. Grierson, who had not forgotten for a moment the truth of his own teaching, was delighted.[19] It was shot silent and sound was added later. It remained a favourite film with Grierson all his life. He looked on the film as a sort of requiem as the *Isabella Greig* was lost at sea, sunk by German bombs when fishing, unarmed and flying the British mercantile flag, in September 1941.

Grierson was to make one other short voyage on the *Isabella Greig*. In 1934 Julian Huxley persuaded Alexander Korda to finance a short film about the gannet, stipulating only that it should have the title *The Private Life of the Gannets*. He lent Osmond Borrodaile to photograph it and, with Ronald M. Lockley, Huxley shot it on Grassholm. He asked Grierson to shoot the slow motion sequence of gannets diving for fish which forms the film's spectacular climax. With John Taylor as cameraman and a cargo of herring and mackerel, Grierson sailed from Granton on the *Isabella Greig*. They were bound for the Farne Islands but got no further than the Bass Rock in the Firth of Forth before the gulls and the gannets thundered down on them. They threw the herring overboard and that took care of the gulls; but every fourth shovelful was mackerel and, being heavier, they sank faster and out of reach of the gulls, concentrating the deeper diving gannets in their thousands. The cameraman got it first time.[20] A job expected to take a week was over in an afternoon. *The Private Life of the Gannets* went on to win an Oscar in Hollywood in 1937.

The Empire Marketing Board, Grierson was to write, 'was a fine chance to make films of ordinary people and the dignities of life in our time. Taking that line, we could have gone on for ever, "bringing alive" to each other the members of our Commonwealth of Nations. The materials were young, dramatic and inexhaustible. With imagination enough, machinery and support enough, one could, on such a commission, have sighted the eyes and established the sentiments of a generation. Propaganda, in our view, is not just a general storming of the imagination, nor are men like Goebbels, for all their powers of organisation, very good. The large gaps of mental distance are made up of an infinite number of smaller gaps. Propaganda, on any considered theory, may be a quiet matter of section speaking to section, specialist to specialist, whether the specialist is a scientist, a fight fan, or a philatelist. Bringing Britain and the Empire alive meant this; and it meant dramatic gambits as various as bringing the countryman alive to the townsman and the research station to the worker. Truth, in the corporate conception, has many facets.'[21]

Whether or not the E.M.B. Film Unit could have gone on for ever is a matter for speculation. Certainly the opportunities were rich and various and would have continued to be, even if, or because, the nature of the relationship between Britain and the Empire (or Commonwealth) was undergoing major changes. In the short period of the movement's existence Grierson had progressed towards his objective of social realism. As he attempted to deal in depth with some subjects he would have been limited or frustrated, as a producer dependent on Government sponsorship. With this constraint the documentary film could not be, in a real sense, 'an instrument of the working class'.

Paul Rotha, whose achievement in documentary complemented Grierson's during the thirties, noted that 'the E.M.B. films of Britain avoided the major issues provoked by their material. That was inevitable under their powers of production. The real economic issues underlying the North Sea herring catch, the social problems inherent in any film dealing seriously with the industrial Midlands, lay outside the scope of a unit organised under a government department and having as its aim "the bringing alive of the Empire". The directors concerned knew this, and wisely, I think, avoided any economic or important social analysis. Instead they contented themselves with attempting a simple statement of facts, dramatising the action material of their themes, but leaving untouched the wider human fulfilments of the job.'[22]

The economic climate in Britain was becoming cold, too cold for the survival of even such promising growths as the E.M.B. The Ottawa Conference of 1932 had made it clear that each member of the Empire must stand by itself in weathering the Depression. Canada, South Africa and the Irish Free State had opposed even a consultative body on economic questions of common interest. The Board's life ended officially on 30 September 1933.

But it was not to be the end of government film-making in Britain. Sir Stephen Tallents (he had been knighted in 1932) was invited by Sir Kingsley Wood, who had succeeded Clement Attlee as Postmaster General, to join the staff of the Post Office. Tallents said he would be happy to do so but would come with much better heart if he could bring with him the Film Unit and Film Library. Kingsley Wood agreed, subject to Treasury consent, and Tallents gave up his holiday that summer to see the transfer through.[23] There had been an approach made to Grierson from a commercial source to take over the unit and everything else. For Grierson, given the relationship he had established between film-making and public affairs, that was unthinkable. He grasped the G.P.O. eagerly 'for the story of communications was as good as any other and in one sense it was better . . . we had at least the assurance of imaginative backing.'[24]

John Grierson in the 1930s.
A cartoon by Max Anderson
from *World Film News*

6 G.P.O. Film Unit

When Grierson and his unit moved to the General Post Office, the documentary movement was steadily gaining momentum. It could be measured in many ways: the growing acceptance of the documentary idea, the increasing number of film-makers, the growth of the audience outside the cinemas, the stimulus to experiment in the technique of a new art, and the interest being shown by overseas countries in the British example. Grierson's personal activities were multiplying. He was arguing the case for documentary in public and in print; he was allied with Tallents in talks with politicians and public relations officers; and he was the driving force behind the creative effort.

Grierson was aware of resistance if not antagonism in the film trade. He had had an early taste of it when Sir Gordon Craig had attempted to halt the production of *Drifters*. That there was still antagonism in and around Wardour Street became apparent when evidence was given to the Select Committee on Estimates, whose report was published on 2 July 1934. Paul Rotha[1] believes that the inquiry was prompted by the film trade, the British Film Institute and the Conservative Party, each of which had reasons for seeking the suppression of Grierson's unit: the film trade because the economical production of films by a government agency was resented; the Film Institute because it envied the non-theatrical distribution which Grierson had fostered; and the Conservative Party because of suspicion about the radical emphasis in the films emerging from the movement.

In its recommendations the Select Committee sought to limit the activities of the G.P.O. Film Unit to the advertisement of Post Office services. They objected to the making and distribution of films by government departments as being unfair competition with the trade. They urged that the British Film Institute should co-operate with the industry in sponsoring the making of certain types of 'cultural' films rather than that a government department should enter the field of commercial enterprise. 'The continuance and the expansion of the G.P.O. Film Unit would practically stultify the British Film Institute and its functions.'

72

G.P.O. Film Unit

Involved in 'this skein of intrigue and manoeuvre', according to Paul Rotha, was 'a small group of politicians and film trade men who were determined to get rid of Tallents and Grierson and their concept of the documentary film'.[2] The opposition was certainly there and it was to surface at intervals; but Tallents and Grierson considered that the wisest course was to counter it with positive achievement. As a buffer Sir Kingsley Wood appointed a Film Committee, with Tallents as chairman and Walter Elliot, Malcolm MacDonald, Clement Attlee and Humbert Wolfe as members. The close and friendly relations which Grierson had cultivated with the film-trade journals tempered criticism in these areas while the British Film Institute, during this early period of its existence, had little influence.

Nevertheless, Grierson had of necessity to take this latent hostility into account in what he was doing, or planning to do. In one sense he arrived at the Post Office at a fortunate moment. Sir Kingsley Wood had initiated a campaign for a new outlook and he found in Sir Stephen Tallents a man ready to implement and develop his ideas. The adoption of the Film Unit was one of a series of departures which, at more superficial levels, included greetings telegrams designed by Rex Whistler and competitions for 'The Voice of God' to record the new time signal. The call to the Film Unit was to articulate the importance of the Post Office to the public and to bring alive for its quarter of a million employees the complexities of the country's largest organisation. It was a challenge in communication which was accepted with vigour and imagination by Grierson.

There was a move to larger premises which must have suggested to the members of the unit some confidence in the film operation and its future. No. 21 Soho Square, a fine eighteenth-century mansion, originally the town house of the Lords of Fauconberg, was to be the home of the unit until the outbreak of war and was to see the production of such films as *Coal Face*, *Night Mail*, *Song of Ceylon* and *North Sea*. The total staff in February 1934 was eighteen and the unit's gross maintenance cost for the current six months was £4,159 5s. In outlay, at least, as the Select Committee had been forced to concede, it was still a very modest operation.

More important than the new office was the acquisition of a studio for sound recording at Blackheath in south-east London. It was in the process of being equipped for sound by the G.P.O. before the closure of the E.M.B. The sound, a British system in a British government studio, was less than perfect and the early films, *Coal Face* in particular, were to suffer from the inadequacies.

Grierson was excited by the prospect of having sound under their control. He had noted the few experiments made with sound in fiction films—the snatches of conversation used as a choral accompaniment for an unemployed sequence in *Three Cornered Moon* and the monotonous sound of radio police-calls sweeping across the crime of a community in *Beast of the City*. He thought the vers-librists were made for the cinema. He was stimulated by such examples as the monologues of James Joyce, covering the subjective aspects of human action, and the masked changes in Eugene O'Neill between the word spoken and the word thought.

It was while the first tentative experiments in sound were being made that Alberto Cavalcanti joined the G.P.O. Film Unit. Grierson was, of course, familiar with the work of the Brazilian-born director whose *Rien que les Heures* and *En Rade* had been shown at performances of the Film Society in London. Cavalcanti had become disillusioned by the routine comedies which he was directing in France—'talk, talk, talk'—and had come to London seeking some more rewarding kind of film-making.[3] Through his former cameraman, Jimmy Rogers, he learned of Grierson's activities and called to see him. He explained that he wished to experiment with sound. Grierson offered him work for a month or two at Blackheath. The wage of £7 a week which Cavalcanti recalls being paid was above the average for the G.P.O. directors at the time.

Cavalcanti was to stay, not for months, but for years. He knew from experience, not only about sound but also about the whole range of film-making, from short experimental works to full-length fiction films. He helped the young members of the unit to learn their trade; and he in turn found working with them stimulating. His technical knowledge supplemented Grierson's conception of the purposeful use of film. Their contributions to documentary were distinctive and different: Cavalcanti's was to film technique and his preference for the story form was eventually to emerge and to become stronger after Grierson's departure; with Grierson the purpose of a film always came first.

The two approaches were sometimes wildly out of unison, as in Cavalcanti's grotesque comedy *Pett and Pott*—although paradoxically Grierson defended the film, to Tallents and to anyone who found it unsuccessful. I recall being among its critics. Herbert Read praised its use of a large variety of asynchronous devices to heighten the comedy.[4] Humphrey Jennings, who had known Wright, Elton and Legg at Cambridge and who had just joined the unit, designed the sets. To

G.P.O. Film Unit

Cavalcanti *Pett and Pott* was a bit of fun—and probably funnier in the making than in the end product.

Those who worked with Cavalcanti valued his experienced guidance. Harry Watt held that 'British documentary films would not have advanced the way they did from then on without Cav.'s influence. . . . It must have been difficult for Grierson when we technicians more and more turned to Cavalcanti with our problems but he was honest and shrewd enough to realise how much more polished and professional our films were becoming under Cav.'[5] Grierson never underestimated or belittled Cavalcanti's contribution. He was to acknowledge it warmly on countless occasions during his life.

Grierson continued to encourage everybody to experiment with sound. *Six Thirty Collection* used nocturnal noises and conversational scraps picked up in a London sorting-office, arranged and orchestrated. Evelyn Spice's *Weather Forecast* conveyed the drama behind the gale warning.

The most ambitious of the early sound films was *Coal Face* for which Legg and Wright had shot some material but which was to become memorable for the collaboration, under Cavalcanti's direction, of W. H. Auden and Benjamin Britten. Auden, teaching at Malvern and already recognised as a significant voice of his generation, had written to Wright asking if there was a chance of a job at the G.P.O. Film Unit. Grierson, shown the letter, said 'Don't be a fool. Fetch him.' Britten joined the unit as the result of an approach made to the Royal College of Music by Grierson who asked if they had 'a bright young student who could write a little incidental music for a forthcoming film'.[6] An entry in the Post Office records (28 September 1936) shows he was employed at that time, at £8 a week, to write incidental music for *Calendar of the Year* and *The Saving of Bill Blewitt*.

Auden and Britten collaborated first on an investigation for a film on the slave trade which was not made. *Coal Face*, which also did not appear to have much connection with the Post Office, was regarded as an experiment in sound. Commentary and music were composed together and to this were added a recitative chorus of male voices and a choir of male and female voices. Auden wrote a madrigal, sung by the women as the miners return to the surface:

> Oh lurcher-loving collier, black as night,
> Follow your love across the smokeless hill,
> Your lamp is out, the cages all are still,
> Course for her heart and do not miss,

75

G.P.O. Film Unit

For Sunday soon is past, and Kate, fly not so fast
For Monday comes when none may kiss,
Be marble to his soot, and to his black be white.

The value of *Coal Face* as an experiment in sound was less than it should have been because of the indifferent quality of the recording; but it did lead to *Night Mail* and that was justification enough.

Night Mail had modest origins: a film to explain to Post Office employees how the postal special travelling between London and Scotland worked. Grierson asked several writers to make the journey and give him their observations (my diary shows I made the trip from Edinburgh to Euston on 28 September 1934); but Basil Wright, who wrote the script, does not recall making any use of these reports. Grierson insisted that, in the film, the train journey be made from south to north (it could as well have been made in the opposite direction): he knew what crossing the border back into Scotland meant for a Scot and had a joke about being able to feel the bump on the line. Harry Watt was given the film to direct, with Chick Fowle and Jonah Jones as cameramen and Pat Jackson and, later, W. H. Auden as assistants.

When the shooting was finished and the first rough assembly was shown, Grierson was conscious of something missing. 'What we haven't got here is anything about the people who're going to get the letters. We have only the machinery of getting letters from one point to another. What about the people who write them and the people who get them?' He may have had at the back of his mind the sentiment expressed by Carl Sandburg in 'The Sins of Kalamazoo' (an impression independently confirmed in a talk between Grierson and Paul Rotha on 17 June 1970). Hugh MacDiarmid (C. M. Grieve) told me that he had accepted an invitation from Grierson to write verse for the film but having heard Auden's contribution to *Night Mail* he was relieved it had apparently been found unsuitable.

Auden wrote the verse on a trial and error basis. It had to be cut to fit the visuals, edited by R. Q. McNaughton, working with Cavalcanti and Wright. Many lines were discarded, ending as crumpled fragments in the wastepaper basket. Some of Auden's verbal images—the rounded Scottish hills 'heaped like slaughtered horses'—were too strong for the film; but what was retained made *Night Mail* as much a film about loneliness and companionship as about the collection and delivery of letters. It was that difference that made it a work of art.

Night Mail was a genuinely collaborative effort. Stuart Legg spoke the verse, timed, with Britten's music, to the beat of the train's wheels. Grierson himself spoke the moving culminating passage:

> And none will hear the postman's knock
> Without a quickening of the heart,
> For who can bear to feel himself forgotten?

Night Mail was to mark a peak of achievement for the documentary film movement inspired and led by Grierson. Everyone who worked on it took pride in its success. It was certainly to meet George Orwell's requirement: 'The first test of any work of art is survival.'[7] Some forty years after the date of its production (1936) it still had the power to hold and move a large audience.

Earlier there had been other films which, in different ways, had been as notable. Grierson sent for Wright one day and said: 'Wright, you're going to Ceylon.' Wright said he didn't want to go to Ceylon. Grierson: 'Never mind, you're going to Ceylon, so you'd better do your research.'[8] And so he spent the next two months finding out everything he could about Ceylon. An approach to Grierson had been made by Gervas Huxley, cousin of Julian Huxley, who had been organising secretary of the Empire Marketing Board Film Committee before being appointed public relations officer of the Ceylon Tea Propaganda Board. He wanted a film made about the island and its life, bringing in tea.

With John Taylor as his assistant Wright went off to Ceylon, his brief being to make four one-reel films. They shot 23,000 feet of film and took 1,000 stills. The aim, according to Wright, was 'to achieve a co-ordination of all the primary elements of Ceylon into a construction which should carry a conviction, not merely of what Ceylon now superficially is, but of what Ceylon stands for in the line of that vital history which is measured in terms of statues, monuments, religion and of human activity'.[9]

When Grierson first saw the material he told Wright to forget about the four short films, although the film was still constructed in four parts. The experimentation with sound had begun and Grierson assigned the composer Walter Leigh to work with Wright. The crossing of a chorus of market cries and a rigmarole of international commerce with a scene of Buddhist ceremonial was only one of the experiments in sound which excitingly emerged from the completed film. The tempo was deliberately slow, as indeed the magnificent visuals demanded, but also in accordance with Wright's belief that the audience should quieten its spirit and be at peace—should in contemplation bring as much to the screen as was given.

G.P.O. Film Unit

Editing completed, Wright showed *Song of Ceylon* to Grierson.'This is absolutely marvellous', he said, 'except that there's something so terrible at the end you've got to put it right.' Wright, who had been living with the film for months, was furious. After two days, when he refused to speak to anyone, he saw a way of meeting Grierson's criticism. He went back to Blackheath at midnight and, working all night, made the changes. When he showed it in the morning Grierson said: 'What did I tell you? There's absolute genius.'

Working in London with Wright was Lionel Wendt—lawyer, brilliant pianist, fine photographer—who had been his assistant and mentor in Ceylon. There had been uncertainty about what sort of commentary should be put on the film so that there would be no conflict with the poetic visuals. Passing a bookshop near the British Museum one day Wright noticed a seventeenth-century travel book about Ceylon by a Scot, Robert Knox—a book unknown to Wright who thought he had read everything published in English about Ceylon. As soon as he began to read it he saw the problem was solved.

The effect of the slightly archaic prose was heightened when spoken by Wendt in a voice of distant and almost hypnotic sweetness. The selection of Wendt as narrator was made by Wright and enthusiastically endorsed by Grierson and the recording was completed only two days before Wendt sailed back to Ceylon. Wendt kept a journal while he was in London and the entries make clear his estimate of Grierson and his contribution to the film: 'Grierson—absolute genius.' For Wright it was an important moment of creative fulfilment. I recall seeing the film privately in London with Grierson and the director, sensing their pleasure in its success and sharing in it. The pleasure was increased when, at the Brussels Film Festival in 1935, the film was awarded the Prix du Gouvernement Belge.

Documentary was beginning to move into other areas, as indeed *Song of Ceylon* exemplified. It was a movement encouraged by Grierson. It was clear to him that documentary had to go wider than the story of communications if it were to fulfil the task it had set itself. It was equally clear to the public relations officers in industry and in national organisations that documentary was something which could be of value to them. There was, therefore, a fusion of inclination and need.

It was out of this fusion that one of the other seminal films of the 1930s came. In Britain it was a time of unemployment, malnutrition and bad housing. Films could present these problems more arrestingly than any other medium. In *Workers and Jobs*, made by Arthur Elton for the Ministry of Labour, unemployed men had told in their own words what idleness meant to them and their families.

This process of direct confrontation was continued in *Housing Problems*, made by Elton and Anstey for the Gas, Light and Coke Company, whose enlightened public relations officer was A. P. Ryan. The cameraman was John Taylor and Ruby Grierson also worked on the film. Instead of using a post-recorded commentary, they took their unwieldy 35mm camera and bulky sound-recording equipment into slum houses and in one memorable case persuaded a formidable cockney woman to describe a battle she had had with a large, ferocious rat. The result was sensational. Features and leading articles in newspapers were followed by a stunned reaction from audiences, brought face to face with the grim reality of life in the slums. Investigative documentary, commonplace today with television's lightweight sound and picture equipment, was then revolutionary.

Housing Problems was followed by Anstey's film on nutritional problems, *Enough to Eat?*, sponsored by the British Commercial Gas Association whose public relations officer, S. C. Leslie, made an important contribution to social documentary through the films he commissioned. Based on Sir John Boyd Orr's report, *Homes, Food and Income*, it exposed the real state of Britain's health. Exposure was also the purpose of Basil Wright's *Children at School* which revealed the appalling conditions in so many schools in England, its direct reportage far removed in style from the lyricism of *Song of Ceylon*. With Grierson as producer, John Taylor directed *The Smoke Menace* which combined forceful narration and interviews with Professor J. B. S. Haldane to deliver its attack on the pollution of urban atmosphere.

These films were much nearer Grierson's original conception of social documentary than some of the productions which emerged from the G.P.O. Film Unit where there was the inescapable limitation of government departmental sponsorship. In them Grierson, with the help of public-spirited colleagues in industry, was practising the art of the possible. It they could have been made wholly independently of sponsorship they might have been even more outspoken; but to make them at all was an achievement, remembering that the movement towards social realism in the cinema spanned only some six years. The movement had had minimal financial support from the Government. It could not have progressed without Grierson's burning conviction and ceaseless advocacy and the political dexterity in the background of Sir Stephen Tallents.

One of the sharpest contemporary critics of the documentary film movement was Arthur Calder-Marshall. He attacked the G.P.O. Film Unit for its failure to express discontent among the Post Office workers and to criticise faults in the system.[10] He maintained that 'when a film is financed by interests other than that of the entertainment industry, the financiers are out to get results, either in sales or in states of mind. Mr. Grierson is not paid to tell the truth but to make more people use the parcel post. Mr. Grierson may like to talk about social education, surpliced in self-importance and social benignity. Other people may like hearing him. But even if it sounds like a sermon, a sales talk is a sales talk.'[11]

Seen from the slopes of an ivory tower the documentary movement no doubt would appear to have such limitations, given its professed concern with social realism. What other method than the one Grierson adopted could have achieved as much? He had established, however modestly, the principle of government support for film-making. Increasingly he was developing the formula of responsible sponsorship which was to generate millions for documentary film-making in Britain and in many areas overseas. He had founded a film school and engaged the loyalties of a generation of young film-makers. In the expensive medium of film none of this had been done without constant, unremitting effort.

Grierson had always to contend with the anomaly that the resources of state or semi-state bodies were being used to make films which, sometimes at least, indirectly criticised the way the state dealt with social-industrial-economic problems. It was a tight-rope operation. Had his radicalism emerged in the treatment of subjects in a form too extreme for the political party in power the movement would have been toppled. He was later to define his political position as being an inch to the left of whichever party was in office. In other words, he accepted his position as a servant of the government but was intent on pushing the administration, as he was later to do more openly in Canada, as far as he could towards reform. He regarded the survival of the movement as of first importance, for the hope and the potential it held.

Surveying the growth of the movement in *The Times* after the success of *Song of Ceylon* at the International Film Festival in Brussels in 1935 he said: 'The key to development was the belief of some young cinema tiros in the place remaining to be filled by the cinema in social affairs. Their task, as they saw it, was to bring into the field of the imagination the new materials and themes of our modern economy. It gave an opportunity both for social service and for an exciting adventure in the technique of a new art. . . . The artist has found his material and a decent liberty in the public service; the publicist has discovered a new and powerful voice.'[12] This was the situation as Grierson saw it in the mid-thirties.

Grierson always believed in emphasising the positive. When I had written some words of criticism on one occasion in the *Scotsman* he wrote to me: 'A better line is surely to indicate what has been achieved and is increasingly being achieved, despite the youth of the movement and its lack of every support except the goodwill of people like yourself. When you consider it from that point of view the progress is remarkable. Starting from scratch a very few years ago, with *no regard at all* in the theatres for industry, work and workmen, you have the success of Rotha's films, of our own G.B. group (*Industrial Britain* alone doing over a thousand theatres), of our *Weather Forecast* group (each one getting on to a thousand theatres) and particularly the recent circulation of *B.B.C.—The Voice of Britain*, with documentary moving up into the feature spot itself. Add to that the influence of documentary on [Andrew] Buchanan, the arrival of the parallel movement from America in *The March of Time*, and the increasing circulation of people like Mary Field, Roy Lockwood and the Travel Association, and you have an all-in circulation for this documentary approach which is far greater than anyone could have foretold three years ago, apart altogether from the non-theatrical and specialised circulation. The fact is the more impressive when you consider the sponsored origins of most of these films, and the overcoming of exhibitors' resistance in this respect.'[13]

In this letter, incidentally, Grierson gives the lie to the suggestion sometimes made that he measured the success of his films only in terms of their non-theatrical circulation. He was writing before the widespread cinema showing of *Night Mail*.

At the G.P.O. Grierson pushed the idea of communications as far as he could. One of the most ambitious films was *We Live in Two Worlds*, made in collaboration with the Swiss Post Office and directed by Cavalcanti. J. B. Priestley, who provided the narration, took Switzerland as an example of both nationalism and the new internationalism of transport and communications. Priestley thought highly of 'the earnest and enthusiastic young men who were making our documentary films, in which branch of the art we were then leading the world' and contrasted the few pounds a week they were being paid with the 'enormous sums of money being handed over by the City . . . to all manner of fantastic Central European characters.'[14]

A film which, in a modest way, was to signal a change in direction

81

for documentary was *The Saving of Bill Blewitt*. Harry Watt groaned when Grierson assigned him to make a film about the Post Office Savings Bank. 'Organised saving seemed like organised religion, and equally repulsive.'[15] He wrote a story about a fisherman's savings which was eventually filmed in Mousehole in Cornwall, with Bill Blewitt, the local postmaster, playing the leading part. This tentative experiment in the humanisation of documentary led to a more important film, *North Sea*, on the ship-to-shore radio service.

North Sea was at the planning stage when one day Cavalcanti brought Carl Dreyer to 21 Soho Square. He had met the Danish director in Paris while he had been making *The Passion of Joan of Arc*. He introduced Dreyer to Grierson who decided that he should direct *North Sea*.[16] Dreyer was given the log of the incident on which the film was to be based and wrote a script which Cavalcanti summarily rejected. The film was given to Harry Watt who wrote the script and brought to the direction of the film a real understanding of character and situation. By the time it was completed and shown (1938) Grierson and several of the senior documentary directors had left the G.P.O. Film Unit and *North Sea* in more than one sense marked a division. In a letter to me Paul Rotha wrote: '*North Sea* sets a lead to the whole industry and there are some of us in documentary who are just ready to take the step into the semi-story semi-documentary film.'[17]

But the divergence inherent in this developing preference for the story form was still some way off, although Grierson with his shrewd reading of character may have been aware of it. The G.P.O. Film Unit was still the centre of the film activity stimulated by Grierson. It had a reputation, nationally and internationally, as a film school and anyone who wanted to go into films turned first to it.

Richard Massingham, the genial doctor who turned film-maker in *Tell Me If It Hurts* and *And So To Work*, joined the unit to make *The Daily Round* for Grierson. William Coldstream was given an introduction to Grierson by Paul Rotha. At a time of great unemployment and a threatening war situation, Coldstream was questioning the social relevance of his painting—a reason which commended him to Grierson when he made his approach. According to Coldstream, 'Grierson, through his ideas and his organisation, attracted to himself some of the most remarkable of the younger generation of painters, writers and composers. They were all, I believe, drawn to the Unit for much the same reason as myself: the opportunity to work in a new medium which seemed technically and socially appropriate to the times.'[18] Benjamin Britten had been joined by Maurice Jaubert, the brilliant young composer who was to be killed fighting in 1940 when the Germans broke through into France.

Among the more exotic callers at 21 Soho Square was the New Zealand painter and great lover of jazz, Len Lye. He explained to Grierson and Cavalcanti that he had made a film without a camera by painting directly on the celluloid. Always responsive to something new and exciting, Grierson saw and, in 1935, adopted Lye's experimental film, *Colour Box*. In the same style Lye made *Rainbow Dance* and *Trade Tattoo*.

In January 1936 Grierson was adjudicator at the Scottish Amateur Film Festival in Glasgow where he saw a film, *Colour Cocktail*, by a young student at the Glasgow School of Art. Norman McLaren had been experimenting in the same area as Len Lye without being aware of Lye's work: he did not see *Colour Box* until about two years later. Grierson was immediately impressed by McLaren's *Colour Cocktail* (I was sitting beside him when he saw it) and told him that when he had completed his art course there would be a job waiting for him at the G.P.O.

McLaren paid a visit to Russia before arriving at 21 Soho Square in January 1937. He made an experimental sequence for *Mony a Pickle* and later in *Love on the Wing* gave more than a hint of the rich, imaginative flow of animation which was to come.

After McLaren had been there for about five months, working in the cutting-room with Evelyn Spice on *Weather Forecast*, Grierson called him into his office and said: 'How would you like to go to Spain as a cameraman?' Franco's forces had surrounded Madrid. McLaren, whose sympathies were with the Republicans, agreed. Grierson: 'Fine. We'll get you leave of absence for two or three weeks. You'll go with Ivor Montagu who will be directing you and your purpose is to take newsreel footage of what's going on and bring it right back. Montagu is going to edit and we are going to screen it to collect funds for the International Red Cross and the Government side.'[19] The film was completed as *The Defence of Madrid*.

McLaren's assignment was one indication of documentary's growing involvement in international affairs. Joris Ivens was already in Spain, shooting *The Spanish Earth*, and Herbert Kline was making *Heart of Spain* and *Return to Life*. Both were later to know Grierson well.

Meanwhile in Britain the scale of documentary under Grierson's influence was expanding. An approach made by Jack Beddington, director of publicity for Shell Mex and B.P., had given Paul Rotha the opportunity to make *Contact*, a major documentary, for Imperial

Airways. This in turn led Shell International to commission a report by Grierson on the use of films generally. His report was accepted. The main proposal, for the setting up of a central production unit, was endorsed by the Shell directors. Asked to recommend who should run it, Grierson suggested Edgar Anstey, who planned the first programme with Alexander Wolcough, selected and equipped premises, recruited staff and made the Shell Film Unit's first film, *Airport*.[20] Dissatisfied with the slow progress being made Anstey resigned and was succeeded by Arthur Elton whose name was to be closely linked with the unit during its most productive period and who was to give to so many of its films the personal stamp of scientific truth and ordered exposition.

Elton and Anstey, with Paul Rotha and Donald Taylor, were members of the newly formed Associated Realist Film Producers. They needed a base from which to manage the gas, and later Shell, programmes and took 34 Soho Square. A.R.F.P., for which Grierson acted as consultant, offered advice, preparation of scenarios, drawing up of production programmes, provision of directors and arrangement of distribution. It was later expanded and gave place in time to Film Centre. About the same time Donald Taylor set up Strand Films and was joined by Paul Rotha. Basil Wright formed the Realist Film Unit.

Grierson was still the unifying influence. The degree varied and fluctuated but all the documentary film-makers shared a common allegiance to him. Harry Watt: 'Grierson was our guru, our "Chief", our little god, the man who had given us an aim and an ideal, who battled for us and protected us, and at whose feet we sat. We were adult enough to laugh at his foibles and play-acting, to joke about his verbosity and Calvinism, but, basically, we adored him and could not humiliate him.'[21]

One of the initiatives taken by Grierson was the introduction of showings of films on Friday nights in the theatre at 21 Soho Square. The new G.P.O. films had their first screening there and other documentary film-makers brought their new productions to be seen by Grierson and his colleagues. According to Basil Wright, 'if anybody was around, they came along. If Moholy-Nagy was in London with a new abstract film, somehow he'd turn up there with the film. Even if they hadn't got films they'd turn up. . . . Paul Hindemith came for one whole evening and saw films, talked about film music. The Friday night shows were very exciting because anything could happen, and did.'[22] The tradition was valuable. The showings and the discussions which followed helped to maintain the cohesion and momentum of the movement.

G.P.O. Film Unit

Grierson believed also in the value of another tradition—the meetings in the Highlander after working-hours to talk and drink. Paul Rotha thought that this was one of the reasons for the success of that period of the British documentary film, holding it to be the English equivalent of the café life in Paris.[23] Among visitors Grierson brought to the pub evenings were D. W. Griffith, Josef von Sternberg and Robert Flaherty.

The movement needed a public voice. For the theory of documentary *Cinema Quarterly* had proved an admirable journal and there had been praise for its service of intelligent film criticism. Grierson felt that the changed situation called for more information and less theory. Information needed to be up-to-date: information about creative people and creative efforts in the many branches of cinema and in radio and television. And so in April 1936, *Cinema Quarterly* was incorporated in the monthly *World Film News and Television Progress*.

The first issue resembled a tabloid newspaper in make-up. McKnight Kauffer described the change as 'an earthquake' which was no exaggeration. Perhaps it was ahead of its time. But there were representations for a less agitated, more literary form of exposition. In response Grierson promised that they would 'on occasion put on our best academic suiting but, in general, we shall continue to be as practical in our interests as we can'. The paper did assemble an astonishing range of information, presented with flair. What a treat it is, said the *Cinema*, to encounter screen literature 'which is devised and contributed by people to whom the film is a living entity and whose fingers, so to speak, bear the odour of celluloid'.

World Film News served the movement well. It combined clear thinking with outspoken comment, conducted vigorous campaigns (often with the help of cartoons by Vicky) on film finance and censorship, and kept a keen eye on the international scene. Marion Grierson became editor and enlisted some lively aides and contributors—Esmond Romilly as advertisement manager, George M. Carstairs and Richard Mason as research workers, Alistair Cooke as writer. Grierson and Basil Wright continued to write regularly for it and there was a well-edited digest of film criticism. It did not, however, win the circulation it merited. It would not accept advertisements in return for editorial support. In the midst of other pressing matters Grierson sought finance for it, latterly with increasing desperation. The last issue was published in November 1938.

Perhaps in their range and intensity the pressures were becoming too much for one man to carry. Grierson himself would never have made this admission, nor did he turn aside any opportunity to add to documentary achievement. He greatly admired *The March of Time*, founded by Louis de Rochemont in New York in 1935. He admired it for its capacity to get behind the news, to analyse the factors of influence and to give a perspective to events. He recognised that, for the moment, *The March of Time* had won the field for the elementary principles of public discussion. This was something he respected.

Louis de Rochemont asked his younger brother, Richard, to set up a London-based *March of Time* unit. Richard had been given Grierson's name and after meeting him and being impressed by his ideas as a realist film-maker and by his range of contacts in government departments and elsewhere, engaged him as consultant. The association was fruitful for both. De Rochemont had the advantage of Grierson's knowledge and channels of approach. Grierson saw *The March of Time* both as a stimulus to public discussion and as providing an outlet for the energies of documentary directors with a particular interest in political and current affairs. He recommended Edgar Anstey as director of productions and Richard de Rochemont, who had seen *Enough to Eat?*, acted on it and appointed him. Anstey was to spend some two and a half years with *The March of Time*, partly in London where he wrote and directed ten films, and partly at headquarters in New York as foreign editor. Harry Watt made films for *The March of Time* on football pools and tithes.

Grierson did not press his consultancy after Anstey's appointment. I recall him taking a personal interest in an item on the clearances in Scotland—the enforced removal of the crofters by Highland landowners to make way for sheep. The burning of crofts was staged—a highly emotional spectacle for *émigré* Scots. Grierson's association with *The March of Time* continued until the outbreak of war and was resumed in a different form on the other side of the Atlantic.

At the end of 1936 Grierson was in Scotland talking to the film societies in Stirling and Edinburgh. His plea was that the Empire Exhibition, which it had been announced would be held in Glasgow in 1938, should provide the occasion for a Scottish national effort in film-making. His arguments were supported by the newspapers and a campaign was sustained by the societies. To implement his proposals, the Edinburgh Film Guild called for the appointment of 'a committee of representative Scotsmen drawn from all spheres of cultural life and from appropriate cinema organisations'. At the Scottish Office there were minds sympathetic to the idea, among them Niven MacNicoll, the public relations officer, with whom Grierson had talks. In due course the Scottish Office announced the appointment of the Films of Scotland Committee of the Scottish Development Council, with Grierson as production adviser and Alex B. King, the leading Scottish exhibitor, among its members.

Had it not been for Grierson's drive and enthusiasm, backed by his knowledge of Scotland, the production of an ambitious programme in the short time available would scarcely have been possible. The programme had some historical importance: it was the first comprehensive film record of a country's life and achievement. Basil Wright made *The Face of Scotland* on the country's character and traditions and *The Children's Story* on education. Donald Alexander told the industrial story in *Wealth of a Nation* and Mary Field the farming one in *They Made the Land*. Other films dealt with fishing, health and sport. Ritchie Calder said of the series that it would 'tell the world of the other side of Scotland, tear away the tartan curtains of romance and show a nation fighting for its existence'.[24]

But was the world to see this other side? The Scottish films became involved in what Grierson described as 'the battle for authenticity'. His ceaseless struggle to bring to the screen an honest picture of life in Britain had been resisted in areas where the preference was still for the pomp and circumstance of British life. The issue was brought into the open over the selection of films for the New York World's Fair. Selection was in the hands of the British Council's Film Committee and the films chosen reflected the Council's belief in the value of tradition and ceremonial: knee-breeches rather than working-clothes. The battle was fought with some bitterness and was reported in both British and American newspapers: *The Times* and the *New York Times*.

Grierson's films were ultimately shown, not as part of the British exhibit, but in the American Science and Education pavilion. The battle gave proof both of Grierson's tenacity of purpose and of the lingering resistance in British official circles to the export of films regarded, however unreasonably, as being too far to the left. Grierson relished the battle. An admission that the path had not been comfortable was as far as he would go. 'It has taken a good deal of persistence to maintain that a full and true story of British life is more likely to describe our virtues as a democracy, and that the richest picture to present in Britain and other countries lies in the actual bone and substance of British life.'[25]

Grierson had more freedom to assert his point of view after he had resigned from the G.P.O. on 30 June 1937. During his last year there had been a Special Branch presence at 21 Soho Square. Arthur Cain had been placed there as the unit was suspected of being a Communist cell. This appeared to be on evidence no more substantial than (a) the use of Margaret Grierson's car to help a Communist candidate in a minor local election (he lost); and (b) an unfounded suspicion that Ralph Bond was sending to Moscow secret information about B.B.C. equipment while working on *B.B.C.—The Voice of Britain*.[26] Cain's presence was not taken seriously. According to Harry Watt, the members of the unit deliberately made remarks in his hearing designed to arouse his suspicions. 'All right for to-night, Joe? Got the bomb? The job's on.' According to Ritchie Calder, 'Grierson and I had the dubious distinction in 1936 of sharing for different deviations, the same Special Branch "shadow". We materialised our "shadow" and got on friendly terms with him.'[27] Arthur Cain eventually helped with some research for the G.P.O. Film Unit. Later he was to marry Grierson's secretary, Phyllis Long, indispensable for more than her ability to decipher Grierson's handwriting.

Sir Stephen Tallents had been succeeded as public relations officer at the Post Office by Ernest Tristram Crutchley who was the member of the Post Office Board with responsibility for the G.P.O. Film Unit. In his diary a passage under the date of 26 June 1936, reads: 'Wrote a note indicating antagonism to the Treasury view that their Mr. Stewart should control or rather supervise our film work. The Conservative Research Council apparently accuse Grierson and his friends of Communism which is alleged to find expression in their work. For Communism read realism and a certain healthy liberalism and there might be something in it. But I am convinced we can't have Treasury butting in.' On the following day he wrote: 'Find Gardiner in full agreement about the film scare. He had had a frank talk with Grierson and was entirely satisfied.'[28] In Ritchie Calder's opinion, Grierson 'certainly wasn't a party-liner for any party. He was a maverick and a romantic.'[29]

On economic and functional grounds Grierson had had his struggles with the Treasury. As early as 1934, he had been reminded of the narrow remit to the G.P.O. Film Unit and that the founding of a documentary school was not among his functions. Nevertheless, Grierson made his move, not primarily because of any pressure from within, but because he wanted a wider field to work in. He had trained a score of film-makers who were already out and about. He had stimulated a demand for documentary from large industries and national organisations. He had encouraged the leading exponents of public relations to operate at a deeper level of communication. He had done this while in the public service and he was never to under-estimate the support the documentary movement received in both Whitehall and Parliament. He wanted to do more.

The setting up in 1938 of Film Centre (with Wright, Elton, Legg and J. P. R. Golightly) was the device he adopted to meet the growing needs of industry and national and civic organisations and to hold the various units to a common policy. In addition to Shell's film work and the gas, electrical and oil industries, it looked after the needs of Imperial Airways, the Films of Scotland Committee and the other organisations seeking Grierson's guidance in the use of films. Much of this use was outside the cinemas. Over the whole period of documentary's growth, since his first encounter with the Canadian Motion Picture Bureau, Grierson had fostered the non-theatrical showing of films, maintaining that there were many more seats outside than inside the commercial picture-houses. The original E.M.B.–G.P.O. Film Library was joined by similar libraries set up by the oil companies and the other large concerns making their own films.

Approaches began to be made to Grierson from outside Britain. One day the American writer, Ernestine Evans, called on him in London with what seemed to be a very bright idea for the constructive and educational use of films in the public interest. She said that the International Labour Office had some fifty member nations, all interested in working conditions all over the globe.[30] Her suggestion was that each country should make a film which showed what they were best at and that these should be passed out to the world through the agency of the I.L.O.: a Swedish film on safety in mines, a French film on a service of information to farmers, a film from New Zealand on pre-natal care, all contributing by their example to the common interest.

It was a good idea. Grierson and Wright worked out a scheme on this basis and, in September 1937, took it to the headquarters of the I.L.O. in Geneva. Later Grierson put it to the Rockefeller Foundation. It was taken seriously. It was in fact the first blueprint for an international use of film. In each case the answer was the same: the world situation was too unstable for such a plan to be successfully realised.

One other approach made to Grierson was to be much more productive. Vincent Massey, appointed High Commissioner for Canada by Mackenzie King, came to London with, as his secretary, Ross McLean, who had been at Oxford during the early years of the E.M.B. Film Unit. He was interested in films and, in Canada, had helped Donald Buchanan to found the National Film Society. Massey asked

McLean to make a study of the British documentary movement. He met Grierson at a moment of some excitement: the night of the first private showing of *Night Mail*. His report was forwarded by Massey to Mackenzie King in February 1936, with a warm recommendation that it should be carefully studied.[31]

There were many reasons which had nothing to do with its merits, or with films, why action was not taken on it: the death of George V, the accession of Edward VIII, the abdication and the coronation, not to mention the wars in Spain and Abyssinia and other preoccupations in Europe. In the spring of 1938 McLean approached Lester Pearson, then first secretary at the Canadian Legation in London. At the same time he sent a memorandum to the Minister of Trade and Commerce, W. D. Euler, recommending that Grierson should be invited to visit Canada. Eventually, Grierson received an invitation from the Canadian Government to make a survey of the film activities of the various government departments in Canada and particularly of the operations of the Canadian Government Motion Picture Bureau.

At about the same time Grierson was invited to make a survey of film developments in Canada for the Film Committee of the Imperial Relations Trust, set up by the British Government in 1937. Sir Stephen Tallents was a member. The trust had allocated limited funds for the encouragement of educational and cultural film services between Great Britain and the Dominions. It was the beginning of a whole new phase in Grierson's life.

Although he discontinued reviewing films with the end of *World Film News*, Grierson continued to comment critically on the state of British film-making. He wrote on 'The Fate of British Films' in the *Fortnightly* (July 1937) at a time when the future of British film-making was under debate in the House of Commons. It was a typically trenchant, well-informed and constructive review, ending with an expression of regret that the Government had omitted from the proposals made by Lord Moyne and his committee one for a commission which would stand above the conflict of commercial interests. He had no soft words, not even for Alexander Korda, whom he knew well.

Grierson occasionally dined with Korda in his penthouse at Claridge's and, in the presence of Monet and Manet, talk of the films to be made if money and Wardour Street were no object. After one such dinner they discussed a film to be called *Six O'Clock in the Morning*. 'It was to be a sort of *Paradise Lost*, describing the moment of dawn when the forces of light fought with the forces of darkness and there was not to be a human being in it save the one who appeared in the last shot like a poor leper to extinguish the conflict and the grandeur. It was to run a duly impossible minimum of ten hours. It was to cost half a million and I was to work years on it. The brandy, as ever, was excellent. As a clue to the magnificence of our thought there was to be one scene in which a couple of slugs in the tall grass had the delusion that they were in Chartres Cathedral and, of course, no expense was to be spared in having the great Chartres choir singing to the breaking heavens. There was a grain of sense in the concept. We were not just talking of the night life of the badgers and foxes and moles and voles and owls and nightingales; the film was to go deeper, deeper into all the living things of nature above and below the soil dependent or independent of the light.'[32]

Grierson counted the growing of things among his many and sometimes surprising enthusiasms. He had left his house in Merrick Square after the death of his mother in 1936 (his father had died in 1928 while he was making *Drifters*) and he and Margaret had gone to live in Kent at the Mill House, Fairbourne, Harrietsham. He had ten acres, three in apples, five in strawberries and the rest in nuts and plums and cherries. The small holding was to become well known to all the members of the unit and to Grierson's friends. According to Harry Watt, 'all of us were asked down for a pleasant day in the country, and ended up working our tail off in the fields. We always got a feed and a good drink, and it was rather fun, but, as usual, we were being pleasantly exploited.'[33]

Grierson took his strawberries seriously. With some advice from the Ministry of Agriculture research station at East Malling and by discreet questioning of prize-winners at local shows, he entered his strawberries at Folkestone, 'The Largest Soft Fruit Show in Great Britain', and won a prize, received, he claimed, from the hand of David Lloyd George. To keep the birds off his strawberries he would get up at 5 a.m. and walk round the policies with a gun. Sometimes he would shoot a rabbit for the pot. There was a large pond at the farm on the opposite side of the road and occasionally, in the early morning, out of the strawberry season, he would go out in a boat on the pond. He was an excellent fisherman but here at least he never caught anything. He loved cooking, and would continue to do so all his life. To him growing and cooking were 'the only arts and aspirations which join and do not divide'.

7 Canada, Australia, New Zealand

Grierson sailed for Canada at the end of May 1938. He left a country ill at ease and apprehensive. In March Hitler had occupied Austria. Czechoslovakia was his obvious next target. Chamberlain had succeeded Baldwin and his Government was applying its policy of appeasement. The country was in the grip of a creeping paralysis. A kind of helplessness hung heavily in the air during a summer which was to end with Munich.

Perhaps the voyage did something to lift Grierson out of the encircling depression. Certainly, when he arrived in Montreal on 17 June his energies had been recharged and he was ready to devote them at their maximum power to the task he had been given. His first contact was with Raleigh Parkin, Vincent Massey's cousin, who had been alerted about Grierson's visit in correspondence with Lester Pearson. Parkin picked up the telephone in his Sun Life office and a gruff voice said 'This is John Grierson.' Parkin said he had been looking forward to meeting him. Grierson: 'Can I come up now? I'm at the dock.' Parkin agreed and invited him to dinner, asking as an afterthought, 'Do you like strawberries?' 'I grow them', growled Grierson.[1]

Grierson spent the evening with Raleigh Parkin and his wife Louise. There was a steady flow of introductions, some to men who were to have a considerable influence on Grierson's activities during the next six or seven years. One was to Brooke Claxton, a lawyer who knew Ottawa politicians and departments well and was one of three people (the others being Graham Spry and Alan Plaunt) who were responsible for creating national broadcasting in Canada. Another was Davidson Dunton, editor of the *Montreal Standard* and a close friend of John Bird, editor of the *Tribune* whom Grierson was advised to meet in Winnipeg. Grierson was impressed by the young progressive Canadian point of view of Frank Scott and his associates in Montreal. There were also introductions to people in the United States, including Stephen Clark, one of the founders of the Museum of Modern Art, who had a remarkable collection of Matisse in his New York home: an indication that Grierson's interest in painting was as strong as it had been on his first visit to North America.

92

Canada, Australia, New Zealand

As Grierson moved west he met more and more of the men who were prominent in Canadian life. In Ottawa there was Charles G. Cowan, head of the British-American Bank Note Company. He was an original member of the National Film Society of Canada, founded by Donald Buchanan, Ross McLean and Donald Fraser: a man of the utmost goodwill, deeply respected in the business world of Ottawa, whose advice and guidance were greatly valued by Grierson. In Winnipeg he met J. W. Dafoe, editor of the *Winnipeg Free Press* and a substantial figure in Canadian life. Grierson was introduced by George Ferguson who succeeded Dafoe as editor and was to become editor of the *Montreal Star*. George Ferguson and his wife Mary were among Grierson's closest friends in Canada and were to remain so until his death. In the home of the editor of the other Winnipeg newspaper, Grierson was shown the work of a painter who had some pretensions to Impressionism. 'Very like Matisse, isn't it?' said the editor's wife, in front of one canvas. Grierson looked at it for a moment, half closed his eyes, and said 'Not enough.'[2]

Ottawa was the main location of Grierson's investigation. He met the Prime Minister, Mackenzie King, and there was an immediate warm understanding between men who shared a Scottish origin and much else besides. He had discussions with R. B. Bennett, Howard Ferguson, Sir Edward Beattie and Ministers Euler, Howe, Crerar and Rogers; with newspaper editors in Ottawa, Toronto, Winnipeg, Edmonton, Regina, Calgary and Lethbridge; with the presidents of the Manitoba and Saskatchewan Universities; and with many leaders of educational and civic activities. On one point they were all agreed: that the film should be used to diminish sectionalism and give Canada a sense of its relationships at home and overseas. 'In most discussions, I presented the notion that the most important federal media were those which imaginatively brought alive one part of the country to another, and dramatised relationships as distinct from differences, and that from a physical point of view, radio and film were the most important of these.'[3]

Grierson's exploration of Canada was in no sense confined to government, official and newspaper areas. For the first time in Canada he was using the aeroplane to get around (New York to Regina, eleven hours, Lethbridge to Winnipeg, less than five) and he saw below him 'impossible miles of the prairies telescope into the life of a people'. He was fascinated by the use of aeroplanes for prospecting in the north. He felt the excitement at Edmonton as the planes flew out over the waste lands of yesterday and brought their riches under the hand of man. In a mail plane he sat beside radio and meteorological engineers who were mobilising weather reports across thousands of miles and building, like brick layers, the edifice of safety. He drove in a bus a hundred miles into the country to meet farmers suffering the effect of eight years of drought. In Calgary for the Stampede he thought the cowboys, riding so easily in and about the milling crowds, were 'just Scottish cattlemen who happened to be on horses' and that the town was like Perth or Stirling when the Highland Show was on—'The same untidy tangle of landsmen on holiday, the same capacity to be at ease with themselves.'[4]

Asked what he thought of Canadian films he said: 'I have seen many Canadian films and most of them were about National Parks and people on holidays. I didn't, so help me, believe that Canada could be just the big innocent, baby-hearted, holiday haunt it pretended to be in its pictures. I thought maybe somebody did some work once in a while and that Canada's work might just conceivably have something to do with the real Canada. That in fact is my interest in the world. I would like to see more and more films about real people.'

It was quickly obvious to Grierson that his activities in Canada were not welcomed by Frank Badgley, head of the Motion Picture Bureau. Badgley was aware that there was considerable criticism within Canada of the quality of the films made by the Bureau and that Grierson shared this criticism. Grierson for his part admired the distribution achieved by Badgley for his films—films which had largely made possible the establishment of the E.M.B. Film Library in Britain. But the Bureau had been left behind by the pace of film development. It was staffed largely by veterans of the First World War. Badgley had friends in the government prepared to back him. Grierson knew that this was a moment for tact. As always he presented the case in a positive way: the Motion Picture Bureau must be strengthened so that it could retain its position as a world leader.

Before returning to Britain Grierson paid a visit to New York to investigate the use of Canadian material in American newsreels. He discussed the situation with the editors of Movietone, Paramount, News of the Day and Universal and found that they used only two or three Canadian items a year. They were offered 'pedestrian accounts of Queens of the May, Boys' Brigade sports, mumbling publicities for local politicians, bridge openings, parades, provincial recreation centres, etc.' Whatever interest these had in Canada, they were useless in the United States and Britain. Grierson analysed the situation in a tersely expressed letter to the Minister of Trade and Commerce, pointing out that the international circulation of newsreels was one of the most powerful and important means by which a country makes itself known across its borders.[5] This conviction was to be reflected in future Canadian film-making policy and practice.

Grierson completed and delivered his report to Vincent Massey and W. D. Euler in July. An abridged edition, prepared in August in London for the Imperial Relations Trust, ran to sixty-six pages.[6] The report was frank and far-seeing, incisive in its detail and imaginatively constructive in its recommendations. Grierson had wasted no one's time, not least his own.

Grierson saw government film propaganda as serving four objectives: general knowledge, trade publicity, departmental information and national prestige. He had found three main weaknesses in Canada: lack of a considered directive for Canada as a whole; lack of a strong creative film unit to carry out the policy and interpret it in imaginative terms; and the parochialism of the different departments. Of the Motion Picture Bureau he said that what should be a dynamic force in government propaganda had been conceived as an ordinary executive civil service department. It should be released from its inferiority complex. He recommended the setting up of a continuing committee to keep Canadian propaganda film policy under review, that the hand of the government film officer should be strengthened and that the Motion Picture Bureau should be given creative manpower. He was firm in his criticism: 'The technical capacity of the Bureau is far in excess of its creative capacity; and the first is useless without the other.' Grierson also suggested ten subjects for prestige films, including the St. Lawrence Seaway and the administration of the Arctic.

There was much more by way of detail in the wide-ranging report. Grierson's plea was for a planned co-ordinating policy, a strong film unit, and for freedom for creative interpretation. Part of the report related to complementary action to be taken at Canada House in London.

The report was favourably received by the Canadian Government. When action on it appeared to be delayed over-long, some stimulus was injected by Donald Buchanan and Charles Cowan of the National Film Society. On 14 October 1938, a cable was sent inviting Grierson to return to Canada to indicate the terms on which the co-ordination he had recommended could be carried out. Grierson returned to Ottawa in November and began the task of obtaining the common understanding between departments which he considered essential. They needed to be convinced that it was in the national interest as well as their own to have centralisation of film production and distribution; and the Government needed to be convinced that such centralisation should be backed by legislation. Ultimately, at a meeting of departmental representatives in mid-January 1939, Grierson's plan was approved.

The bill to create a National Film Board was drafted by Grierson who had the help of J. F. McNeil of the Department of Justice to give it the necessary legal form. The Board was to have as chairman the Minister of Trade and Commerce, and to consist of one other minister, three civil servants and three members of the public, drawn from journalism, radio and general education. A film commissioner was to be appointed as the Board's executive officer, the appointment to be for three years only. The Board was to formulate the policy of government film-work. The Motion Picture Bureau was confirmed as the principal production agency of the Government. The first duty imposed on the commissioner was to 'advise upon the making and distribution of national films designed to help Canadians in all parts of Canada to understand the ways of living and the problems of Canadians in other parts'. Here clearly was Grierson's hand.

The bill was introduced in March 1939, and the National Film Act received the Royal Assent on 2 May 1939. Meantime Grierson had returned to Britain. Munich had come and gone, Chamberlain's 'Peace in our time' had lasted six months, Czechoslovakia had been occupied and the British guarantee had been given to Poland. War with Hitler's Germany had become inevitable.

Against the broad backcloth of a world moving irreversibly towards war there were personal evidences of its impact on individual filmmakers. In the spring of 1939, Herbert Kline, editor in New York of *New Theatre and Film*, was in London to show Grierson *Crisis*, the film he had made on Munich and its aftermath. He was preparing to make the film which would have *Lights Out in Europe* as its title. He met Grierson in the Highlander in Soho, with his cameraman Alexander Hackenschmied (Hammid), his associate producer Peter Mayer and his wife, Rosa. They had 'a marvellous get-together'.[7] Grierson invited Kline to show him his rushes. The director received much helpful criticism from Grierson, Paul Rotha and Basil Wright. Rotha wrote that *Crisis* and *Lights Out in Europe* had been struck off in the heat of the moment. What was significant was that 'Kline gave importance to the documentary camera by focusing it on the decisive events of the period when many of his colleagues were turning out "social" films which to-day seem mere paltering.'[8]

18. John Grierson in his Ottawa office during his early years as Canadian Government Film Commissioner

9. John Grierson as fisherman. At J. R. Booth's fishing lodge, The Hincks

20. John Grierson's other relaxation—sailing

21. John Grierson with
Stuart Legg in Canada

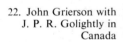

22. John Grierson with
J. P. R. Golightly in
Canada

23. John Grierson greeted
at La Guardia airport,
New York, by Margaret
Grierson on his return
from a visit to Normandy
in August, 1944

24. John Grierson and Ralph Foster examine posters for the National Film Board of Canada's 'Canada Carries On' series at Ottawa during World War II

25. **Battle of the Harvests** (1944) Produced by the National Film Board of Canada. Directed by James Beveridge
26. **Trans-Canada Express** (1944) Produced by the National Film Board of Canada. Directed by Sydney Newman

27. Frances Flaherty, Richard Leacock (camera) and Robert Flaherty on location for **Louisiana Story** (1946–8)

28. Sir Julian Huxley and John Grierson representing UNESCO at the Freedom of Information conference, Geneva, March 1948

29. John Grierson with Lady Huxley and Sir Julian Huxley at a UNESCO reception in Paris, 1948

31. John Grierson with Sir Stephen Tallents

30. John Grierson with Forsyth Hardy in Princes Street Gardens, Edinburgh at the opening of the first Edinburgh International Film Festival, August 1947

32. The presentation of honorary membership of ACTT to John Grierson, 1968. Left to right: Ralph Bond, Forsyth Hardy, William Brown, Charles Oakley, Sir Alexander B. King, George H. Elvin, Dr. John Grierson, George Singleton, James Sutherland

33. John Grierson with Sir Arthur Elton, Bt.

34. Norman McLaren at work on an animated film for the
National Film Board of Canada
35. **Neighbours** (1952) Directed by Norman McLaren.
Produced by the National Film Board of Canada

Canada, Australia, New Zealand

Another visitor to Film Centre in January 1939, was Jiri Weiss, the Czech film-maker, who showed Grierson his film *Sold Out Country* (later titled *The Rape of Czechoslovakia*, with a commentary by Cecil Day Lewis). He returned to Prague in mid-February and on 13 March received a telegram from Grierson inviting him to return to London and advising him that a travel ticket could be collected at a Czech travel bureau. Weiss replied that he would use the ticket at a later date —and realised two days later, when the Germans marched into Prague, what the message meant. He slipped out of Prague on 29 March and got as far as Bentheim on the Dutch border before he was arrested by the Nazis. A decent civil guard closed his eyes and Weiss succeeded in crossing the border to Oldenzaal where he spent a week in jail. Film Centre again arranged a British visa and travel ticket and, via Harwich, he reached London. 'Grierson saved my life', Weiss told me in New York. 'I was sorry when he went back to Canada. Possibly, in hindsight, it was wise. He was a great initiator, a spark to fire on, and that was his function.'[9]

In the midst of many preoccupations, national, imperial and international, Grierson found time for a visit to Glasgow where, on 18 May 1939, he opened the Cosmo, a specialised cinema built by George Singleton, a leading exhibitor in Scotland. He was to come to know the cinema well and to work closely with its owner in the development of film production in Scotland.

Grierson's visit to Canada, in so far as it had been made on behalf of the Imperial Relations Trust, was part of a larger plan to obtain information about film activities also in Australia, New Zealand and South Africa. During the spring and summer of 1939 he was actively involved in preparations for a visit later in the year to Australia and New Zealand. He was still in close touch with Canada. While in Ottawa he had been approached by Norman Rogers, Minister of Labour, to recommend a producer to undertake two films on a new youth training plan. He had recommended Stuart Legg who left for Canada in February and who also had the help of introductions from Raleigh Parkin. By July Legg had researched, written and directed the films: *The Case of Charlie Gordon*, which Grierson found 'a very human document with a Canadian accent and a Canadian face on it', and *Youth for Tomorrow*, an analytic account for non-theatrical showing. Legg had moved rapidly over the country, from Glace Bay to Peace River, and, once the Motion Picture Bureau had accepted his speed of working, he carried them with him.

Grierson left Britain in July. He sailed to New York where he spent some days packed with activity of one kind or another. He did not have time to see the World's Fair properly but he did have time for a parachute jump and a trip up the North River in a speedboat at forty-five miles an hour. The temperature was over ninety but the heat did not limit his exertions.[10] He had discussions at Paramount with the news-reel and short film departments. At the Guggenheim Foundation he had a meeting with the director, Henry Moe, and discussed the building up of more effective systems of national and international communications and the need to have experts with a deeper knowledge of the use of the new dramatic media in creating opinion. The Guggenheim fellowships were just being opened to Canadians and Grierson thought one might be allocated for the purpose he had in mind—a possibility he was to discuss with Norman Robertson and others in the Prime Minister's Department in Ottawa.

Inevitably Grierson was keenly interested in what was happening in documentary in the United States. Pare Lorentz had made *The Plow that Broke the Plains* and *The River*, Paul Strand *The Wave* and Joris Ivens *Power and the Land*. Willard Van Dyke and Ralph Steiner had produced *The City* to show at the World's Fair. Documentary was edging its way tentatively into the American film vocabulary but these films were isolated efforts, not part of a movement as in Britain. Efforts were being made to give coherent purpose to the various activities. While in New York in 1937–8, Paul Rotha had done some valuable missionary work on which he had reported in detail to Grierson. Grierson himself had submitted a memorandum to the General Education Board of the Rockefeller Foundation outlining a scheme for the intensive circulation of documentary films in the United States and stating that the co-operation of the American Committee on Intellectual Co-operation had been assured. Mary Losey (Field), who had seen Grierson in London in 1938 and who was associated with him in his work for Louis de Rochemont, left *The March of Time* to organise the American Film Centre. She spent some time with Grierson reporting on these developments as he passed through New York on his way to Canada.

In Ottawa in August Grierson was disappointed to find that so little had been done since May: no Board, no commissioner, no films. Although the news from Europe gave him little stomach for the job he immediately started stirring things up. He had meetings with the Minister of Trade and Commerce, the Minister of Labour, the Prime Minister's Department and the Canadian Film Committee. He found the Ministry of Trade and Commerce reluctant to bring in livelier spirits which might lose them their traditional precedence in film matters. Frank Badgley, he sensed, was anxious to be appointed commissioner. Grierson feared Badgley did not have the imagination to see the possibilities and use the weapon which had been forged for him but characteristically made a powerful effort to help him by setting out in a long memorandum a programme of action full of sound advice, both on procedure and on subjects for films.

Grierson had moved west by the time the Government announced the members of the Board. The chairman was W. D. Euler, Minister of Trade and Commerce, who had as government colleagues T. A. Crerar, Minister of Mines and Resources, V. I. Smart, Deputy Minister of Transport, J. Parmelee, Deputy Minister of Trade and Commerce, and R. S. Hamer, Department of Agriculture. The other members were Dr. W. C. Murray, retired president of the University of Saskatchewan, Edmond Turcotte, editor of *Le Canada*, and Charles G. Cowan. Members of the Board felt, as Grierson did, that the commissioner should be a Canadian, and one who knew the country well and who knew how to produce and distribute films. Grierson himself recommended E. A. Corbett of the Adult Education Association who declined on the ground that he had insufficient experience in films. He urged that the appointment should be offered to Grierson.

From Winnipeg Grierson had sent a long report to Tallents. He went to Vancouver and was in Hollywood when the German troops crossed the frontier into Poland. Grierson sensibly took account of the new situation by postponing his visit to Australia. Margaret had now joined him from England in readiness for the voyage. Although he was in 'the city of unreality, stardust, and people's dreams' he did not feel a world away from the war. He saw Hollywood as one of the greatest potential munition factories on earth—a great instrument of war propaganda. Among the Hollywood magnates there was nervousness and uncertainty. A third of their world market had vanished overnight. The first orders to the studios were to throw out all serious subjects and to concentrate on light-hearted froth which would, in theory, help the people to forget their worries. Grierson saw a number of the studio heads, including Walter Wanger at United Artists, and persuaded them —or those who needed persuading—that they should do something to keep the decent human values alive and maintain men's sanity, so that when peace came they would know how to make it stable. This was his theme when he spoke on 13 September to a packed audience at the Academy of Motion Picture Arts and Sciences.[11]

In a letter to Sir Stephen Tallents Grierson expressed his concern about the effectiveness of British propaganda in the United States. 'It cannot be sufficiently emphasised', he wrote, 'that we have not yet got hold of American opinion. The isolation sentiment is strong and minds are doubtful of the rights and wrongs of the European issue.' He thought that, in the information service, a mistake had been made in overestimating American direct interest in British affairs. There was little conviction that Britain was in earnest. Stories of Mayfair wearing decorative gas masks and maintaining the snobberies even in war were being greeted with giggles and 'I told you so's.' He told Tallents that he intended to see what could be done in Australia and New Zealand and thought that, even in these unhappy days, the Imperial Relations Trust might find a great opportunity for building relationships within the Empire.[12]

Grierson was invited by Lord Lothian to go to Washington to discuss his film ideas and by 25 September was in the Shoreham Hotel. Over the next few weeks he was hard at work. He moved between Washington and New York, having discussions, not only at the Embassy but also with the British Library of Information and the Committee on Intellectual Co-operation and its associated groups. He drafted a plan for an international film centre for the circulation throughout the United States of film documents of a constructive democratic sort. The plan was forwarded by the Embassy but its reception by the Ministry of Information in London was frosty. It was thought it would disturb commercial distributors. There was also resentment of telegrams Grierson had sent *en clair* instead of in code through the Embassy.

Grierson was disappointed by the London reaction but not surprised. All the reasons for doing little, or for doing precisely the wrong things, in this matter of projection he thought he knew by heart. In the early period of the war the British Ministry of Information was an ineffectual department and by the time it had been reformed, under Churchill and Brendan Bracken (with Jack Beddington at the Films Division), Grierson's drive and dynamism were engaged elsewhere. 'I had this American job well sighted', he wrote to Tallents, 'and could have done a valuable service. I could have commanded co-operation and even enthusiasm on this side on a large scale and, in one's own field, made the prevalent picture of a muddled and perhaps rather devious England clearer and more straightforward.'[13]

Early in October, while Grierson was still in Washington, Charles Cowan called Stuart Legg and asked if he had any suggestions which might help to solve the impasse over the film commissioner. Legg pointed out that Grierson was in Washington, his Australian visit having been postponed, but he did not think he would accept the appointment. The Board's chairman invited Grierson to come to Ottawa and spend a couple of days. On 11 October the Board formally recommended to the Government that Grierson be appointed for a period of six months. Grierson had a commitment to the Australian Government and was anxious to return to Britain; but he felt he could not stand aside and see the organisation he had created stillborn. He agreed on Friday 13 October, and the appointment was confirmed on 16 October.

There followed three months of whirlwind activity such as the somewhat sleepy civil service world of Ottawa had never known. Stuart Legg was appointed to the Motion Picture Bureau and seconded to the National Film Board as production supervisor. From W. D. Euler's staff Janet Scellen was loaned as Grierson's secretary. Ross McLean accepted Grierson's invitation to join the Board and arrived from Western Canada on 11 November. Later that month arrived Donald Fraser, secretary of the Canadian Film Committee, and James Beveridge, who had met Grierson in London in 1939 when he visited the documentary units. Raymond Spottiswoode, English author of *Film and Its Techniques*, was brought in from Hollywood and Evelyn Spice joined from the G.P.O. Film Unit. A. Phileas Côté was engaged to organise distribution. Stanley Hawes was invited to come from London. The small unit was housed in the west block of the government buildings in Ottawa and Grierson had his first clash with officialdom when he insisted that the offices be painted grey, not the conventional bilious green. He won.

On production Grierson was given *carte blanche* by the Board. He scheduled two important documentaries, one on the people of Canada and the other on the Undefended Frontier to the south—a picture of Canada's North American relationships and responsibilities which he hoped would make a wise contribution to understanding. He initiated a programme of films for French-speaking Canada, in the belief that the time was ripe for a *rapprochement* between French Canada and the West. Six films for schools on the human geography of Canada were scheduled. He began planning with N. L. Nathanson, head of Famous Players, the circulation of a monthly reel on the lines of *The March of Time*. A similar offer from Columbia Pictures gave Grierson access to the whole theatre system of Canada. He responded to a plea from George Ferguson in Winnipeg for a film urging farmers to plant trees as wind breaks to keep the soil from being blown away: 'I've got your film in hand on the importance of breaking wind on the prairies.'[14]

In New York Grierson saw Louis de Rochemont and persuaded him to devote an issue of *The March of Time* to *Canada at War*—a film to present to people in the United States, in Britain and in other countries the scale of Canada's war effort. He had the authorisation of the Prime Minister's Department for the undertaking and had an assurance that the final content of the film would be under his control. With Grierson's departure for Australia becoming imminent, Ross McLean was assigned to the production and he spent some time in New York, working with Lothar Wolff. A film on such a subject would always have been a political issue. It was to become a much bigger political issue than anyone imagined.

On 18 January 1940 Mitchell Hepburn, Premier of Ottawa, launched a bitter attack on Mackenzie King, denouncing the Federal Government for its failure 'to prosecute Canada's duty in the war in the vigorous manner the people of Canada desire to see'. Mackenzie King accepted the challenge. Parliament was dissolved. The people were to judge at a general election whether or not Canada's war effort was adequate. The Prime Minister had made a contribution to *The March of Time* film in which he spoke positively and impressively about Canada's role in the war. He and Ross McLean were well aware of the contribution the film could make in the general election campaign. It was due for release in March, just before voting would take place.

Grierson had recommended that during his absence Colonel John Cooper, head of the Canadian Motion Pictures Distributors' Association, should act as temporary film commissioner. He had in mind that such a gesture would ease the distribution of the Film Board's productions. Colonel Cooper, politically in sympathy with Mitchell Hepburn, realised the value of *The March of Time* film and, by pressing heavily on J. J. Fitzgibbons, president of Famous Players, had its release held back. After protesting to Cooper, Ross McLean saw Walter Turnbull, the Prime Minister's secretary, who warned Cooper that a strict interpretation of customs regulations might result in long delays in the import of the Paramount films distributed by Famous Players. In six hours Mitchell Hepburn was told the film would go out. But the Ontario premier was not defeated. He had the film banned by the Ontario Board of Censors. Louis de Rochemont announced that there had been only one other banning of an issue of *The March of Time*—by Hitler. *Canada at War* was advertised as 'See the film banned in Ontario'. At the Federal election which followed, Mackenzie King and his Liberals captured twenty-five seats in Ontario.[15]

It was a significant outcome. Grierson had emphasised to Tallents that 'there are powerful factors of detachment in the Canadian mind at this time. I see no signs that they are intimately appreciated on the other side. The acquiescence of Canada in this war is, I feel, not to be estimated as the full-blooded co-operation of the last. I shall put the distinction this way: One does not talk of "winning the war" but of "relating the Canadian nation to the new circumstances created by the war". Preparedness is not exactly a preparedness to do or die at the behest of the somewhat distant Prime Minister of a distant country—but a matter of being "strong in ourselves". In other words, Canada's first interest is to make itself more of a nation and less of an appendage to anyone—and articulate its own particular destiny better than it has managed to do before.'[16]

Meantime Grierson was far away from the political imbroglio over *Canada at War*. He left Ottawa on 25 January, the day Parliament was dissolved. He and Margaret sailed from San Francisco at the end of the month on the S.S. *Mariposa* of the Matson Line.

By the time he reached Honolulu on 6 February he had a large bundle of letters, typed by Margaret, to post. So much for the 'leisure of shipboard'! One of them was to Raleigh Parkin.[17] In this and in others he expressed his concern to have a shot at restating the problem of education in the modern world and seeing education anew in terms of wider horizons, more urgent problems of civic comprehension, etc. This would mean, wrote Grierson, stating the problem of comprehending the corporate factor in modern society. It would mean presenting the importance of the democratic approach to education. It would mean developing the idea of education as a system of communications, not only from the state to the citizen but also from the citizen to the state, and between civic groups themselves. These were ideas to which he was often to return in the next five years.

The other recurring theme in his letters was that England was failing in its leadership of the democratic idea. He argued that a use of the dramatic media of information was more than just a way of conveying thought or policy. It was the machinery of expression itself (the medium is the message?) and a country could not think out the terms of modern existence without it. 'You say it, and therefore you are it; and without saying it you have not its reality.'

Grierson arrived in Auckland on 16 February and spent 'a month of hard hither and thither' in New Zealand.[18] He saw everyone that mattered, from the Prime Minister downwards: the fact that Peter Fraser had been born in the north of Scotland helped Grierson to establish a quick rapport. He was surprised to find that there was more knowledge about the documentary movement in Britain than he might reasonably have expected in a country twelve thousand miles away from Soho Square. His writings in *Cinema Quarterly* and *World Film News* were well known and his work in Canada had been followed with an envious interest. He was fortunate in having an early introduction to Stanhope Andrews, editor of *National Education*, who was steeped in his thinking before they met and who in the ensuing four weeks was to see more of Grierson than anyone else in New Zealand.

His driving energy and his capacity to grasp quickly the essentials of a national situation made it possible for him to produce his report for the New Zealand Government well within the time he had allowed himself. It was characteristically comprehensive and clear in its analysis. As in Canada, he found some government use of film, mainly the production of travelogues and advertising films for the Tourist and Publicity Department. They were made at Miramar, a suburb of Wellington. He was scrupulous in giving credit for the work being done at Miramar, often in difficult circumstances and with much interference; but, understandably, he had higher expectations of government film-making in New Zealand. Wherever people were doing anything of human or national significance, there was a subject for a film.

New Zealand films, he argued, should reflect the contribution the country was making to the world—and he was not thinking of butter and lamb. New Zealand, he said, was a young hopeful country, making brave experiments in social construction. Housing, child welfare and public health were three fields where, he thought, New Zealand's achievements could lay claim to international validity. New Zealand, he suggested, was fortunate to have the Maoris. He made a plea that some of the grace and poetry of the Polynesians should be brought into the dominion's films: it would be a great tragedy if the pakeha had all the plumbing and the Maori all the poetry.

In his recommendations, as was his wont, Grierson was cogent. If they occupied fifteen pages, that was because he left little uncovered.[19] It was clear, he said that there should be a more directive policy in both production and distribution—a central planning and animating body. He argued for professionalism: a good single group of creative and technical men, helping each other, sharing each other's experience and building up a team spirit, would obviously be more precious in the long run than a series of amateur or semi-amateur units with different measures of initiatives and ability. He suggested that creative aids to production should be employed on a temporary basis, with a limited permanent staff, and he gave as examples of the usefulness of this procedure his calling at will in Britain on the ideas of writers like Shaw, Wells and Priestley, poets like Auden and composers like Leigh and Britten. 'The highest single fee I ever paid was one hundred guineas to Priestley. Shaw and Wells worked for a nominal fiver.'

Grierson's recommendations were carried out in principle if not in detail. A National Film Unit was set up, with Stanhope Andrews in charge. Responsibility for the unit's policy was vested in a wartime Director of Publicity, attached to the Prime Minister's office. A film magazine, the *Weekly Review*, was shown in almost every theatre in New Zealand. Its directors and cameramen produced for this format some admirable documentaries in New Zealand. They also went overseas with the New Zealand forces. In time the National Film Unit gained for documentary film-making in New Zealand a reputation, given its much smaller scale, comparable to Canada's. Oxley Hughan and Michael Forlong were to make films of quality.

When Grierson sailed for Sydney on the S.S. *Monterey* he had the promise of new policy, new creative approach and real backing for co-ordination of government film activities. 'All of which, you may take it', he wrote to Basil Wright, 'means as sweet a job of mass conversion as Paul the Apostle ever himself imagined.'

Grierson reached Sydney on 18 March. He quickly sensed that Australia was going to be much less responsive to his ideas than New Zealand. 'It's a gay country with a pleasant sense of sin after New Zealand', he wrote to Basil Wright, 'and none of its problems is more important than horse racing. Which is a good thing when you think of it, but not greatly contributing to the more earnest notions of Empire integrations and so forth.' Sydney he found a flashy town. 'Males are incredibly tall and handsome, females look fed on the best and are dressed to the nines; the shops glitter; the hotel lounges flash; the beaches blaze on brilliant thousands. Everyone is either at the races or on the merry-go-round.'[20]

In contrast to New Zealand, where problems of socialisation had forced them to consider problems of national education and the proper use of the media, he found in Australia few people tutored enough in the idea as a whole, or effective enough, to bring the various forces together and mobilise a documentary movement out of the country's actual and appreciated needs. 'I know what will happen when I get down to planning the siting of this curious little act of ours in Australia. I shall as usual have to relate it, not to the real objective needs of Australia, which are, as anywhere else, human management, responsibility, illumination, and humility before the Lord; but to the *felt* needs which, I can lay a million to one now, will turn out to be sectional, selfish, political, vulgar and dishonest. Nevertheless, I shall relate the process to these very needs, and it will be the wise thing to do, for the process is itself the seed of conversion, or as much of it as is vouchsafed to us to administer. I shall not, of course, talk documentary, for if I guess rightly Australia is a generation away from any such conception. I shall talk war information, the cohesion of the national effort, the contribution to be made to an Empire plan of the highest authority. I shall discuss with consummate ease the need for focusing the popular mind on the national purpose, and away from what it now may consider its immediate interest; and each dark mind will leap to a vision of its own, thereby, advantage.' With typical confidence he added 'But out of it, I know, will come that "obligation to inform" and "obligation to realise" which will before long have a very different result.'[21]

With its centres of population widely separated, Australia is a difficult country to attempt to cover quickly. Grierson doggedly worked through his timetable, always seeking the main areas of influence and the liveliest minds. He found a very progressive Minister of Education, D. H. Drummond, in New South Wales and spent a lot of time with him. Out of this came a Films Committee (still in existence as the New South Wales Film Council) for the distribution in the state of informational and documentary films. In Victoria he found the progressive group was the University Extension Board and in South Australia the teachers. He expected Films Committees to be formed also in these states but this hope was not to be realised until the end of the war. To visit Queensland, which he found already ahead on school films, he made a twenty hour journey by train from Sydney to Brisbane —no sleepers, sitting up all night, coal strike and saving coal. 'This I do for the Empire. The compensation in Australia is the landscape. It staggers the eye with flat green the light can't penetrate or sissify. What the light gets at is the solid mould of the landscape and the twisting mould of the trunks and branches of the gum trees. In South Australia add the cockatoos and the parrots.'[22]

Grierson was not impressed by Canberra. 'A great moment of wrongness, glorifying its 300 miles of distance from the cities, and the people, and the real things, by hiding its own few houses from each other, spreading its Government offices miles away across the country-side and making the cypress the symbolical Federal tree. It's all very pretty, with shrubberies in square miles, flowers to make a fortune, only there's nobody to see them; but in Government it means worse than nothing. Politicians and officials spend half their lives getting about, and finish up making virtue of getting nowhere. It doesn't matter much, with only seven millions in so rich a country, but you will appreciate it doesn't promise well for the organisation of informational services. The Federal Government, through inertias constitutional, geographical, *laissez-faire* and of sheer impotence or incompetence, can do little.'[23]

On 8 April Grierson submitted a preliminary memorandum to the Prime Minister. It dealt in the main with what had been done in Canada 'because its problem is in many ways similar to the Australian one'. Having in mind Grierson's reactions it was comparatively restrained. Even in the accompanying letter he said nothing stronger than, 'The national handling of the film instrument appears, to the outsider, somewhat inadequate', although he did add, 'In the development of production for non-theatrical audiences you are, I think, well behind other leading countries.' On 25 April, just as he was about to leave Sydney, Grierson received a letter from the Prime Minister's Department, saying that the Federal Cabinet had considered the possibility of making effective use of films to further national interests and had appointed a sub-committee of ministers to deal with the matter. The sub-committee comprised the Prime Minister, the Treasurer (Mr. Spender), the Minister for External Affairs (John McEwen), and the Acting Minister for Information (Sir Henry Gullett). The letter, signed by C. C. Dawson, Commonwealth Publicity Officer, concluded: 'I am most enthusiastic about the proposals you have advanced and I now see a real chance of effective action being taken in Australia. For our young country, imbued with British ideals and occupying a strategic position in the Pacific, the film can be of the greatest value as a medium of propaganda.'

Responding to the invitation to submit a comprehensive memorandum, Grierson spent the days between Sydney and Auckland compiling, with Margaret's help, a long and detailed paper, setting forth his analysis and recommendations. As he knew there was some resistance to his ideas in the film industry, he treaded warily. 'Without prejudicing the essential nature of the film business (i.e. light entertainment), the use of its screens can be mobilised to give an orderly and regular service to the nation, at least during war-time', and added that the other half of the story was the utilisation by film of all branches of education and public discussion. He recommended the setting up of a government film committee for the co-ordination of government film interests and the mobilisation of the film medium for national needs and the appointment of an executive officer.

The long memorandum, drawing on conversations Grierson had had with ministers and others in Australia, was completed in time for it to be posted when the S.S. *Mariposa* called at Auckland on 29 April. When it was considered by the Cabinet sub-committee the members were uncertain what to do about the recommendations. The Minister for External Affairs, John McEwen, suggested that they should be turned over to the newly appointed Director of Information, Sir Keith Murdoch. The Prime Minister agreed and they eventually reached the director of the Films Division, whose work they criticised. Six months later he reported that no action was necessary on Grierson's main proposals: 'The Department has already taken adequate steps through the National Films Council to regiment the theatrical interests of the Commonwealth in publicising the war effort and in maintaining the morale of the citizens of Australia.'

Grierson's proposals for Australia eventually reached fruition but not until after the war when the Australian National Film Board was established and film councils or centres were appointed in the states. Ralph Foster, representative in Australia of the Canadian National Film Board, was appointed first head of the Australian Commonwealth Film Unit and was succeeded in 1946 by Stanley Hawes. 'Those of us who knew Grierson regard it as a monument to him. He made it possible for us, and through us for many who did not know him and who may not even have heard of him, to work in films with self-respect.'[24]

Australia had been the difficult job Grierson expected and when he left he was not very confident about the outcome. He arrived in San Francisco on 14 May and was back in Ottawa by 23 May. Stuart Legg and Stanley Hawes were at the airport to meet him. As the lights of his aircraft became visible, Legg said, with a kind of wry affection, 'Here comes a load of trouble.'[25]

8 By the Ottawa River

In Grierson's absence Stuart Legg had been frantically hard at work on the implementation of the production plans made before his departure. Legg had given priority to the series for theatrical distribution, *Canada Carries On*. The first, *Atlantic Patrol*, on the North Atlantic convoys, was shot by J. D. Davidson and Donald Fraser and was ready in April. When Legg showed it to David Coplan of Columbia Pictures who were to distribute the series it was nearly forty minutes in length. Coplan said it must be no more than twenty and sat with Legg in the projection room suggesting how it could be compressed to its advantage.[1] Legg was grateful for the distributor's advice and acknowledged to me how helpful it was to have someone of Coplan's experience sitting at his elbow.[2] Coplan for his part had long wanted to have a Canadian monthly film magazine to distribute and was pleased to collaborate with a film-maker of Legg's skill and imagination. The commentator was Lorne Greene whose firm, authoritative voice, 'with a built-in cello', was to become inseparably associated with the series. *Atlantic Patrol* was followed by *Letter from Aldershot* and *Home Front*. By the time Grierson returned *Canada Carries On* was showing, 'very, very successfully', in some eight hundred cinemas in Canada.

Action had been taken on another significant decision taken by Grierson: that versions in French should be made of all new films and that some films should be produced in French and versioned in English. *Canada Carries On* was prepared in both languages. The first original French film in the series was *Un du 22ième*.

But there were problems. The Motion Picture Bureau was not accustomed to production on this scale and at this tempo. Frank Badgley had been running it on douce, civil service lines, a nine-to-five operation, innocent of pressures, unaware of deadlines, content to plod along. To Grierson this was anathema. He worked long hours himself. He expected everyone else to do so. His first secretary, Janet Scellen, had been totally unprepared for her dynamic and demanding employer and, worn out mentally and physically in a fortnight, resigned. Grierson assured her (mistakenly) that she would soon have an easier time and

109

she stayed on. Later she was to admit that working with Grierson was worth at the very least a couple of years of post-graduate study and she never regretted her devotion to him and his work. 'He was charming and demanding and difficult. You had to be totally committed.'[3]

Grierson's temporary appointment expired in July 1940 but was extended in stages until November and eventually until January 1941. In his letter of resignation to James A. Mackinnon, who had succeeded W. D. Euler as chairman of the Board, he commented on the conflict between the civil service attitude to their work and the creative freedom he felt they must have. He recommended that the Government should bring the Motion Picture Bureau within the administration of the National Film Board and should let the film commissioner and his executive relate government procedure to creative practice.[4] Among those who reacted immediately to his letter was Leonard Brockington, personal adviser to the Prime Minister and former chairman of the Canadian Broadcasting Corporation (his voice was often to be heard on radio in Britain during the war). He sent a memorandum to the Prime Minister, reminding him of the valuable creative work Grierson had initiated and concluding 'While, no doubt, Mr. Grierson has some temperamental weaknesses, as all creative people have, he is recognised as a world authority, and I believe his resignation to be a national calamity.'[5]

There were differences in emphasis in letters Grierson was writing at the time to Britain. To Basil Wright he wrote: 'I'm due to depart from here at the end of January. I have given them hell over the year, meaning mostly Frank Badgley and his veterans. I've been sorry to do it, and in a small town like this it seems almost sadistic; but it was a case of either/or. Frank could neither see the purposes, nor had the energy for the required initiative. . . . Well, after a year, I thought I had done enough, so I announced I was kissing them all good-bye, my job of initiating the National Film Board could be regarded as done, and I was now handing over to Canadians.' After referring to the forty films made in the first year of the Board, compared with the one and a half made by the Motion Picture Bureau in the preceding year, Grierson continued 'To this add the selfish reason that this was coming to look like a job instead of a revolution, and I don't like jobs.'[6]

From the terms of his letter to Wright, Grierson was obviously sincere in his wish to be free 'for some little things I have in mind to do'; but in the press and in Parliament there was growing resistance to the idea of his resignation. 'Why Lose a Genius?' asked the *Winnipeg Free Press* in a powerful leading article. 'Canada was very fortunate in securing John Grierson's services. This man is a genius, a creative, forceful, unorthodox, dynamic Scot with a wealth of experience in film-making and a tremendous, continuous stream of ideas pouring from his mind. . . . He is himself of the greatest value. But his chief importance lies in his faculty for inspiring the efforts of others.'[7] Even louder protests were made in French Canada. In twelve months the Board had made thirty-four films in French—more than the Motion Picture Bureau had made in twenty-five years. 'Down in the bistros of Montreal and Quebec they clutched me to their Canayan bosoms and cried "Le Gouvernement doit faire l'impossible pour conserver M. Grierson à son poste." '[8]

The battle rumbled on, long beyond January 1941. Grierson's health began to crumble under the strain. He saw a doctor who told him to lie on his back and that he was as good as ninety now. 'I started walking like an old bastard of ninety, very slow and dignified up everlasting steps, but I lied on no back.' He went to New York and Washington and then on to Mexico. The elevation in Mexico City was supposed to be bad for hearts but it did him a great deal of good, especially the bullfights. He went to Acapulco 'and lashed around for a week in a temperature of 120°, and struggled with two or three sharks'. Later he flew to Hollywood where Stuart Legg met him and they lined up a dozen films to be made in co-production. 'I was pretty well dead and am pretty well alive again', he wrote to Basil Wright on his return to Ottawa. 'I've got the old fight on my hands, and coming to a head again. If I win, there'll be a set up here the young dream about in their dreams. . . . The issue is the same—youth and activism against the bureaucrats and the mediocrity and complacency and death of the spirit they represent.'[9]

In Ottawa the conflict was still unresolved. The permanent civil servants were ranged behind Frank Badgley. In the Prime Minister's office the wise and politically skilful Walter Turnbull advised the Prime Minister that it would help if the representation of the Department of Trade and Commerce on the Board were limited to one, the chairman; that the secretary should be drawn from another department, and that the Board should have its own Treasury representative. Within the Board Charles Cowan won support for Grierson's proposals: that the Board's statutory authority be recognised in practice as well as theory; the film activities of the Bureau be brought under the Board; the present director of the Bureau continue as an officer of Trade and Commerce retaining the stills section; the organisation of the Bureau and the re-classification of its staff to be undertaken by the commissioner.

The recommendations were accepted and Grierson was persuaded to continue as commissioner for a further six months, until August 1941. On 11 June 1941, the Cabinet passed an Order-in-Council transferring the Bureau to the Board. The powers defined by the National Films Act to the Minister of Trade and Commerce were transferred to the Minister of National War Services. Frank Badgley, defeated, rejected the idea of retaining the stills section and a further Order-in-Council, on 8 August 1941, transferred this also to the Board. The reorganisation was complete. For Grierson it meant that he could at last control the implementation of his ideas. No more time was to be wasted in bureaucratic procedures.

During the months of indecision—but scarcely inactivity—Grierson was in close touch with his associates in London. This was as much a reflection of his uncertainty over his own future as of the feeling in London that, although he was in Canada, he was the active leader of the documentary film movement. There was a steady flow of letters from Basil Wright, Arthur Elton, Paul Rotha and John Taylor. In January 1940, they had begun to publish *Documentary News Letter* which was to continue 'the policy and purpose of *World Film News* by expressing the documentary idea'. Grierson was a member of the editorial board and contributed as opportunity allowed from Canada, as well as commenting critically on the issues as they appeared. It received some financial support from the International Film Centre, founded in the United States with the help of the Rockefeller Foundation with Donald Slesinger as executive director. It was from the first number a notable success, achieving a large readership in Britain and overseas among those who sensed in its contributions a solid concern with the impact of the war on the social scene.

Both the newsletter and the private letters to and from Grierson in Ottawa reflected the continuing struggle over the direction of the Films Division of the Ministry of Information in London. The appointment of Jack Beddington promised to inject a sense of purpose into production. Thomas Baird was put in charge of distribution and the future of the non-theatrical system built up by Grierson at the E.M.B. and the G.P.O. was secure. Grierson was told by Arthur Elton, 'I think you should stay out of the mess here. You are doing better over there.'[10] Later Elton was even firmer: 'Stay in Canada and make the thing flourish there. There is nothing I want to see happen more. You are about the only common sense focus left to us in the outside world.'[11] He noted that 'the powers of reactionary and malicious reaction are still entrenched in the official side of our life' (something Grierson

112

would understand), although Beddington was beginning to get things pretty firmly into his grasp.

The physical distance between Grierson and the members of the documentary film movement in Britain did not seem to matter. His influence was obvious in their thinking and in what they were struggling to do. It was no transient thing. Grierson always knew what was happening, both in the units around Soho Square and at the Malet Street headquarters of the Ministry of Information. When he learned that Paul Rotha, having completed his film on *The Times* (in the initiation of which Grierson had been involved), was temporarily out of production, he cabled inviting him to come to Canada. Rotha declined. In a long letter to Grierson he explained his motives: 'All the old complacency, reactionism, muddled thinking, lack of will to progress, which we have known during the whole development of documentary for ten years is now crystallised in the Films Division. . . . You may have your toes on the threshold of a new growing point for documentary and I pray to high heaven that great new things may come from Canada, but we cannot give up the situation here. The battle for propaganda must be fought to the bitter end.'[12]

In the same letter Rotha said he had asked Grierson's sister Ruby to give him a considered summing up of the whole situation when she saw him in Ottawa. She was due to sail on the *City of Benares*, carrying evacuated children to Canada, and had been working with John Taylor obtaining material for a film on the subject commissioned by the National Film Board. She had by then directed a number of films. *Documentary News Letter* considered that 'Her co-direction of *To-day We Live* established her as one of those few directors whose passionate sympathy with the life and spirit of ordinary people has formed the real main artery of documentary progress.'[13] She was as much admired for her personal qualities—her good humour, her fierce enthusiasms and her physical and spiritual energies. On 17 September 1940, the *City of Benares* was torpedoed six hundred miles off land. Of the ship's complement of 406, including ninety children, 248 were rescued. Ruby was not among the survivors. Nor was she in a lifeboat rescued five days later.

Grierson was crushed. His eyes revealed the depth of feeling stirred by his sister's death. A letter of sympathy from John Marshall at the Rockefeller Foundation received the briefest acknowledgement: 'Many thanks for your note, but neither wind nor water can undo it.'[14] The sadness was out of sight but not, for a long time, out of mind. Many years later, when the hurt had gone, he paid a tribute to what

113

Ruby had done when working on *Housing Problems*. 'The trouble with you', she had said to her brother, 'is that you look at things as though they were in a goldfish bowl.' Grierson: 'Yes I do. But so what?' Ruby Grierson: 'I'm going to break your goldfish bowl.' And so Ruby said to the slum-dwellers in *Housing Problems*: 'The camera is yours. The microphone is yours. Now tell the bastards exactly what it's like to live in slums.' The result, said Grierson, was a film which became very important to them.

In Canada, with the months of difficult reorganisation behind him, Grierson was launched on what would be the most productive period of his life. As film commissioner his base was now secure. He had the personal backing of the Prime Minister. Mackenzie King, who had been impressed by Grierson's *élan* and vitality, had responded, as one radical to another, to his ideas. The relationship became 'What Grierson says goes.' The Prime Minister did not pay much attention to ministerial sensitivities. When he wanted something he did it, in his own way, without much regard to whose responsibility it was or what the lines of authority were. Therefore when he wanted Grierson to have freedom to put his ideas into practice, an understanding of the situation was disseminated from the Prime Minister's office by J. W. Pickersgill and Walter Turnbull.[15] It was informal but effective.

The Film Board was located in an old sawmill by the Ottawa River, at the corner of John and Sussex Streets. Here Grierson began to build up a film-making organisation which by the end of the war was to grow to over eight hundred. Ross McLean was there to carry the burden of the day-to-day administration which Grierson then and later found irksome. Grierson recognised that McLean had a lot of influence on the place. 'He represents as well as anyone what Canada is about nowadays and keeps it marching into a dream of the Canadian future which in these parts excites almost everyone under forty.' Stuart Legg, austere, gifted, studiously conscientious, was meeting the formidable demands of the monthly *Canada Carries On* series and satisfying Grierson's blunt instruction: 'Bang them out, and no misses.' The quiet and steady Stanley Hawes, initially assisting Legg, was put in charge of army training films and films dealing with labour relations. Raymond Spottiswoode was combining the teaching of new apprentices with film production. Donald Buchanan, an indefatigable worker whom Grierson thought was never sufficiently appreciated in Canada, was building up, on the model of an experiment made in Scotland, the chain of rural circuits across the country. Grierson provided the overall direction, co-ordination and inspiration.

By the Ottawa River

New faces began to appear. Grierson showed an uncanny judgment, often exercised in a way which would have seemed eccentric to a staff recruitment officer. Tom Daly, freshly graduated from the University of Toronto and uninterested in films, used without much enthusiasm, a letter of introduction and became convinced, under Grierson's questioning, that he knew nothing about anything, not even his native city. Something in his manner registered with Grierson and Daly joined the Board where his devotion to careful research and his visual memory quickly proved his value.[16]

Stanley Jackson, a schoolmaster in Winnipeg, was summoned to meet Grierson at the Fort Garry Hotel and found him with George Ferguson and two or three other prominent Winnipeg citizens. Fascinating talk. Grierson probing, getting to know the country. Jackson said not a word, nor was a word addressed to him. The experience was repeated later in Toronto, with Morley Callaghan the novelist and Jean Bigisth the historian present. Drinks enjoyable, talk fabulous. There was a third hotel meeting, silent as far as Jackson was concerned. Then a call from Grierson, on a Friday: 'I want you in Ottawa on Monday.' Jackson thought 'The man's mad.' Later, when Jackson had established himself at the Board as a researcher and writer of quality, Grierson said: 'You have a great distinction, Jackson. You're the only person I've ever hired in my life without hearing him say a single word.'[17]

Grierson knew what he was doing in bringing in young people from the universities. He wanted an intellectual discipline in the Board's films. But the scale of the work was increasing at such a pace that he needed a leavening of film-making experience. His efforts to bring over Paul Rotha and Edgar Anstey were unsuccessful. He did, however, seek out Norman McLaren, who was in New York doing some work for the Guggenheim Museum. Grierson assured him that he would not be asked to make propaganda films for the war and persuaded him to come to Ottawa—where at the Film Board he was given all the freedom he wanted and where his genius was to enrich Canadian film-making over a span of thirty years.[18] Guy Glover, who had met Grierson with McLaren in London, joined the Board as an animator with McLaren but was soon assigned to *Canada Carries On*. Later he became head of the French unit.

Irving Jacoby, an experienced director of short films, had worked for a time with Grierson in London on *World Film News*. Grierson brought him from New York. In collaboration with Morley Callaghan he directed *Hot Ice*, an authentic description of the game of hockey as

115

it is played and breathed by youngsters everywhere in Canada and so successful a film that it ran for twenty years. Jacoby followed it with *High Over the Border*, a film of depth and beauty on bird migration in the western hemisphere.

Some of the filming for *High Over the Border* was done by another experienced film-maker, Julian Roffman, a Canadian whom Grierson invited to join him in Ottawa. They had met in New York in 1938. Roffman idolised Grierson, openly admiring his flow of stimulating ideas and the faith he placed in young people. He was put in charge of films for the armed forces. Like Grierson he never lacked confidence: when he described to Alfred Hitchcock, in Ottawa on his way to Hollywood, his plan for a two-minute musical to recruit women for the Army and Hitchcock said it couldn't be done, Roffman replied: 'You can't do it. But I *can* and I *will*.' And he did, with Grierson's blessing.[19] Roffman in turn invited another Canadian from New York, Leo Seltzer, whose first film was on minesweepers between Halifax and Newfoundland.

Grierson brought in other talents. Joris Ivens, who had helped to build documentary in the Netherlands and had been working in the United States, was brought to Canada to make *Action Stations!* on the conflict between the Canadian Merchant Marine and German submarines. His talented countryman, John Ferno, edited *High Over the Border* and worked on other films for the Board. When Grierson learned that Boris Kaufman, Jean Vigo's cameraman on *Zéro de Conduite* and *L'Atalante*, was in New York, he invited him to come to Canada to help both in shooting and in teaching the young apprentices. He enjoyed the experience, he told me in New York. 'Grierson had confidence in people once he had selected them to work for him. This confidence was inspiring and gave a freedom of action. Every creative artist likes to work this way.'[20] Alexander Alexieff, another Russian who had worked in Paris (*Night on the Bare Mountain*), was brought to Ottawa to collaborate with Norman McLaren on *Chants Populaires*. For George L. George there was also a French connection. He had met Grierson in Paris in 1930—'a man absolutely resolute in what he wanted to do'—and when they met again in Hollywood in 1942 George was making French versions of M.G.M. films. Grierson invited him to come to Ottawa where he reluctantly accepted the position of production manager but was happier when actively involved with Stuart Legg on *The World in Action*.[21]

Grierson's Ottawa acted as a magnet for young people all over Canada. 'Grierson not only created turbulence and excitement where

116

he went', wrote James Beveridge, he also 'goaded all his people to bring out the best within them. The times were ripe: there was fervour and idealism. Grierson caught this particular flood-time in Canada, and brought a charge and excitement to the business of communication which left its mark for years to come, among two generations of film-makers.'[22] Sydney Newman had been a successful artist before Grierson engaged him. It was the beginning of a long and fruitful friendship: Newman was later to become film commissioner and to have Grierson's help at a difficult time. Grierson conveyed to them his sense that there was something uniquely marvellous in Canada—that they were not American or English or Scottish. 'He gave us all a sense of time and place and importance and dignity and a kind of respect for the craft—but always the craft as subservient to the message.'[23]

Michael Spencer, who was later to be in charge of the Canadian Film Development Corporation, joined Grierson and worked as a cameraman and editor before going to Europe with the Canadian Army Film Unit. Alan Field had newspaper experience before joining the Board to work on *Canada Carries On* and eventually supervise the news-reel division. Graham McInnes, radio commentator and art critic, was recruited as a script-writer and collaborated with F. R. (Budge) Crawley in making *Canadian Landscape* before directing and producing many fine films for the Board. He recalled Grierson as 'the very picture of sulphurously creative disruption', telling them after the fall of France that there would be rough times ahead for the people of Britain. 'We must oppose discipline to discipline. Ours to theirs. But you discipline a democracy by creating the collective will from within; not by imposing it from without.'[24]

In a short film made by the Board about the fall of France, Grierson introduced a sequence which was later reckoned to be one of the simplest and most successful pieces of Allied propaganda. At Compiègne Hitler, in delight at his victory, did a sort of first step of the Highland fling. By slow motioning and repeating the gesture, Grierson made it appear that he was dancing a jig. 'Any slow motioning of a dancing gesture tends to look sissy and that of course was the intention', he said. 'I don't believe myself that the enormous note taken of the so called Jake came from the film at all. What happened was that when we had the gesture in front of us in slow motion we produced a page spread of stills and circulated it all over America. Every still of course tends to have its own sissifying suggestion. I myself think it was the page spread so widely circulated which did the trick.'[25]

The expanding Film Board could now have a music department.

Lou Applebaum and Maurice Blackburn wrote the music for many of the Board's early films. Grierson did not know much about music, with the exception of jazz, but he had a sense of rhythm and was a good judge, at the cutting copy stage, of where music would help a film. He would sometimes make impossible demands—as of Lou Applebaum to make a new arrangement of 'La Marseillaise' on the spot 'with more trumpets. It's too soft.' He knew what he wanted and he wanted it done right away.[26] He couldn't wait. Another musician to join the Board was Eugene Kash. Many years later the Toronto conductor spoke movingly to me about the memories Grierson had left with him. 'There's an inner flame in just a few mortals that can ignite the talents and energies of young people on which they can build their futures and those of us who came into contact with Grierson had every right to place him beside milestones of the twentieth century in great thought and action in any medium.'[27]

Grierson was protective about the staff he was building up. A belief in the value of their work for the future of Canada was central to his philosophy. He did not want to see them drawn into the armed forces. He had an argument one day in George Ferguson's room at the Château Laurier in Ottawa with the minister responsible for man-power. 'I think we're getting after the Board', the minister said. 'It seems to me there's a lot of military man-power available there that could be put to work.' Grierson took him seriously and argued that it was essential to have skilled film-makers in wartime Canada. 'Well', said the minister, 'I'll just take a few of them.' Grierson: 'You take them if you want them. But mark my words, you'll ruin the Board and you'll get nothing but a couple of indifferent platoons.'[28]

At the back of Grierson's mind was the thought that one day they might have to go. So he started hiring women. Janet Scellen was working long, hard hours as his secretary, deciphering his handwriting, dashing after him with telephone messages, and admiring his skill in extracting funds from government departments for film projects. Evelyn Spice (Cherry) had returned to Canada, bringing the experience she had gained in Britain. In Winnipeg Grierson was interviewed by 'one of the most beautiful women in Canada', Gudrun Bjerring (Parker), working for his friend George Ferguson on the *Winnipeg Free Press* and brought her to Ottawa as a writer. After about four months she was making films, successfully, for the Department of Health and Welfare.

Beth Bertram left the University of Toronto library to work first in the Board's film library, was later taught how to handle negative by

118

Margaret Grierson, and was eventually to be in the important post of director of personnel where, one day, she rejected an application for a job made by Pierre Trudeau.[29] Through Donald Buchanan, Grierson met Margaret Ann Bjornson (Lady Elton) in Winnipeg and engaged her. After a spell in the negative room, Spartan, spick and span, the pride of the Film Board and much admired, she moved into Stuart Legg's *World in Action* office as research assistant, idea woman and expert at locating shots. She thought the sense of being overworked and underpaid was important to the staff. 'They liked being driven. They felt they were engaged in doing the job of the century.'[30]

Marjorie McKay, who passed an examination for economists in Vancouver and came into the Film Board by accident, remained to bring some order into the accounting system. Later she was to write the first *History of the National Film Board of Canada*. From the eastern seaboard came Margaret Perry whom Grierson was later to put in charge of the Nova Scotia Travel Bureau. Laura Boulton signed a six-week contract to make a film on the people of Canada—and remained for three years to produce a series of fifteen, among the most popular of all the Board's films.

More and more women were being engaged by Grierson. Some like Daphne Lilly (Anstey) and Jane Marsh (Beveridge) went into production. Helen Watson (Gordon) went into distribution to run the rural circuits. Many years later she met Grierson in India where 'he only then seemed to be realising, in Calcutta twenty-five years later, that the early enthusiasm and organisation procedure had put a very special foundation under the National Film Board.'[31] Margaret Carter, sent by Grierson to organise United States distribution from Chicago, was told, 'You have the whole United States to play around in. It's up to you.' Bette Brunke, who was brought in with Marion Meadows by Grierson from the University of Toronto, told me: 'He had an eye for everybody's potential. He seemed to be able to spot creativity.'[32]

There were, of course, interruptions. When one of the women came and told Grierson she was getting married he would leap out of his chair and say: 'Ditched again by a fucking woman. What do you do? You spend six, nine months, a year training them and then they get up like God-damned breeding cattle and walk off into the stable!'[33] In a calmer mood he would sum up: 'They may brag about what the men did at the Film Board, but let me now say that they wouldn't have been worth a damn without the women. The women were the stronger half.'[34]

Amidst the proliferation of production and the spreading distribution, there was never any doubt in Grierson's mind about the main focus. It was in Stuart Legg's unit and the regular issue of *Canada Carries On* and *The World in Action*. The films in the first series were devoted to Canadian achievements—'what Canadians need to know and think about if they are going to do their best by Canada and themselves.' *The World in Action* looked outwards. 'We are concerned in these films', said Grierson, 'primarily with the relation of local strategies to larger world ones.' Here was a powerful demonstration of the still comparatively new concept of geo-politics. A number of factors contributed to the phenomenal success of *The World in Action*. There was the knowledge of world events and movements which between them Grierson and Legg commanded. There was Legg's almost uncanny prescience which again and again suggested he had inside sources of information. There was the availability of a vast amount of material: footage from the British Ministry of Information, the U.S. Signal Corps, the Free French news-reel and all the captured material from Germany, Italy and, later, Japan. There was the advice given at key moments by James Reston of the *New York Times* who said to Legg on one occasion when he was desperately trying to see a way out of chaos: 'Remember there is a reason in history for everything.' In style there was a minimum of reflection and a maximum of certainty. There was the experienced guidance of David Coplan about what audiences would accept in a twenty-minute film. If he said, 'Do you expect me to sell that crap?' it was back to the cutting bench to see how the drama could be heightened or the conflict sharpened. And there was Grierson's supreme confidence as a salesman.

Stuart Legg thought of the films as screen editorials. Taut and remorseless they were the pattern of event rather than the event itself. Their themes were summed up in the titles: *Food—Weapon of Conquest*, *The Battle for Oil*, *The Strategy of Metals*, *Hitler's Plan for Empire*, *Global Air Routes*. Two weeks before Pearl Harbour *War Clouds in the Pacific* was released in Canada. Legg's prescience meant that the Canadian Film Board had scooped *The March of Time* and other United States news-reels by anticipating Japan's involvement in war with the United States. The film contained some shots obtained by arrangement from *The March of Time*. Louis de Rochemont entered an action in the District Court of New York, barring the distribution of the film in the United States. There was a meeting in New York between Grierson and his lawyer and Louis de Rochemont and the lawyers of Time–Life Incorporated. It could have been an awkward impasse but the solution was less dramatic than some accounts have suggested. Grierson's lawyer pointed out that the shots from *The March of Time* could be replaced by similar material from other libraries but it would be more convenient to leave them in, in return for an acknowledgement to *The March of Time*. The suit was dropped.

War Clouds in the Pacific was shown in thousands of theatres in the United States and did more than any other single film to draw attention to the work of the Film Board. *The World in Action* was eventually to play in some seven thousand United States theatres. It was a formidable achievement, especially in a market so closely protected. In another sense it was an all-important outlet for a Canadian view of world events.

Grierson did not underestimate the value of non-theatrical distribution as a complement to what was being done in the theatres. In July 1941 he was on his way to Hollywood to arrange for Walt Disney to produce four films persuading Canadians to hold on to their War Savings Certificates. He stopped in Chicago long enough to see Wesley Greene whom he had met in 1938 and who had his own successful International Film Bureau.[35] Greene accepted Grierson's invitation to come to Ottawa as co-ordinator of distribution. Grierson showed his appreciation by giving him Janet Scellen as his assistant. He was joined by the experienced Donald Buchanan, just back from Bermuda where he had been receiving the captured Axis footage. Together they built up a system of travelling projectionists to cover the rural areas and later other circuits, organised by Gordon Adamson, to reach the workers in the factories.

This completed for Grierson the scheme of nation-wide communication he wanted. 'We have made a big business of our moods of relaxation; we have not concentrated nearly so much on our moods of resolution. Yet, on the face of it, it is in our moods of resolution that we may be expected to build the future. These moods are worth organising, just as deliberately as the movies, the newspapers and the show business generally, have been organising our moods of relaxation. In Canada we are well ahead in this new film development, out among the leaders.'[36]

By the summer of 1941 Grierson felt that the Canadian film operation was sufficiently well organised for him to pay a visit to Britain. Mackenzie King had left Canada for Britain on 19 August and Grierson followed not long afterwards. He was in Edinburgh on 3 September but most of the time he spent in London. He did not find the documentary movement in particularly good heart. It still lacked a strong, positive lead from the Ministry of Information. Among the units there were jealousies and other personal antagonisms which were aggravated by war conditions. He found it a little difficult to make contact. Paul Rotha arranged a meeting of some of the younger film-makers where Grierson was 'boldly cross-examined' and where he was 'interested in the fact that they couldn't take anything constructive out of what I said'.

The constructive line, he suggested in a letter written from Lisbon to Basil Wright, 'does not merely come from repeating single positives like tempo, objective reporting, etc., etc., but more deeply from the conception of order. It will mean on the one hand having a clearer idea of what to do with the social themes that come to hand: getting in a more factual approach, seeing the thing as a whole, seeing where it came from and where it leads, and where it relates to what is basically happening. It will mean, on the other hand, developing themes now hardly touched and finding new themes: particularly in the Services, and particularly where leadership and organisation of any positive support is developing. And not least there may be something in giving a new emphasis altogether to youth and the new generation.'[37]

Grierson was sick at heart at leaving his colleagues. 'I was afraid from the beginning of this whole business of coming back, whence perhaps my drastic effort not to get too involved.' The Canadian show, however, was bigger than most of them had realised. *The World in Action* series was the first really international thing the documentary movement had managed. 'Nothing, except our own limit of wit, can prevent it growing into a powerful instrument, the like of which the Ministry of Information just hasn't thought of.'

Ostensibly neutral Lisbon, Grierson found, was not a capital to linger in. 'We waited an hour to-day to have eight passports examined by a police official who was damned if he'd be courteous to anything from England, even the Duke of Alba. We haven't much left evidently to impress a Portuguese cop. The local sheets, I see, give first place to the German communiques.'[38]

One of his first engagements on his return was an address on the film industry in wartime at the National Board of Review conference in New York in November. Grierson was punctiliously polite. The cardinal sin in employing the film industry as a vehicle of public information was to bore people away from it, he said. He spoke of the success of *Canada Carries On* but explained that they had been diffident about showing the series in the United States. 'We thought you might think we were trying to do something to you and we wouldn't hurt you for the world'—an attempt at humour which, according to his friend Martin Quigley, Jr., did not meet with audience response. Had his talk been given a few weeks later it might have been heard with more appreciation in a country at war.

In Ottawa the Film Board was still growing. Among those who joined at the time of Pearl Harbour was Alan Adamson whom Grierson had met in 1939 as an undergraduate in Winnipeg in the company of Donald Buchanan and Margaret Ann Bjornson. Of his first meeting Adamson remembered being struck by 'these terrible eyes, glaring at you. He looked like a man who was living an immensely exciting, ravaged kind of life, burning himself up at immense speed.'[39] He also remembered Grierson saying 'It's not going to be the same this time. The ordinary Britisher is not going to allow himself to be pushed around by the officers. They've learned from people like Jimmy Cagney how to defend themselves.' Adamson had a job in the Manitoban Department of Education, looking after films and radio for schools, but wanted to work for Grierson who had become for him a kind of intellectual exemplar.

By this time Grierson and Margaret were established in a house at Cooper Street from which he liked to work. Here Grierson summoned Adamson after about three days and he was little out of his sight, from breakfast until midnight, for the next four months. About four in the afternoon, when Adamson was soaking with sweat and tension and exhaustion, Grierson would be sitting there 'with the most malevolent look of sadistic joy on his face'. Like so many others before and after him, Adamson reached an understanding with Grierson, 'this small, passionate, angry, caustic, militant, radical Scot, this teacher whose pedagogical secret was example, who may not in the end have been sure of what he was to exemplify, but who made the air vivid by signing it with his vitality.' For a brief period Adamson saw more of Grierson than any other member of the Board and came to know him better than most.

On 26 February 1942, Grierson was back in Hollywood, attending the fourteenth annual awards banquet of the Academy of Motion Picture Arts and Sciences at the Biltmore Hotel. He received the Oscar presented to the Film Board for *Churchill's Island* and made the presentations of the special awards for documentary, given for the first time that year by the Academy. One was for *Target for Tonight*, directed by Harry Watt. Grierson's speech was admirable in form and content.

He congratulated Hollywood for having, under the influence of the

Academy and other forces, 'come progressively to grips with public responsibility and public purpose'. He had a friendly dig at Brendan Bracken, British Minister of Information, who found that a Soviet delegation in London, given the opportunity to see some British documentaries, said they would prefer to see Chaplin's *The Dictator*— and laughed all the way through *three* non-stop showings. He noted the wartime service being given by Walter Wanger, Darryl Zanuck, John Ford and Frank Capra. And, because the occasion was something of a milestone for the documentary film, he cited the names of the pioneers in documentary. From the United States, Robert Flaherty, Ernest Shoedsack, Merian Cooper, Pare Lorentz and Louis de Rochemont. From England, Basil Wright, Stuart Legg, Arthur Elton, Paul Rotha and Bruce Woolfe. From France, Cavalcanti, Benoit-Lévy, Jean Painlevé and Jean Vigo. From Holland, Joris Ivens. From Belgium, Henri Storck. From Germany, Walter Ruttmann and Leni Riefenstahl. And from Russia, Vertov, Eisenstein and Pudovkin. 'Without each and all of them, we would not to-day be celebrating the relative maturity of the documentary film, nor would we be facing the growing tasks which the war has imposed upon us, with the same confidence and usefulness.' Grierson the diplomat.[40]

On his way back to Ottawa Grierson stopped, as he often did, in Chicago and saw Rudolph and Fritzi Weisenborn. Their son, Gordon Weisenborn, who had had some success as a stills photographer, inheriting his father's skill in composition, was invited to join the staff of the Board.[41] He arrived at the same time as Grant McLean whose father, A. G. McLean, was controller. After a short period of inactivity they went together to Grierson to protest that their talents were not being used. Grierson's response was typically direct and immediate. 'You will see on my desk here a camera. An Arriflex. The first time anyone outside Germany has seen one. I'm going to give you this Arriflex and 400 feet of film. Weisenborn and Grant, go out and make a movie. No pans. No tilts.' They concocted a plot for a film to be called *A Sunday in Hull*. When it was shot and edited they showed it to Grierson. As the lights went up Grierson said 'That's the greatest bunch of stills I have ever seen. McLean, go to the camera department. Weisenborn, go to editing.' Weisenborn worked with Tom Daly, editing *The World in Action*. McLean became one of the longest serving, and most independently minded, members of the staff.

When so many new people were being engaged it was inevitable that there should be some failures. For a man with a reputation for toughness, Grierson found it difficult to be ruthless in firing them. His method was to give them a dauntingly difficult assignment, in the hope that they would feel inadequate and quit. Two such film-makers, about whom Grierson felt he had make a mistake, were sent to the Arctic to make a film. Julian Roffman recalled being in Grierson's office when they re-appeared. 'My God,' he said 'you're back.' 'Yes', they said, 'we've finished the film.' Grierson: 'Well, get back and do another film.' To Roffman he said later: 'I'll get rid of them if it's the last thing I do.' Roffman felt that he often played one man against another in order to get them to do better, prove themselves. Maximum effort was what he wanted from everyone.[42]

By now the staff numbered nearly two hundred. Grierson thought they were on the whole a good crew, with plenty of energy and good-will. He did not think he had yet discovered enough people of first-rate power to hold down the wide field they were being progressively given. Two, perhaps three, series of films had really good people behind them. 'The others slip and slide in only relative competence and it's a problem to know how to give the natively not-so-good the kind of production approach that lets a producer sleep easily at nights. We have now as many as seventy films on the stocks at one time, and of all sorts and kinds. Legg has emerged as the most powerful news editor and commentator in films in North America, but we could do with half-a-dozen of him.' Grierson knew that he had paid a price for the elimination of the old gang under Frank Badgley. The reaction went deep and it was not to be forgotten. He enjoyed the personal support of the Prime Minister. He knew he had done more for Quebec than the other information services 'which may come in handy one day'.[43]

Grierson now had an opportunity for reflection—the first for a very long time. In April 1942 his health had broken under the strain, coupled with the hard Canadian winter, and he had been sent off with Margaret to recuperate in the sub-tropical heat of Sarasota, Florida. 'A blessed relief it is from the vicious Canadian winter, and nicely impossible in purple skies, green seas and blazing white beaches, with decorative pieces of flamingo and what not.' Writing to his brother, Dr. Anthony Grierson, he said: 'The health thing is a bother, but my own fault. I did a hell of a job in the past year and between you and me the sort of job that tears your guts out. . . . The actual difficulties of organisation have been enormous. We've had to build personnel where there was none creative and all the technical departments have had to be raised from the dead. It has meant a lot of cruelty and if I'm exhausted it's with a sense of my own bloodiness. But I don't think a big unit was ever made so fast and so spontaneously. Right now we're probably doing as much as the M.o.I. with all its ready-made units and we're moving in on national education on fifty fronts, like the German army. Give me a year and I'll have taught progressive democracy to a nation as it hasn't been taught for a couple of generations.'[44]

It was impossible for Grierson to remain idle for very long. After what he called his forty days in the wilderness when he was pretty miserable, accepting the tropical blessings as sourly as a beachcomber, he came to, with all his usual fire. He wrote a long assessment of the documentary situation, 'The Documentary Idea, 1942' for *Documentary News Letter*. He wrote at length to his friends in Britain and Canada. But by far the most demanding piece of writing was some 60,000 words or so for a book, 'Eyes of Democracy'. He had signed a contract with George Routledge & Sons on 1 February 1940. One of the Routledge directors, Herbert Read, was on the selection committee of the Labour Book Service and it was intended that Grierson's book should be one of its monthly choices. In October 1940 he had had to write explaining that because of the demands on him he had not the reserve of time and energy to do a considerable job on the book—'events these days are distorting our calmer purposes'—and hoping that he could do something in the future when times were quieter.

The completed chapters remained among his papers, unseen and unpublished. In the introduction he wrote in a more directly personal way than was his wont: 'I have been a propagandist all my working life because I have believed that we needed to do our democratic mind over if we were going to save democracy. I have believed that in education was the heart of the matter, but that education needed to be revolutionised altogether if it was to become the instrument of revolutionised democracy I was thinking of. . . . I have had to pretend to a whole lot of powers I didn't have in running my education revolution. I have had to be a creative worker and a civil servant and a promoter and an organiser and a critic and a teacher of the youth; and although I hate finance and know nothing about it, I have had to find the millions, often from people I dared not tell fully what I was after lest it would seem pretentious. . . . I have, of course, been paraded at various times as an uncomfortable character for a public servant to be, and certainly I have always fought my battles as though I intended to win them. This was always a difficult situation, for . . . it is only if the State is fighting for democracy that it has a dog's chance of coming through.'[45]

Grierson wrote that circumstances had made the book a hurried job, done on an enforced holiday to clear the conscience about the war and its implications. He hoped it would be read as an effort to teach a lot of young people and incidentally himself on a very important and practical issue of the day. But the book was to remain uncompleted. After his appointment as general manager of the Wartime Information Board, he realised that publication had become impossible. Directors of information should not write books while they are directors of information, he wrote to Routledge. 'I have only to publish this particular one to destroy everything we are doing. For, as with you, our department of information is a notable target for politicians and my written views are too sharply put for this young nation to take easily.' Grierson did not reveal the existence of this uncompleted manuscript when I proposed to him the book which was published in 1946 as *Grierson on Documentary*. I was unaware of it until I found it among his papers.

In a long letter to Sir Stephen Tallents—with Basil Wright, his most regular correspondent—Grierson wrote that the film thing had the appearance of being well founded in Canada. 'There has been a good deal of thought and research behind the films and of a more deliberate and scientific nature than we ever got organised for in England. They have acquired a certain present pertinence and size from considering the more far reaching and difficult patterns of the war. The world strategy of food, for example, which goes back in a curious way to the E.M.B. and John Orr, but less sentimental than Orr. We have certainly diverged a long way from the documentary model now being pursued in England: in the direction of more knowledge of political plan and the design behind the news.'[46]

While Grierson was still absent from Ottawa there had been a near disaster at the old sawmill. One hot summer morning in June, a glass frame covering a light bulb in one of the cutting rooms was broken and there was contact between a reel of film and the exposed bulb. In less than a minute the cutting room was a mass of flames. The negative room was on the ground floor and, in answer to the cry, 'Rescue the negative!' members of the staff rushed through the greenish smoke, grabbed a few tins, and got out. Asbestos wall-board and the immediate closing of heavy fire-doors in the vaults limited the damage. It was a near thing. The immaculate and unapproachable Raymond Spottiswoode, drenched and dirty from working with the firemen, was the acknowledged hero of what might have been a disastrous day for the young National Film Board.

9 Canadian Summit

Through newspapers and more especially radio, Grierson kept himself constantly well informed about the war situation. He had a small, high-powered radio and at night he often fiddled with it, listening to all sorts of stations. On the night of 19 August 1942—the day of the Dieppe Raid—he was listening with Irving Jacoby to a German station. He knew the psychological importance of the raid to Canada, where the people were longing to hear of Canadian troops in action and where the newspapers believed they were about to satisfy this longing with news of a Canadian success. Grierson listened to the German account of raiders repulsed, men killed and guns captured. He sensed that this was not Nazi propaganda but the truth. Immediately he was in touch with the newspapers to alert them about the German version and to advise them to restrain their headlines. Events proved his intervention to be timely.[1]

Some months later there was a sequel to the Dieppe Raid which demonstrated Grierson's positive attitude to propaganda. Canadians had learned with anger that prisoners taken at Dieppe were manacled hand and foot on Hitler's express orders. Grierson proposed to Mackenzie King that the Film Board should make a film on how German prisoners of war were being treated in Canada. Alan Field, supervisor of the news-reel divison, produced the film and a crew under the direction of Ham Wright filmed young captured German sailors, bronzed and healthy, working cheerfully in the sunshine, playing soccer and eating from plates heaped with good food. Only one print of the film was made. It was delivered to the Swiss Red Cross who arranged for it to fall conveniently into German hands. Later Grierson learned that it had actually been shown to Hitler—and that the Canadian soldiers had been released from their chains.[2]

Grierson had the Dieppe Raid in mind when he addressed the Institute of Inter-American Affairs at the Museum of Modern Art in New York on 11 October. American newsreels, he said, were rightly proud of having something to say about their American troops at Dieppe. 'But imagine what the reel looked like to Canadians. It was a

Canadian action but somehow, all at once, it had become an American action, and to people who had just come from reading their own casualty lists.'

Whatever the source—his return to full health, the opportunity for reflection in Florida, or the growing strength of his position in Ottawa—there was a new note of authority in this address. He felt he could enunciate for the United States the principles of international relationship. 'There is a feeling, right or wrong, that the United States has a degree of imperialism in its composition which bears watching.' He hoped it was not the good neighbourliness of the benevolent squire to his villagers that the United States was thinking of. Internationalism, he argued, began at home. It would be one of the surest signs of world leadership in North America if, in their films, they had the implicit assumption that North American citizens were natural citizens of a wider world. 'We should seize every opportunity we can, particularly in the field of newsreel and actuality, to turn our national stories into international stories and accustom the native mind to thinking in these wider perspectives.'

Grierson chose this occasion to give his own reading of the internal situation in Canada—what was sometimes stupidly referred to as 'the problem of French Quebec', the problem simply being that the Frenchman would not speak or think or believe like the Anglo-Saxon. He thought of the problem as an Anglo-Saxon problem rather than a French one. 'The French learn to speak English; they go to great lengths to understand the Anglo-Saxon viewpoint, but you may take it that the last thing we Anglo-Saxon Canadians do is to return the compliment. . . . We take what we can from French Canada but, in the last resort, we give it little in return. So elect do we feel as Anglo-Saxons that we do not think to do so. It is a basic weakness in our character and attitude and among all those who have fallen under our influence; and it would be the greatest possible contribution to international understanding if we only set ourselves still more busily to unlearning it.'

Grierson was often to return to this theme, in public and private discourse, and action was to emerge from his beliefs. Meantime in Ottawa moves were being made which were going to add very substantially to his burdens and responsibilities. Canada's information services had been much criticised. Charles Vining was asked to prepare a report and as a result the Bureau of Public Information was replaced by the Wartime Information Board which followed the pattern of the National Film Board in that it had a governing board consisting of a

E   129

chairman, vice-chairman and eight senior departmental officers representing the informational needs and problems of the government services, and an executive instrument, headed by a general manager who had to give regular accounts of his stewardship but for most of the time enjoyed considerable freedom.

Vining accepted appointment as general manager and, in partial fulfilment of his own recommendations, established offices in Washington, New York, London and Canberra, as well as in Latin America. Vining's health was indifferent—some people suggested that the thought of actually running the organisation he had created was too much for him—and he resigned in January 1943. Before he left he recommended that external and domestic informational activities should be combined under a single administration. He suggested that Grierson should become general manager, a suggestion welcomed and acted upon by Mackenzie King. Grierson accepted the appointment, on a temporary basis. The Wartime Information Board occupied the handsome, newly completed Supreme Court building, the best building in Ottawa, much to the annoyance of the judges and the civil servants—something in which Grierson found malicious enjoyment.

Sir Stephen Tallents was among those who wrote congratulating Grierson on his appointment. 'Nothing has galled me more in recent years', he said, 'than my failure to get you in this country the opening that your real genius for such work demanded (I always hoped that you understood what a weight of partly vicious and partly rapine opposition had to be borne). And no tidings could have given me greater satisfaction than those of Canada's offering you a real opening for the exercise of qualities which, I like to think, I recognised when you called on me years ago at the E.M.B.'[3] Grierson replied at length: his letters to Tallents were always carefully phrased. The appointment had surprised him, he said. The French had welcomed it. 'Being Scots, and a natural-born pluralist in a country that has made a political philosophy of pluralism has helped. . . . "Cet Écossais, notre cousin." ' He thought the Prime Minister had had a good deal to do with it and was personally pleased.[4]

Canadians, Grierson suggested in a penetrating passage in the letter, had a fantastic sense of want, although they did not realise it. The want was articulated in a thousand different directions. 'Partly it's young-nation staff; partly a growing sense of destiny *vis-à-vis* the United States to the south and Russia over the right shoulder; partly it's a sense that the pluralist political shape they are dedicated to, is too difficult, and a craving for what seems a greater and more dramatic simplicity in others; partly it's a sense of the common economic illness. The last appears especially ridiculous in a country that has far more production power, agricultural and industrial, for its twelve millions than any country on the earth; yet, paradoxically, it is closer than most to the primitive dreams of personal fortune that go with a pioneer state.'

Grierson indicated his intention in his new post to put the media under their own steam and concentrate on easing the sources of information, even when it laid the department open to public criticism. On the press side, he said he would sooner demobilise and send back to their papers men in the Services than build up at the centre. Radio was in the hands of a fellow villager of Grierson's, Dr. James S. Thomson who had been with him at school in Stirling, had gone to Canada as Professor of Theology at Pine Hill Divinity Hall, Halifax, and had become President of the University of Saskatchewan. The big job, Grierson thought, would be to get a centre of good thinking into the Canadian Broadcasting Corporation and a production staff which would recognise a continuing purpose when they saw it. Grierson confessed that he could not get very excited about the war effort *per se* and felt that any information regarding it must somehow try to get behind the shot and the shell. He expected to concentrate instead on a new activism in education and a sense of education in action and by action. He hoped to get all the relevant departments behind the schemes, so that all information was tied to common ends. He thought that if the planning were extensive enough, a few reactionary let-downs would not affect the bearing of the whole.

Inevitably there were difficulties. Grierson found that he had inherited an office with no policy and no internal morale, and enemies everywhere. The Wartime Information Board had interpreted its co-ordinating authority as a sanction to master-mind the departments. The press was suspicious of an instrument which might appear to the people as something over their heads and come between them and the sources of information. Parliament sensed the same danger. No one, Grierson found, had drawn a sufficiently clear distinction between Information on behalf of departments, departmental heads and the party, and Information related to Government initiative which was necessary and carried general sanction. In time Grierson found both a friendlier press and Parliament than before. The more he became tangled in Information as a whole, the more staggered he was at the power it could so easily exercise, without the safeguards as in

Britain of a strong press, a strong sense of local initiative and local criticism, and a relatively critical educational system.[5]

Grierson found another problem in the physical size of Canada. Great sectors of the country were a thousand and two thousand miles distant from the Federal capital. When restrictions and sacrifices of one kind or another were imposed, there was always a big lag, by reason of distance, in comprehension and co-operation. There were also vast differences in psychological reaction between the English-speaking and French-speaking citizenry and a tendency to translate natural prejudices into general complaints of governmental distance and misunderstanding. Writing to his brother-in-law, Duncan McLaren, Grierson said that the difficulties of the Information job had already bumped off three general managers and that he expected an attempt would be made to bump him off. 'But we'll see about that, because this time the animal is going to be very malevolent and will defend itself, you may take it. They're not bumping me off, just because of their bloody geography.'[6] Such pugnacity was another indication of his return to his natural aggressiveness.

Never allowing an idle moment to slip his grasp, Grierson was writing to Duncan McLaren in a Vancouver-bound plane, flying over a smooth white landscape. 'I never thought there could be so much snow in the world, or for so long. It's getting so they have to dig out the telephone poles to keep the wires working. If there isn't a Chinook, or whatever they call it, by the time we get to Calgary, and a spot of black earth in Victoria, I'll give up. But I expect there will be and, like Alyosha, I shall feel the sticky little leaves with my hands and water the earth with my tears of sheer thankfulness.' It was forty below zero. But he knew that in two or three months' time the earth would break and blaze into a flurry of summer 'and melons and peaches and pomegranates (pomegranates are an exaggeration) will spring from nowhere and overnight, out of the fatted soil'.

Grierson could carry the double burden of Information and the National Film Board not only because of his own energy but also because he had able deputies. At the Film Board Ross McLean looked after administration while Stuart Legg directed the creative effort of a large number of workers. At the Wartime Information Board Grierson had an assistant general manager Davidson Dunton, former editor of the *Montreal Standard* who had joined the organisation shortly after its establishment. 'Grierson was full of ideas', he told me in Ottawa, 'and we were all stimulated by him but he did not do much of the day-to-day administration of the Board.' According to Dunton, Grierson always had very ready access to Mackenzie King. 'The Prime Minister had a great deal of faith in him, a great deal of confidence. Grierson represented a side of King—and a very good side of King—an interest in humanity and people and proposed advancement and change. It's a side of King which isn't always recognised. I remember Grierson saying: "If things get tough, I'll go and see the P.M." He did, and things were all right.'[7]

One of the films made by Grierson and Legg gave particular satisfaction to Mackenzie King. *The War for Men's Minds*, a daring four-reeler, was based on the Lincoln theme: 'When the common people rise to find their liberty, not the gates of Hell will prevail against them', and it was, in Grierson's opinion, 'a fiercer statement of the progressive, democratic outlook than any government source has publicly attempted'. Matching the thundering rhetoric of Legg's commentary was a memorable score by Luigi Agostini, with a magnificent march in deference to Grierson's ideas about music. The Prime Minister was much excited by the film and sent a personal copy to Roosevelt with whom he was linked in the commentary as one of the two voices of North American leadership. Grierson was proud of the film, proud of its order, its compassion, and its hope in images of disorder and savagery as horrifying as Bosch or Goya.

During his year as general manager of the Wartime Information Board, Grierson made a number of speeches in the main Canadian cities: he regarded it as part of his duty to move about the country and whether it was snow-bound or baked by the sun made little difference. In October 1943 he was in Winnipeg, making a major speech on 'Propaganda and Education' at a Canadian Club occasion. He had a gift for refreshing and recharging his basic thinking with contemporary reference and example and did so to great effect in this long statement of his beliefs and attitudes. He was concerned as so often with the power of education to affect the relationship between people and government and he criticised educators for having failed to realise their duty and their responsibility.

Reasons for the failure he found in the extent to which education was unrelated to an active and participant citizenship and its incapacity to absorb the complex materials of civic observation and action. He did, however, think that those who had been working progressively together had something to show for their labours. 'I knew the day when it was revolutionary to think of making "peace as exciting as war" and I think I was the first to hear an audience applaud the film appearance of industrial workers as though they were applauding the national flag.

For there was a time when the ordinary was rejected as boring and when we were told firmly that people wanted to escape from the contemplation of their own lives and their own problems.' He went on to describe how that obstacle had been overcome by putting 'glistening patterns of vigour and skill and mass industrial achievement against the sky and men to-day accept them as part and parcel of the testament of beauty'.

In another speech on 'The Necessity and Nature of Public Information' he dealt with Canada against a broad world background. The war, he said, had given to Canada a degree of international significance she did not have before. 'She has with a spurt become an industrial nation of great importance. She has developed her native air-mindedness into a power to be reckoned with in any country's language. She has discovered in the new world of air spaces and air routes that she is in cold fact on top of the world.' He referred to the responsibility to neighbours and said 'it is more important than ever before that Canada's story be known to the nations. Her place at the council table and her place in the world, materially and spiritually, depend on the predisposition of other nations to hear her voice, understand it and respect it. That carries with it a great deal of prior work in creating that disposition.'

To a unique and remarkable extent, Grierson accepted that duty and directed the work. To him the test of a good information service was not to be found in the slickness with which it drummed up public attention but rather in the wide reaches of education lying behind the immediate news. It was in the creation of national unity and the promotion of concord between one part of a country and another. It was in the promotion of better industrial relations, better knowledge of food and nutrition, better preparation of youth for a life of good citizenship. His message, expressed in different forms and on many occasions, was that an active and participant citizenship, while required for the conduct of war, was necessary for dealing with problems of social relationship identical with those which so profoundly concerned them in peace-time.

One of Grierson's obsessive interests, at both the Information and Film Boards, was the North. He thought Canada was neglecting its importance, as a source of minerals, for air routes and in other ways. As late as 1953, Louis St. Laurent, the Prime Minister, referring to the North as a whole, was to remark in Parliament: 'Apparently we have administered these vast territories in an almost continuous state of absence of mind.' In Ottawa in May 1943, Grierson met Hugh

Keenleyside, one of the most active members of the North-West Territories Council, and found they thought alike about the neglected potential of the North. Keenleyside suggested that the Wartime Information Board should engage Trevor Lloyd to prepare a report. Lloyd, who had already done some filming for the Film Board in 1942 of the Canol Oil Project in the North-West, found there was more information about the Canadian Arctic in the Arctic Section of the Arctic, Desert and Tropical Information Centre in New York and spent some time there before producing his report for Grierson.[8] Out of this active concern with the North, in which Grierson's friend Raleigh Parkin was much involved, came not only such films as *Guards of the North* and *Look to the North* but also the idea of the Arctic Institute.

When Grierson was satisfied that the Wartime Information Board was operating as effectively as any government information service can in a democracy, he proposed that he should return to the National Film Board on a full-time basis. Arnold Heeney, Mackenzie King's close adviser, considered that Grierson should remain at the Wartime Information Board, particularly in view of the many changes in the previous twelve months. The Prime Minister spoke to L. R. LaFleche, Minister of National War Services and chairman of the N.F.B., and it was agreed that Grierson should remain in the dual capacity until January 1944.

In his letter of resignation to the chairman, Grierson gave his reason: 'I have done the job I was brought in to do. I remind you that I came in for six months under special assignment, and that at the end of that time the National Film Board was asked to extend my leave until the Board's work had been established. The place is now in good order, with well-established relationships and a sound, if modest, program of work.' After expressing his gratitude to the chairman for the hundreds of things he had done to ease a sometimes troublesome journey, he concluded: 'I am interested in the many possibilities in the information field; no one, I think, more. But I want to serve it intensively rather than extensively. I can manage W.I.B. and the National Film Board as a *tour de force*, but all along the line there are creative problems to which I can give only a mere executive's attention. It would suit me well if I could give more intimate attention to some of them.'[9] He recommended Davidson Dunton as his successor. His resignation was accepted but the Committee of the Privy Council recommended his appointment as special adviser on information.

During the second half of 1943 Grierson had Basil Wright with him in Ottawa. Basically Wright was there because Grierson felt there was an increasing ideological gap between Britain and Canada and he wanted Wright to study the Canadian scene and not least the Quebec issue. Wright was also exposed to the lightning strong arm methods of the Film Board which contrasted much with the leisurely approach of the Films Division of the British Ministry of Information.[10] He helped some of the young directors, including Tom Daly, Sydney Newman and Gordon Weisenborn. Wright's visit (he had also been in Canada briefly in 1942) was welcomed by Grierson: their friendship was a strong, unchanging element in his life.

Towards the end of Grierson's service at the Wartime Information Board, pressure had been brought to bear on him to accept the position of chairman of the Canadian Broadcasting Corporation. His friend, James Thomson, had resigned. In a letter to Grierson Thomson wrote: 'I now realise how lonely I was in Ottawa—and how far out of the regular beat of my interest and affections. . . . I found few in Ottawa to whom I could talk on things that really were interesting. All this self-disclosure adds up to a very sincere gratitude for the hospitality of your mind, heart and spirit that you opened up for me. I believe I can say honestly that you were the only man I regretted to leave behind in Ottawa—that is spoken in no spirit of flattery or superlative.'[11] He hoped that the choice of successor at the C.B.C. would fall on Grierson. But Grierson declined. To add control of broadcasting to the control he already had of information and film would have been too much. 'No man should have such power', he said.

At the same time he accepted another involvement—appointment as one of the foreign advisers to the Commission on Freedom of the Press, set up by the University of Chicago in December 1943, under the chairmanship of its Chancellor, Robert M. Hutchins, and with William E. Hocking of Harvard, Harold D. Lasswell of Yale, Archibald McLeish and Charles Merriam among its members. Grierson was to make a vigorous contribution to the Commission's deliberations over the next few years before its report, *A Free and Responsible Press*, described as 'a singularly important document in the literature of American communication', was published in 1947.

In December 1943 Grierson was elected honorary chairman of the Permanent Film Committee of the National Council for Canadian-Soviet Friendship in Toronto. To a seer this might have appeared a cloud no bigger than a man's hand. At the time, however, no sinister significance was attached to the address he gave at the Canadian-Soviet Friendship Congress. He acknowledged what the documentary movement had learned from the Russian films whose directors, after they had celebrated the great themes of the revolution, found they had to make dramatic patterns out of the ordinary processes of peaceful life. And he hoped they might find in the daily life of Canadians something of the same size, scope and challenge to the imagination. There was nothing here to cause any alarm on Parliament Hill in Ottawa.

At the Film Board there was a sense both of relief and of stimulus when Grierson returned full-time and at full power. The films were pouring out: a greater flow than in Britain and a richer one than in any other country in the world. The staff was still growing, as the scale of production and distribution increased.

When Ron Dick ('Somebody from Dundee can't be all bad' was Grierson's welcome) joined the Board early in 1944 he found the place a kind of whirlwind: the long hours, the pace of activity, the sense of ceaseless merry-go-round. Grierson used every minute of his time. He always wanted to know what people were doing, how they were getting on, if they were worried about anything. He could move from a large meeting in his office on some important development to the cutting room without any thought of levels. Dick found a natural discipline in the place. 'Somehow or other you were infected with the feeling there was a cause. Somehow or other in the midst of the bloody war we had to come out with a vision of just a bit more for more people. Call it socialism, that's obviously the term. Somehow that was taken care of.'[12]

Grierson was no hidebound bureaucrat, with a fixed set of rules for running his organisation. In the cutting room he might have a quick word with, say, Gordon Weisenborn and something would be said which roused the Grierson theoretical. 'The next thing you knew,' Ron Dick told me, 'he would be sitting on the floor with his legs crossed and there would be a twenty minute harangue in which he was at his toughest and most brilliant and you were expected to come back at him, to get into these dialogues. Work would stop. I can remember a whole hour's session like that. The fascinating thing was that there was no apology, no "I know I'm taking up time and I shouldn't be doing this." We didn't feel when it was finished that a moment had been lost. The whole principle and the theory of documentary which we were all learning, feeling our way and being confused about, Grierson himself was still exploring.'

Grierson felt that film had a wonderful quality of clarifying, synthesising, simplifying, popularising and a kind of spiritualising. It could provoke and excite people. He saw it as an extension of the educational process. To Ron Dick his attitude seemed to be: 'I will take people from here and here and here and make them into something. They'll grow into film and then film will make them do something.' If it had not been for Grierson and the Film Board, and the war, and the Canadian Government's persistence in wanting the National Film Board, and their listening to Grierson's advice, a great many of the early people in the Film Board would have become teachers. They had in the main no film background. Grierson seemed to feel that if they had the instinct of wanting to communicate, they would be excited by the fact that they were not merely communicating with a class but could reach out through the film medium to a large audience.

To some outside observers Grierson sometimes appeared to be a kind of Svengali with the power of hypnosis. He did have a compelling presence and he was certainly surrounded by a group of hero worshippers, who would happily work all day and all night if they were asked to do so. But the relationship was one of mutual confidence and there was a belief that whatever was done was appreciated, that it was part of a team effort. Grierson had a natural sense of authority. Yet Ron Dick felt it was done in a democratic way in which you felt that somehow or other you were part of the thing, you were part of an important operation in which you had real rights. His ability to get work out of people was astonishing. 'I've never seen anyone who commanded this strange mixture of affection and almost reverence, but in this friendly popular way.'

The debates which, on occasion, began during the day at the Board were often continued, or new ones started, at 30 Cooper Street in the evening. Grierson loved lively, hard-hitting argument, as those who foregathered in the Highlander in Soho during the 1930s knew and as another generation was to know some twenty years later at McGill University. He would often be deliberately provocative. There was no knowing if the proposition he appeared to be defending one night would not be attacked the next.

One night Grierson started talking about concepts and conceptual analysis and very soon got on to his favourite subject of Kant. He got into an argument with Ernst Borneman who did not accept his estimate of the philosophical system of German idealism. Grierson spoke of the Hegelian Right and the Hegelian Left, of Bauer and Feuerbach, and said that half of what Marx wrote could never have been written had it not been for Feuerbach. He had the group spellbound. Ron Dick found not a trace of a lecture by a man with a philosophical cultural background. It was an expression of passionate belief. 'Those are the people you should be reading', said Grierson, 'not your little North American so-called left-wing nobodies. Get back to Hegel and read Feuerbach and all those people who lead down to Marx.' One at least of those who heard him acted on his injunction and never regretted it.

It was part of Grierson's policy to build up the French unit at the Board. Vincent Paquette, the first French-Canadian to be employed in production, was joined by François Zalloni, Maurice Blackburn, René Jodoin and Jean-Paul Ladouceur, among others. A significant later appointment was of Paul Thériault as adviser and consultant to the commissioner and to all branches of the Board. Thériault, a French-Canadian of fourteen generations, came to know Grierson well and through him Grierson added to his knowledge and understanding of French Canada.

Thériault came into the Board through the influence of Guy Glover, Alan Adamson and Margaret Ann Adamson (Lady Elton).[13] They said to him: 'Grierson has brought together all the mavericks of the country and if he can find them he goes outside and picks additional mavericks. Life is glorious fun and we hit right and left and shock the blasted Establishment every way we can.' Thériault, intrigued, was very nervous when he was ushered into what he had expected to be the august presence.

'He surprised me no end. I expected to see a six foot man of Homeric build and here was this Napoleonic little man, obviously extraordinarily intent. Inside you could see there were all kinds of volcanoes fuming and exploding in every direction, but under rigid control. It was within the scope of his intellect to re-invent and fashion a kind of objective dialectic which had nothing to do with Karl Marx and was completely identified with him, to filter the reality of his time in terms of the mass media. In any case you felt—and he used this very subtly to put you off your anticipated footing—a sentiment of love-hate, repulsion and at the same time intense attractiveness. I thought "My God, this is obviously a man of enormous talent. What scope it has I don't know. He's arrogant, tolerant and pitiless. If I go to work with him it will be like living crucified most of the time. Since he's so violent but under control and since I'm violent, there will probably be a short connection." '

But it was not to be a short connection. Few forgot their first meeting with Grierson and most, I found, could reconstitute the experience with vivid precision. Grierson said to Thériault: 'I feel that the Francophone element is under-represented at the Board and that our film distribution circuits are not working very well in Quebec. I will give you two

139

Canadian Summit

months to survey this and prepare a report. In no circumstances are
you to reveal that you are working on this survey.' Thériault worked
like a madman, eighteen hours a day, seven days a week. Eventually he
finished the report, a fifty-page document, at 4 a.m. on the day it was
due and later took it to Grierson. Grierson: 'You are absolutely sure
of every fact?' Thériault: 'I stake my life on it. I have checked and re-
checked.' Grierson: 'That's magnificent.' Without reading a page of
the report he took it and, to Thériault's fury, started tearing it up.
Thériault: 'You God-damned son of a bitch. I should flatten you.'
Grierson: 'Stay calm, stay calm! Don't you understand? Now *you*
know what it's all about. I don't need to know. I knew already. You
remember your recommendations? From now on you're footloose.
Implement them!' He had made his assessment of Thériault. Why
should he waste time briefing him? Thériault had to discover for
himself. Grierson knew that when he was thoroughly prepared he
would do what was necessary.

What arrogance! To Thériault this was the poet hiding behind the
hard shell. Grierson was not prepared to accept gratitude or any feeling of affection because to do so he would have lost some of his
cherished autonomy. Thériault found him at once enigmatic and dis-
concerting. 'You think you nail him and then you speak to four other
persons and what you thought you held has evaporated. Isn't poetry in
a sense inseparable from this type of mystery?' There were ambiguities
about him which made Grierson 'the grand-daddy of all apprentice
sorcerers. You never were the same after you had met this granitic and
enormously gifted Scotsman.' Thériault added: 'I have yet to meet a
French Canadian who has known Grierson and has worked with him
who has anything but a rather warm, fraternal and deep feeling of
animation and friendship for the man.'

And so the French unit was built up. Guy Glover, familiar enough
with the whole spectrum of the arts to be of value not only as an inter-
locutor but also as a teacher, was already there. Pierre Juneau came in.
In six months they had a group of talented people. Grierson was looking, not for outstanding scholars but for people with a certain level of
literacy but not contaminated by the system—people with native
creativity. Then he launched them like weapons. 'They were so unhappy that they were able to do very well out of sheer pain', Thériault
told me. 'No one came to pat them on the shoulder. He was pitiless.
No comforting, no babying—this was his own way to pass on to us his
Scottish life. You have a tendency to cry when it hurts. You must
also learn as human beings. You must be stoical. You must have

discipline.' Out of the concern, frustration and agony came an annual programme of production with themes built on elements in the other culture so that the country could discover them for the first time on a national scale.

Grierson called in Thériault one day and told him he had arranged for Jean Benoit-Lévy to be a consultant adviser to the Film Board. When he saw the little towns in Quebec Benoit-Lévy said: 'After all the horrors I have lived through in the past three or four years everything is so peaceful. A man I have met only once or twice before should give me this blessing of peace—I don't understand that man.' Benoit-Lévy was unable to function creatively in the North American milieu and before the end of his visit Grierson knew. It was a spontaneous, beautiful gesture to the dedicated, conscientious director of *La Maternelle* and it mattered not that there was no film to show for it. Georges Rouquier, director of *Farrebique*, was also brought over from France and Grierson made an attempt to get Jean Grémillion. Here was evidence of the loyalty of the documentary community.

Thériault resigned from the Film Board in 1952. He opposed the Board's move to Montreal. 'Montreal needed a creative institution like the Film Board as a man with two pairs of legs needs two more.' He had no regrets. The agonies of his seven years there were enough to fill three or four lifetimes. 'We did do something which shook the country and I don't think it's ever been the same. I think you can find the genesis of the quiet revolution in Quebec. You can trace it to the documentary films of the Film Board which were shown regularly in innumerable little parishes and suddenly, before television came, they opened the window on the universe in these communities. They had an impact I am absolutely sure.'

Among Grierson's visitors when he returned to the Film Board was J. P. R. Golightly who had been appointed the commissioner's London representative in March 1942. His visit produced at least one story which passed into the Grierson–N.F.B. legend. As Grierson told it, Vancouver was cold and wet and the whisky, when you could get it, was down to a mickey (13 oz) a man-month. Grierson found himself one dark January evening, shivering and soaked through at the end of a long queue and hoping for his dram from the British Columbia liquor commission. As he stood there the voice of Golightly struck him as in a dream and the figure of Golightly materialised out of the fog.

'Is it you, Golightly?'

'My dear Grierson! What a delight to see you! But whatever are you doing in this fearful queue?'

'What every other honest man in this god-forsaken province is doing, you idiot: hoping for the sight of whisky before night falls.'

'But, my dear fellow, that's all nonsense. Come along with me and you'll have all the whisky you could ever desire.'

'Golightly, you don't seem to understand. This is British Columbia. There is a war. Whisky is down to 13 oz a month.'

'Nonsense, dear boy. Come along with me.'

Grierson did, and found in Golightly's hotel room two cases of the finest Scotch whisky. In Grierson's version there followed an endless, picaresque tale of Golightly's passage into the North-West Territories (he was ostensibly studying non-theatrical distribution), of an unlikely flight in a 1928 aircraft through a blizzard, of a forced landing in zero visibility at Whitehorse, of being snowed in, of the discovery there not of gold but of unlimited supplies of whisky, of six days of uninterrupted drinking, of loading the aircraft with Scotch and then, pilot and passenger equally incapacitated, an uncertain flight down to Vancouver. All of which Golightly accepted—in Grierson's telling— as though it was the commonplace stuff of an ordinary Canadian winter. When Grierson told it, the tale lasted a good hour.[14]

In August 1944 Grierson visited Brittany and, on the day before the Canadian breakthrough to Falaise, drove in a jeep to a Canadian encampment near Caen. His mission was to see and talk to film and still photographers in the front line. On the journey they kept to the country lanes. 'It was one of those beautiful evenings which everyone who knows France will remember to the end of their days—the old quiet Normandy of rich cornfields, large cows and large horses, straight scraggy hedges of poplar, elm and willow, quiet reedy streams, orchards, soft gray farmyards—and as we sped along, a mere mile or two outside the terrible tide of war, the contrast seemed strange and unreal.' The armies were smashing their way through the French towns and villages and the people had lost much. Yet Grierson found that their liberation, so dearly paid for, meant more to them than anything else. He found the experience deeply moving, and so he thought did every soldier. There was an air of simple, deep understanding between these common people from different lands that, after all the mistakes and misunderstandings of the past, he never expected to see. 'We have obviously entered upon something more than a military operation. We have entered upon an international crusade and I only hope we shall forever keep it that way.'[15]

Among the cameramen Grierson met in Normandy was Michael Spencer. On one of the three days of his visit he took Spencer to Mont

St. Michel and, acting as guide, explained to him and the driver of the jeep the finer points of the abbey's architecture. An unexpected diversion in the heat of war, but characteristic.

Grierson flew to London and, in the black-out, heard the bombers go over, droning endlessly for a couple of hours. He knew where they were going and what they were going to do and the mathematics of war seemed to him at that moment very dramatic.

While in London Grierson took the opportunity of showing three films from *The World in Action, Labour Front, Global Air Routes* and *Fortress Japan.* Grierson said that the aim of the series was to give the current military and political scene its international interpretation. The series, he added, was showing in some six thousand cinemas in the United States and would shortly be shown generally in Britain through United Artists. The films were warmly and widely welcomed and there was praise for the skilful editing and the lucid compelling commentaries —both the work of Stuart Legg.

Grierson saw some of the new British films, had talks with the film-makers and cast a sharp eye over what was happening in the documentary world.[16] He formed the opinion that Britain was not nearly so co-ordinated in documentary films as it ought to have been and that if there were only two government agencies, the Ministry of Information and the British Council, there would still be one too many if they did not work to a common plan. Too many departments and too many assorted sponsors, he found, meant unnecessary complication, delays, frayed tempers and a general loss of national effectiveness. He recognised that it was all too easy to view the situation from Canada where government sponsorship was centralised and where they were into a stage of something like a common outlook and a unified effort.

He also thought it had been a wonderful thing to see that, in spite of the war and the special difficulties of film-making in Britain, the documentary people had remembered the essentials of social reference and had not been fooled into the fallacy that fighting films gave anything more than one layer of reality. He had the feeling—and in this he was especially percipient—that the documentary group as a whole was not close enough to the centre where political planning and social planning was being thought out and legislated. He urged the units to keep before them documentary's primary sense of public service but warned that 'the original bright blue eyes are not enough, and hardly a thing we said ten years ago means a thing to-day.' He was to find, before very long, that his diagnosis of the situation in Britain had been cruelly accurate.

Canadian Summit

Back in Canada Grierson was thinking more and more in international rather than national terms. This preoccupation emerged both in the treatment of the subjects chosen for *The World in Action* and in the public pronouncements Grierson felt free to make, now that the Film Board organisation was running smoothly. Stuart Legg led the team working on *The World in Action*, still increasing on merit its wide circulation. The contrast between the propaganda pictures of the First World War and these films, clarifying issues and setting them in a world perspective, was noted by many critics. 'These films are an attempt to give the people a great hope and a great faith in themselves and in a brave new world', wrote Theodore Strauss in the *New York Times*. The Film Board, he added, was achieving this end only because its purposes were clearly conceived and their execution systematic.

As the films were concerned so often with political themes or issues about which Parliament was sensitive, there were inevitably moments of embarrassment. One of these occurred over *Balkan Powder Keg*, which criticised Britain for its treatment of Yugoslavia and Greece. Mackenzie King saw the film and while he did not think there was anything amiss in it, asked that it should be withdrawn until he thought about it. He knew that Winston Churchill was contemplating using the Canadian Corps in a Yugoslavian landing which was contrary to an assurance he had given in Parliament that his Government had no wish to interfere in the internal affairs of liberated countries. The film was withdrawn. When it was released almost a year later there were again protests in Parliament, on the ground that it appeared to be anti-British and pro-Russian, and it was again withdrawn.

Another issue of *The World in Action* to cause embarrassment was *Our Northern Neighbour*, dealing with the Soviet Union as an ally. It was courageous of Grierson and Legg to attempt a comment. Wisely they avoided any specific reference to the basic clash of communist and capitalist ideologies; but the commentary device of concentrating on the common man in Russia, 'thinking hard about what awaits *him* when victory is won', did not deflect the criticism of those who did not think it was the duty of a government body to release films concerning the foreign policy of any country. Grierson noted that the principal complaint came from the Soviet Legation in Ottawa—'and I expected it. They do not hold my particular form of objectivity in veneration any more than they like my memory of Dostoevsky.'[17]

Such temporary embarrassments did not deter or divert Grierson. He was determined to pursue his internationalist line. In April 1944 he made a major speech at the International Labour Organisation conference in Philadelphia. It was a powerful piece of pleading, his main argument being that if the I.L.O. was pledged to the improvement of working standards and working conditions throughout the world, it was of necessity pledged to the duty of world education in the matter of standards and conditions. At the same time he accepted an invitation from the head of another international organisation, Governor Herbert Lehman, to design a film programme for UNRRA. In December 1944, he was in Hollywood, speaking to the California Club about how films would fit in to the further planning of the Los Angeles District. On the way back he spoke on 'Films as an International Influence' at the Vancouver Advertising and Sales Bureau.

In February 1945 he was in New York, speaking to the United Nations Information Council of Columbia University. In May he spoke at the National Conference on Adult Education in Winnipeg and in June, at a conference of the Arts, Sciences and Professions in the Post-War World, his subject was 'The Challenge of Peace'. While the film had stuck stubbornly, he suggested, to the drama of personal habits and personal achievements, the documentary had done something to open a window on the wider world and outlined the patterns of interdependency more distinctively and more deliberately than any other medium whatsoever.

Despite this intense activity Grierson was in good health. The end of 1944 found him writing to J. P. R. Golightly admitting that he had been on the wagon for seven weeks. 'My eyes are clear and sparkle in the happy sunshine of this beautiful winter climate. I eat like a horse and have gained ten pounds. I walk smartly to work at nine o'clock every morning and work till midnight. Little children in the street point at my rosy cheeks as I stride blithely past. You may take it I am very pure. I may even give up smoking to-morrow. . . . Naturally I have no sympathy any longer with the foibles of my fellow men. I went to eight parties over Christmas and spent a contemptuous half hour at each, hauling a very angry Margaret away with me. The astonishing spectacle repeats itself of people—including Margaret—getting down on their bended knees and praying me to take to drink again. Like Norval on the Grampian Hills I am, of course, adamant. Some wag, who heard I had gone teetotal decided very logically I would not need liquor any more, broke into the house two nights ago and pinched everything I had.'[18]

As it became clear that the end of the war was approaching, Grierson called in one of his producers, Nick Balla, and asked what he was doing about it. Balla said there was not much time to make a film for Canada. Stuart Legg had already completed *Now the Peace* on the need for international economic planning and joint military effort to resist aggression. Grierson gave Balla five days, or 120 hours. With Stanley Hawes, Bob Anderson and Stanley Jackson, Balla worked with little rest or respite for three days and three nights. Anderson wrote the commentary which was spoken by Leonard Brockington. Within the limit set by Grierson the compilation film was completed. On V–E Day copies were in theatres all across Canada and that night Canadians saw *Salute to Victory*.

It was the last demand of its kind Grierson was to make and it was met as uncomplainingly and wholeheartedly as any of the others made over the period of his commissionership. As Tom Daly told me of an earlier similar occasion when a compilation film had to be made at very short notice, 'Faced with felt need you can do many things. You don't stop to wonder. You just go ahead. It is exhilarating to find you can work like that.' This was the effort Grierson could inspire through his own tireless, driving energy.

During the summer of 1945 Grierson was preparing in various ways for the end of his term as film commissioner. He was very much concerned about the future of the Board and of the people he had brought into it. He knew that by flouting civil service procedure and practice he had earned for it some resentment and antagonism. While he was commissioner and while he had the protective support of Mackenzie King the danger was limited; but when that no longer applied? To Grierson the Film Board was not like any other department of government. It did not merely administer an Act: it provided services of a creative or imaginative nature. It needed imaginative and creative workers and it needed a commissioner who could hold them, hold them together and get the creative best out of them. Grierson had the quality of creative leadership to achieve this. He knew that civil service regimentation would disrupt the Film Board as he had conceived it.

Grierson thought the new commissioner should be someone from the inside who knew the policy of the Board, had proved his understanding of it and who had the heart and the will to extend it in relation to the new times ahead. He should be someone who enjoyed the confidence of the creative elements in the Board and who would work for his men and not over them. He must have taste and both believe in the first-rate and Canada's capacity for it. Grierson put forward three names: Ross McLean who had been in from the beginning, who had taken the weight of the organisation during his absences and whose weakness was that, tender-minded, he shunned the surgical operations which in a creative organisation and a changing scene were sometimes necessary; Malcolm Ross, who was a good administrator with a continuing capacity for drive but whose experience of production was limited; and James Beveridge who had made a notable success of the Royal Canadian Air Force film unit in Europe, who had a deep affection for film, film-making and film-makers and who, Grierson thought, could hold together the imaginative elements of the Board. He reminded the Minister of National War Services that, at twenty-nine, Beveridge was no younger than he had been when appointed to the E.M.B. and that the film was a young man's medium looking to the future.

With this responsibility fulfilled Grierson announced his resignation early in August, to take effect on 7 November 1945. In his announcement he said: 'It is not the easiest thing in the world to give up what is probably the best and happiest job of its kind anywhere. There are, however, new things I ought to do in the field of documentary films. . . . In particular, the production of films on international themes and the international exchange of films of common social interest ought now to be strengthened, if the new interest in international relations, especially on this continent, is to be adequately fed. This is now, and I hope properly, my principal interest.' He referred to the Board's policy of having placed the international interest on a level with the national one, not without 'occasional criticism from unimaginative isolationist quarters', and added that he could not reasonably ask the Board to go as far in this line as he himself wished to go.

He said he proposed to produce for international theatre circulation two monthly series of films, one dealing with international affairs, the other with scientific and technological developments in various parts of the world. He hoped to maintain his association with the Canada Foundation (of which, as the Canadian Committee, he had been an original member) and the various movements in Canada for educational progress. Of the young Canadians he had trained he said 'There is no group anywhere of its kind more spirited or with greater prospect.' And he trusted 'that the Board and the Government will continue to consider film as the lively and important medium it is, and a powerful instrument in serving the public imagination and building Canada's future'.

Grierson had in part been prompted to issue his statement because of advance press speculation about his future, including the suggestion that he was about to go to the State Department in Washington. He apologised for the apparent discourtesy when writing to Mackenzie King and he went on: 'I have to thank you more than I can say for the honour of serving your administration. In seventeen years of public service I have worked under many ministers, and some notable, but it has been one of the richest public lessons in my life to watch the enormous patience and skill, and participate in the progressive spirit, of your leadership. In the four years since you added your personal blessing to our film operation, we have built one of the strongest and most articulate organisations of its kind anywhere, the international repute of which is as good as any. For my part, it could not have been done without the constant feeling that I understand your mind a little, had your personal confidence and could rely on your generosity. Under these unwritten but nonetheless decisive auspices we have, I think, done a progressive work for the war effort, for Canada and for internationalism.'[19]

The Prime Minister dictated a reply but did not mail it as he felt it was an inadequate acknowledgment. On 8 November, on board the *Queen Mary*, returning from a vacation in Britain, he had at last an opportunity to send Grierson 'some real expression of my feelings in the matter of the service you have rendered Canada and, in particular, the National Film Board in the years of your association with the government. Particularly have I been anxious to express to you my appreciation of the kindly interest you have taken at all times in matters which were of special interest and concern to myself. Though my contacts with you have been less frequent than I should have liked them to be, I know that in you I had, at all times, a friend at my side, and one to whom I could look for a fair interpretation of my aims and motives. For all of this, I am most grateful to you.'

There were not many idle hours for Grierson before he left. Outside the Board he had meetings to attend in Chicago of the Commission on the Freedom of the Press, now busy preparing its report, and in Ottawa of the Canadian Committee before it became the Canada Foundation. At the Board the organisation was at its peak of productivity: a staff of about eight hundred, over 250 films made in 1945, some four thousand prints placed in eighty-three Canadian film libraries across the world, a monthly attendance of over 250,000 on eighty-five rural circuits and a similar number reached by circulation from libraries, Canadian films shown publicly in twenty-five overseas countries, *The World in Action* in over six thousand theatres in the United States alone. Tom Daly was ready to take over *The World in*

Canadian Summit

Action from Stuart Legg and Sydney Newman was in charge of *Canada Carries On*, Norman McLaren was winning world-wide recognition for his animated films. Malcolm Ross, Ralph Foster and Jack Ralph held posts of responsibility. The Film Board was still attracting many of the brightest minds in the country. The creative urge inspired by Grierson still charged the atmosphere.

Grierson and his wife left Ottawa on 13 October. On 19 October they sailed from New York on the Danish freighter *Erria* and disembarked at Liverpool. Among their fellow passengers were half a dozen Canadian girls competent in either French or German who were going to serve as interpreters for the British Army in Germany. To Grierson they represented the younger Canadian generation which, thank God, still believed in the impossible. In this company Grierson was completely relaxed, delighting in his love of conversation, his feeling that everybody had something to tell him. The sessions at the captain's table were unfailingly lively and rich in laughter. There was no suggestion that the man who was the mainspring of the wide-ranging conversations had just ended the most demanding five years of his life. Nor was there a hint of the wounding experiences the next twelve months would bring.

10 A Dream Crumbles

En route to England Grierson had ample time for reflection. His job in Canada was done. The National Film Board was going great guns. He had gone originally on a mission for the Imperial Relations Trust and had become Canada's first film commissioner more by accident than by design. But Canada was only one part of the larger plan. New Zealand already had a film unit resulting from his recommendations. Australia had acted belatedly and had accepted his nominee, Ralph Foster, as its first commissioner. There was a stirring in South Africa. The National Film Board example was influencing other countries such as China and Czechoslovakia. Grierson did not feel at all diffident about any assessment of his achievement against the hopes and plans of earlier days.

His departure had predictably prompted approaches and soundings from many quarters. There had been invitations from Hollywood and New York, including the setting up of a political intelligence service for one of the major companies, the control of the Encyclopaedia Britannica film venture into American and international education, and the establishment of a film, radio and television set-up for *Newsweek*.[1] Rank had cabled to learn of his plans. There had been a sounding stimulated by David Coplan in London, from the American Motion Picture Producers' Association. Grierson thought it possible that the Rockefeller Foundation would ask him to salvage the American Film Centre and International Film Centre, on the single understanding that he would again farm in Kent and be occasionally around. But it was the international idea which dominated his thinking and he felt that the big momentum for the wider international development of documentary lay in the United States.

Grierson expressed something of what was in his mind in a letter written to Charles Cowan on board the *Erria*.[2] A truly international conception of international exchange, he wrote, one supplementing the various efforts of the national information services to impose themselves on other countries, 'must be done by functional internationals of our own making—the documentary people of the world

150

if they will get together'. He noted that, in the meantime, he had registered International Film Associates in Washington, that registration in London and Ottawa would follow and that Flaherty and Benoit-Lévy had agreed to join the first list of associates. He thanked Cowan for his friendship, encouragement and understanding and said that without him he wouldn't have stuck it. The mediocrity of spirit of the civil service made him physically sick. 'I wonder sometimes if I shouldn't have contented myself making a few films of my own like Flaherty, taking my time, and be damned to organising national instruments of information and enlightenment, and such. What a crew to impose on a creative intention!'

Among the cablegrams Grierson received on board was one from Cowan. At the meeting of the Board on 2 October Cowan had moved a resolution putting on record appreciation of Grierson's service to the Board and to Canada and recommending the Government, as tangible evidence of its appreciation, to pay him a gratuity of three months' salary. It seemed a modest gesture but Cowan's cable advised him that it had been refused. In a letter written from London to Brooke Claxton, chairman of the Board, Grierson said that, personally, it did not matter. 'What does matter is that no government can, for its own sake, afford to be pettifogging towards public servants who, because of the nature of their persuasion, give their total resources to the public service.'[3] It gave an early indication of the latent hostility which was to emerge over the next twelve months. By any reckoning it was a petty piece of ingratitude. The high sounding words on his departure now had a hollow ring.

Another cable invited Grierson to be the guest of the British Government while in London. He was asked to prepare a memorandum on the future form the Government's information services might take. A first paper dealt comprehensively with government informational film-making. Grierson did not spare either the direction of the government film operation or the film-makers. It was a powerful document which should have had results.[4] A second paper, on which Paul Rotha worked with him, dealt with the relation between any proposed government film corporation and the British documentary film movement. It should be the first step of such a corporation, they suggested, to safeguard and develop the industrial security of the independent documentary units which had preserved their immunity from monopolistic control. It referred to distribution guarantees for documentary films, the need for a training and apprenticeship scheme, the reconstitution of the British Film Institute and the importance of liaison with any film office set up by the United Nations. It was completed on 22 January 1946, the day before Grierson returned to New York via Montreal.

While in London Grierson fulfilled a promise made to Brooke Claxton to put down some notes on the Film Board and its nature. He did so in an extraordinarily frank document which, in its blunt criticism and uninhibited naming of individuals, was indiscreet, especially in view of what was about to happen in Ottawa.[5] The failure of the Canadian Cabinet, he wrote, to realise what the C.B.C. and the National Film Board meant to Canada was at once a betrayal of government leadership of the nation and a betrayal of the creative workers within these organisations. 'Neither can give of their best unless their role is both recognised and honoured. The attitude to both has been inadequate.' He said of Claxton that he represented a generation of ministers which was capable of understanding the relation of government to the educational and imaginative processes of the nation and thought he might be 'a gift from the Gods after the mediocre and dreary succession of Chairmen the Prime Minister so carelessly imposed on me'. He left Claxton in no doubt about his opinion of James Mackinnon, LaFleche and McCann. The curse of all creative services within governments, he said, had been too close a responsibility to Treasury sanction in the method of expenditure and in the matter of employment of personnel and he supported this from his observation of what was happening in the United Kingdom. It was an explosive letter, with good advice and hurtful comment fairly evenly balanced. For it to be on file in Ottawa was a kind of time bomb.

The main purpose of Grierson's visit to London was to discuss the launching of The World Today, Inc., with Basil Wright, then producer in charge of the Crown Film Unit and special adviser on films to the director-general, Ministry of Information. Wright was wholly in sympathy with Grierson's aims for the new enterprise whose broad aim was to support the objects and activities of the United Nations. Later in 1946 Wright formed, with John Taylor and E. P. Moyna, International Realist, Ltd., to ensure the adequate representation of British affairs, opinions and life in the series of films Grierson planned to produce and to contribute a number of films to the series. Grierson invited Wright and Moyna to visit him in New York to discuss the plan and project in detail.

Back in New York Grierson proceeded with his preparations for The World Today, Inc. With the help of a grant from the Rockefeller Foundation, he had brought Stuart Legg and Raymond Spottiswoode

A Dream Crumbles

from Ottawa. Later they were to be joined by Guy Glover, Julian Roffman, Gordon Weisenborn, Roger Barlow, Mary Losey, Margaret Ann Adamson (Lady Elton) and several others from the National Film Board. Grierson took a very fancy duplex apartment at 200 West 57th Street, chosen to impress potential sponsors or people who might be persuaded to invest in The World Today, The others were much more humbly accommodated at De Luxe Laboratories, 450 West 56th Street —according to Weisenborn, 'a despicable place: four or five offices all leading into one another and all painted green. There were no windows and we sat in these little cubby holes and it was just terrible.'[6]

The World Today, Inc., was founded on a distribution arrangement which Grierson negotiated with Edward Raftery, president, and Gradwell Sears, vice-president, of United Artists who, according to the company's announcement, had 'decided to develop a new policy in the matter of short films and to use its world-wide organisation to distribute films of a dramatic nature which will describe and discuss the international scene'. A contract was signed whereby The World Today was required to supply United Artists with thirty-nine short films each year for four years, in three series, each portraying a different aspect of the international scene. The three series were *Worldwise*, explaining and interpreting great events on the international scene; *Wonderfact*, evaluating scientific and technological developments in terms of everyday life; and *Venture*, highlighting human skills in the realms of sport and outdoor achievement. One film in each series was to be delivered each month.

At the same time Grierson announced that the foundation, International Film Associates, was doing research and surveys for UNRRA and the Hudson's Bay Company. Grierson's plan, which he had evolved in much discussion with Stuart Legg, was clear: to capitalise one of the main assets they had developed in Canada—a series on international events on the lines of the highly successful *World in Action*, with a distribution guarantee—and a documentary organisation embracing sponsored non-theatrical work and other film-related activities.

All the omens seemed favourable. Success was not going to be easily won; but Grierson brought with him to New York all the experience he had gained over some twenty-five years, his proved skill in promotion and his tireless energy in pursuing a chosen objective. He had with him people who believed in what he was doing and who, in this belief, were prepared to work as hard and with as little reward as they had done at the Film Board. There was still a missionary zeal about the enterprise.

153

A Dream Crumbles

Something of this confidence Grierson expressed in a letter to me written after he had received his copies of *Grierson on Documentary*. 'We are coming along fine but not speedily, and it may take a full year before the total plan is capable of development. It involves not less than a total articulate library of public enlightenment covering all the basic fields of public interest—international affairs; economics and finance; public health and community planning, intercultural affairs, the nature of art, etc. The most interesting present sign is that, apart from the United Nations contract, half-a-dozen of the big groups, including the Presidential Committee for Financing Foreign Trade, have asked us to work out major plans for the sponsorship of films based on long-term approaches to national and international education. But, of course, there is much to be done in the education of even the higher realms of sponsorship. It has, indeed, barely begun in this country.'[7]

Absorbed in these demanding activities—raising finance, arranging distribution, preparing production, approaching sponsors—Grierson was unaware that in Ottawa events were contriving to undo all his work. Always an avid newspaper reader, he must have noted references to Igor Gouzenko, his decision to defect to the West and the information he had taken to the Canadian authorities concerning a Soviet spy-ring operating in Canada. If he did, the references held no special significance for him. He was probably unaware of Mackenzie King's alarmed reaction to the alleged attempts being made by the Russians to gain information on the manufacture of the atomic bomb and of the Prime Minister's meetings with Attlee in London and Truman in Washington; but, with the ending of his official link with the Canadian Government, these were no longer matters of direct involvement.

The Royal Commission 'to investigate the facts relating to and the circumstances surrounding the communication, by public officials and other persons in positions of trust, of secret and confidential information to agents of a foreign power' was appointed by Order-in-Council in Ottawa on 5 February 1946, under the Judges, Robert Taschereau and R. L. Kellock. Among the material produced by Gouzenko was a notebook with an entry by Motinov, assistant military attaché at the Soviet Embassy: 'Research Council—report on the organisation and work. Freda to the professor through Grierson.'

'Freda' was Freda Linton who had been Grierson's secretary at the National Film Board from May to November 1944. She had come from the International Labour Office in Montreal and had been interviewed, not by Grierson but by Beth Bertram, the personnel manager.[8] After six months she had been transferred to Distribution and had spent six weeks in the Washington office while Mary Losey was at the San Francisco Conference. She was found by Malcolm Ross 'annoyingly inefficient' and 'not overly intelligent, always asking for bigger and better jobs, more money'. When on the point of being released she had resigned in September 1945.

Giving evidence, Gouzenko explained that the work Freda Linton was doing at the Film Board was unsatisfactory to Moscow. They wanted her placed in a more important department, the National Research Council, with Raymond Boyer, another alleged agent ('the professor') and suggested that Grierson's influence should be used to get her into this position. Dr. C. J. Mackenzie, president of the National Research Council, had an office next to Grierson's. It proved impossible to sub-poena Freda Linton. She had left her home in Montreal for an unknown destination.

When Grierson was called to testify to the Commission he was, perhaps understandably, flummoxed. He knew that Freda Linton had been his secretary for six months but vaguely thought of it as having been in 1942 or 1943. He did not know of her having left the Board. In answer to the suggestion that his good offices were to be used to get her into National Research he replied: 'I must say it is the most sterile document in this sense, that the Linton girl asked for no offices and no services in that matter. I merely think of her now as an ambitious girl who certainly wanted to get on in terms of the Film Board.' When the theory was repeated Grierson asked: 'It is a presumption, I take it, on the part of the Russian Embassy, or somebody there, that I would be of service to them?' 'Yes.' Grierson: 'The basis of the assumption, I say, is not very considerable.' He said he knew the Russian ambassadors on the usual diplomatic level. He said in conclusion that he did not think the entry in the notebook had any reference to him, either through Freda Linton or directly.

There was further interrogation about two suspected agents employed at the Wartime Information Board. One of them Grierson described as a 'Left-wing sympathiser, a friend of the Soviet Union, and so on' and amplified this by adding that 'he is an excellent student of Plato, to begin with, and certain matters of liberty in Plato are not so conveniently associated with the communist doctrine.' Of the other he said he was very close to the Left-wing. 'There are certain gradations between the social democracy and communism, and it is almost a matter of high definition. I don't know whether the fellow leans to the social democrats, or to the communist.'

Grierson was recalled on 13 May to give further testimony. On this occasion he was asked directly: 'Are you a Communist or Communistically inclined?' Grierson replied: 'I have been a public servant now for a matter of eighteen years: I was trained in the classical Whitehall school. I have been first and last a public servant, that is a civil servant. Now, that meant in the Whitehall sense that you have no party affiliations. A party should not affect one's public job, particularly in the kind of work I have done, because I have always been concerned with government information.' Later in his testimony he said: 'In the matter of political philosophy the issue is this: those of us who have been trained and who are dyed-in-the-wool liberal democrats say that there cannot be any economic freedom if there is no political freedom. On the other hand, those who believe in international socialism say there cannot be any political freedom unless there is economic freedom.'

The Commission did not pursue such niceties of political definition. 'Would you say that the effect of all that is that you are not a member of the Communist party?' Grierson: 'Oh no.' Asked if he subscribed to any of their views Grierson replied: 'I am entirely a person who is concerned with the establishment of good international understanding. Therefore I am concerned with the floating of all ideas. I mean, I get as much from Gobineau as I get from Marx.' Grierson denied the allegation that there were Communist cells masquerading as study groups at the Film Board and said that the atmosphere there was of progressive thought.[9]

By a supreme stroke of irony, Grierson was, next day, addressing the International Conference of the Junior League in Quebec on 'The Political, Economic and Educational Implications of the Atomic Bomb'. If the members of the Commission could have been present they would have heard as penetrating an analysis of the post-Hiroshima situation as they could have wished. It would be the rashest folly, he said (and this, of course, was long before it had been established that the Russians had the atomic bomb) to base North American foreign policy on the thought of alien inferiority. 'There is, I submit, no way but to forget atomic energy as a weapon of war and banish the possibility of war from our hearts and minds altogether and get down solidly to the business of peace.'

For someone who had just come from a grilling about Communist sympathy, he dealt courageously with the international manners of the Soviet Union, expressing dislike of their secrecy and suspicion and atmosphere of conspiracy but suggesting that the West had given them reason to be secretive, suspicious, silent and conspiratorial. Towards the end of the address came a plea which might have been addressed to the Commission: 'Strangely enough, at a time when statesmen, churchmen and political philosophers are calling for an understanding of Russia by us and of us by the Russians, any attempt to do so becomes the badge of subversive activity. There will be none of that science of human relationships which is to save mankind, if we frustrate and stifle the generous thoughts of our youth or by any action of church or state bar them from the fullest knowledge of the ideas operating in the world today, whether they come from Russia, Rome or from George Bernard Shaw.'

His high-minded courage was of no avail. In Ottawa the politicians whose lives he had made uncomfortable or whom he had spurned, as in his letter to Brooke Claxton, now had the weapon they wanted. In Parliament Claxton had to parry question after question about Communism in the Film Board and pro-Soviet bias in the films. Gordon Fraser suggested that the Film Board needed fumigation. The smear spread. As Grierson well knew, the more you jump on a cow pat the bigger it grows. The enemies Grierson had made through his ruthlessness and arrogance brought out their grievances and gave them an airing in an atmosphere the Royal Commission had made receptive. At the Rideau Club, of which Grierson was a member, there was an extra spice in the lunch-time conversation. Mackenzie King did nothing: having appointed the Commission of inquiry he was bound to let it run. Even some of Grierson's closest friends doubted the wisdom of his conduct at the inquiry. Was it discreet to give the members of the Commission a lecture on political philosophy when all they wanted were plain answers to all too plain questions?

Inevitably Grierson did not agree with this reading. He thought the method adopted by the Canadian Government to deal with the espionage inquiry had come near to disaster. He considered it a direct threat to three of President Roosevelt's freedoms—freedom from fear and freedom of speech and of conscience. Writing before the Royal Commission's report was published, he said it would be extremely useful if the Prime Minister were to restate in unmistakable terms the liberal and progressive attitudes with which he had been associated throughout his political career—a serious misreading of Mackenzie King's attitude and inclination at the time. Confidence, Grierson asserted, needed to be restored inside Canada and between Canada and the United Nations. If it were restored, he believed, 'it would not be possible for the filthy insects and worms to creep out of the woodwork and reveal themselves again for their bigotry and prejudice and evil will.' If these vicious things were permitted to continue without being repudiated, he could see nothing but growth of suspicion and doubt and animosity between individuals and between organisations and communities in the State.[10] If there were many who thought like Grierson they did not conspicuously raise their voices.

The poison released in Ottawa was to run wide and deep. Grierson was forced to make some effort to check it. His old friend George Ferguson, editor of the *Montreal Star*, spoke to Louis St. Laurent, Minister of Justice and Attorney General, who later wrote to him: 'I am at a loss to understand the report which you state is now current in certain newspaper circles in the United States to the effect that Mr. Grierson was a leader of the spy ring now before our courts. It appears to me that Mr. Grierson's name can have become linked with the espionage case only because of the fact that he was called as a witness before the Royal Commission. . . . I sincerely deplore the loose and ill-founded conclusions pointing to Mr. Grierson as "head of the spy ring" or as consciously connected with it in any way. I can only suggest that certain persons have been too ready to make false capital of the fact that he was called before the Royal Commission for the reasons outlined [The appearance of his name and the involvement of Freda Linton].'[11]

One voice, however influential, was not enough to raise. Back in New York, where the climate which would produce McCarthy was now forming, Grierson had this slippery handicap to add to the others he was encountering. Money for The World Today was proving difficult to raise.[12] Mary Losey's husband had helped and there was also money from Arthur Meyer, Maynard Gertler and Elliot Pratt. After the spy trial others tended to be unresponsive. This made it increasingly difficult to put into commission the ambitious plans for the series of films for United Artists. By February 1947, only one film, *Wonder Eye*, directed by Guy Glover, was completed and the distribution contract was terminated. Short films on current affairs were no longer as attractive to cinema exhibitors or audiences as they had been during the war when there was a hunger for information about events affecting people's lives. Further, television with its immediacy and direct communication was increasingly meeting the public need for news and comment. The dream of a series of films circulating as widely as *The World in Action* crumbled and with it went much of Grierson's bold plan for a world documentary organisation centred on New York.

All was not lost but each small gain needed prodigious, out-of-scale effort. Stuart Legg produced and Raymond Spottiswoode directed *Round Trip* for the Twentieth Century Fund, the prestigious United States research organisation representing the social interests of big business. Spottiswoode also produced a film for the Motion Picture Producers' Association on new techniques for teaching class-room subjects. Julian Roffman made *Seed for Tomorrow* for the National Farmers' Union. Gordon Weisenborn was loaned to Nick Read's Southern Educational Film Production Service in Georgia to direct a film, written by George Stoney, for the North Carolina State Board of Public Health. Roger Barlow directed the first film for the United Nations, *People Speaking to People*. Stuart Legg produced several other films on international and economic themes.

Grierson himself was constantly in action, talking to people of influence, conferring with sponsors, giving public addresses. In private he would reveal, as he did to Raleigh Parkin one night over dinner in Sardi's in New York, how bitter he was about his treatment by the Canadian Government.[13] In public his resilience concealed how much he had been hurt. There were meetings with old friends—James Bridie, Gilbert Harding and Donald Ogden Stewart on successive nights in New York.

In June he went to Buffalo to address the American Library Association Conference on 'The Library in an International World'. He was still preoccupied, as most thinking people were, with the threat of atomic warfare: 'Our passion for human enlightenment has been at least equalled by our passion for killing by the million the very people we enlightened' and he spoke of an educational crusade in which the end was the internationalisation of men's minds and whose raw materials were the common interests of humanity.

In July he was in Hollywood. On the return journey he visited the Tennessee Valley Authority and was fired by the imaginative conception and grand scale of the plan. Later he was in Washington, having talks with Walter Evans about the production of films for the U.S. Navy. In Washington he was also seeing Eric Johnston of the Motion Picture Producers' Association who was impressed by what he had achieved in Canada.

While the non-theatrical enterprise, International Film Associates, did at first produce a modest return in what, in the United States, was an intensely competitive field, the comparatively small amount of money Grierson had raised for The World Today was rapidly disappearing. He had hoped for something like half a million dollars but never raised more than fifty or sixty thousand. Fredric March contributed five thousand. Later this contribution was to be itemised as evidence of Communist sympathy when Hollywood embarked on its own witch-hunt. A mood of depression was intensifying among Grierson's associates. Underpaid, they knew that the financial basis of the whole operation was unstable. Few commissions for sponsored films were being obtained. At the same time they were conscious of the political consequences of the spy trial. They were aware that the mail was being examined by the F.B.I. Soon they would experience interrogation.

As the blight of anti-liberal feeling spread in the United States, the Canadian connection made them suspect. They felt menaced. Grierson asked his old friend, Bosley Crowther, film critic of the *New York Times*, when they met one day in a hotel room, to talk in a low voice as he was afraid of bugging. He was being pursued, he said, by elements inimical to him. It was a painful time for Grierson and his associates: feeling the ground everywhere crumbling under their feet, never knowing when or in what form the next chock would be pulled out, was a devastating experience. The gloomy office and the sense of not knowing what was happening did not help.

One day there was a call from the president of the board of C.B.S., William S. Paley. Would Grierson have lunch with him? A feeling of excitement ran through the office. Saved! Saved! When Grierson returned he said, 'We just chatted.' Three weeks later there was another call and another lunch. 'I don't know what it's all about', said Grierson on his return. A third call and Grierson was invited for the weekend to the president's home in Westchester. On this occasion there *was* an explanation. The World Today, which Grierson had copyrighted, happened also to be the title of Edward S. Murrow's show—but the C.B.S. lawyers had never copyrighted it. Out of the negotiations came a proposal that Grierson should be head of C.B.S. News. But nothing came of it, either because Grierson negotiated for more and more and out-negotiated himself or because of the creeping political paralysis.[14]

There were many indignities and diminishments to be borne, not only by Grierson but also by those who had loyally followed him from Ottawa. To some of them it seemed he was unaware they too were suffering. In his ruthlessness he thought they should take what came. The difference was that, isolated in his apartment, he knew what was happening while they did not, unless the making of a film were involved and that was happening all too rarely. Their loyalty was strained. There was a great difference between a government-financed, on-going organisation like the National Film Board, operating in a country with modest film-making capacity, and an underfinanced private company in a much larger country, struggling against powerful organisations like *The March of Time* and other established film-makers and unable to expect support on a national basis. Grierson was desperately anxious to succeed but the combination of factors defeated him.

While Mary Losey was with him one day there was a telephone call from Ellen Wilkinson, Minister of Education in Attlee's Government. Would he be interested in the post of head of information at UNESCO? He responded positively.[15] It was a *faute de mieux*. He flew to London on 22 November and from 26 November until 10 December was in Paris attending the first General Conference of UNESCO. William Farr, learning that Grierson was in London, had suggested to Julian Huxley, the director-general, that he should join the British delegation which, after some discussion in Whitehall, was agreed. David Hardman headed the delegation, with J. B. Priestley as delegate and Ritchie Calder, Grierson, Edgar Anstey, Helen de Mouilpied, Jacquetta Hawkes, A. D. Ritchie, Paul Rotha and Basil Wright among the experts.

In the programme and budget for 1947, the section on mass communications had been drafted by William Farr, René Maheu and Philippe Desjardins. The British experts, led by Grierson, tore the draft to pieces. The Belgian chairman, Jan Kuypers, said: 'Go away and draft what you think the programme should be and bring it back to-morrow morning.' The British experts, with William Farr and two secretaries, went to the Georges V Hotel where Grierson, with his customary dynamism, organised an all-night session at which each expert redrafted a section before all commented on it. By 4 a.m. the work was done. Later in the day it was approved. It was a typical Grierson exercise.[16]

In a contribution at the conference Grierson made clear his conception of the free flow of information: 'We must at any cost encourage mutual understanding between nations, which pre-supposes that each can speak not only to its neighbour but to all countries in the world. We must work to remove all barriers to the free circulation of information. It must be a two-way traffic, and information must be carried from one country to another and from all countries to any one country for the sake of normal and mutual understanding between all.' There was to be much debate about the free flow of information at UNESCO conferences over the following two years.

Before the end of December 1946 Grierson was back in New York, still undecided on his course of action. He went to Washington to have discussions with William Wells, head of the visual media branch of UNRRA. International Film Associates had a contract with UNRRA. to supply information and distribution outlets for films and to implement the recommendations when this was possible. It was a major undertaking in which Grierson was much involved, with Raymond Spottiswoode and Mary Losey. Another organisation which Grierson was advising in Washington was the President's Committee for Financing Foreign Trade. Here discussions had reached a stage where the Committee had before it a detailed information programme involving among other items the appointment of The World Today to implement the plan in so far as it related to film.

But other events in train would make much of this academic. On 15 January 1947 Julian Huxley cabled Grierson (at 48 West 11th Street) offering him the post of adviser with special responsibility for mass media and public relations. On 20 January Grierson replied agreeing to act as adviser as a personal service and without salary. They met in New York in the first week of February. Grierson explained that he did not want to be part of the administration and that he would feel freer if he rendered his service unpaid. Huxley said such an arrangement would be both impracticable and impossible. Eventually Grierson accepted what had been offered—a salary of twelve thousand dollars, plus entertainments and *per diem* allowances.

On 15 February Grierson returned to London. On the previous day it was learned from the U.S. Consulate in Montreal that Grierson had been refused a visa to the United States. The State Department in Washington stated that Grierson was unable to qualify under existing laws and turned aside other queries, holding that such rulings were confidential. The action was taken, newspaper correspondents understood, on the advice of the Federal Bureau of Investigation.[17] Grierson's grand American plan was finally shattered. The ambitious projects were left stranded, to die off one by one. His associates drifted away as their commitments ended, some back to the Film Board in Ottawa, some into independent film-making, some to London. Stuart Legg was to remain in New York until the summer of 1948 when he returned to London and joined the Crown Film Unit.

For Grierson the wound was deep and painful. Ever since his Chicago days he had had an affection for the United States. He loved America's jazz, its newspapers, its writers and its boundless, omnipresent vitality. He knew the country well, from Seattle to Sarasota, from Long Beach to Long Island, and he believed that he understood

A Dream Crumbles

the people. To be denied entry to the United States was a cruel blow to his pride. A nifty political tightrope walker, he had been out-politicked. In later years he would never talk about the experience and if anyone rashly raised it he was furious. From these traumatic happenings he emerged a changed man.

It was later that he learned from Mary Losey something which, in these grey days, he would have found heartening. In her office in Washington the phone rang. It was Robert Flaherty, phoning from Louisiana where he was shooting *Louisiana Story*. 'Mary,' he shouted, 'what's this I hear about the State Department and John?' Mary confirmed that what had been published in *Variety* appeared to be true. 'Well, you call that blankety-blank-blank at the State Department and you tell him from me that I'll come up there and wring his neck if they do that to John.' In Mary Losey's words, Flaherty didn't and he couldn't.[18] But his feeling and his wish summed up what many were feeling.

11 Paris, London, Africa

At the Paris conference it had been clear that UNESCO did not have in any department an adequate budget to finance an ambitious programme. It was true of Mass Communications generally and in particular it meant there was no money to make films. The short-term solution accepted in Paris in 1946 was summed up in two words —stimulation and facilitation. UNESCO would concentrate its efforts initially on stimulating others to make films and programmes on scientific, educational and cultural themes it considered important. In London, on his way to Paris, Grierson pursued this idea. It related both to his experience of the expanding British documentary movement in the thirties and to the hopes of international communication through documentary which had so recently been dashed in the United States.

When Grierson arrived in Paris early in March (his appointment in terms of salary dated from 4 February) he summoned William Farr to the Hotel Crillon where he was staying. He had a bad cold and was wrapped in an enormous bathrobe. Strutting about the room he said: 'This is a wonderful French invention. Why can't all hotels have these things?' Farr had the impression from the beginning that Grierson did not intend to remain long with UNESCO in Paris.[1] To help to re-establish his links with Britain, he considered commuting, spending the weekdays in Paris and the weekends at his house in Kent. Later Margaret joined him and they settled into a flat at 4 Avenue Emile Pouvillon, overlooking the Champs de Mars, where they had a Chinese cook and where their hospitality became legendary. Paris in the spring worked its charm on Grierson and later he reckoned he had enjoyed 'the most cheerful summer I have known in years'.

UNESCO was housed in the rather splendid building on the Avenue Kléber, formerly the Hotel Majestic, which had in turn been the head-quarters of the German Occupation forces and of the Americans after the Liberation. When Grierson arrived he had three counsellors: William Farr, in charge of films, René Maheu (who was later to become director-general) in charge of press and Philippe Desjardins in charge of radio. Grierson thought the organisation should be structured in

164

terms of horizontal objectives, not vertical disciplines, and as a result Maheu was given responsibility for the free flow and freedom of information, Desjardins was asked to survey the technical needs of the media and Farr was given the demanding department of stimulation. Grierson felt there was no point in talking about the free flow of ideas in a world where the technical facilities for the transmission and reception of information were so highly developed in some countries and so underdeveloped in a large part of the world. He believed in helping countries to set up systems and to promote the education and training of mass media people.

In addition to mass communication, Grierson had the responsibility of advising the director-general on public information. He found that, in the hands of Harold Kaplan, it was functioning effectively in informing the media about the problems UNESCO was anxious to tackle, what it was going to do and what it had done. He left it to run itself, giving it general directives from time to time. One was that information policy must march hand in hand with practical results and achievements, lest over-optimistic publicity should lead to subsequent disappointment. He felt that UNESCO needed a newspaper published in several languages and sold throughout the world. This was the origin of the *Unesco Courier*, published first as a tabloid and later in magazine form and in fifteen languages. He appointed as editor Sandy Koffler who had been a journalist with the U.S. Army in Italy and had started several newspapers there. Koffler found Grierson an extraordinary man, a strong dynamic speaker who said what he thought and would hammer away until he achieved his aim. Policy for the *Courier* was often discussed at informal sessions with Julian Huxley and Grierson in the bar.[2]

Grierson had a marked dislike of working in or from his office. His favoured headquarters was the Columbia Bar, opposite the Majestic. Here he would sit in the corner ('I always sit in the corner so no-one can stab me in the back') and summon people to see him. Sometimes he would disappear for two or three days at a time and on his return would phone Farr: 'Bill, can you come over? I think I've got it', and there would be the solution of a problem which had been occupying them. Grierson always found it easier to talk in a pub than in the formal setting of an office. In one Parisian pub—unlikely to have been the Columbia—he had long conversations with a man, about painting and everything else. One day Grierson was asked for his name and when he gave it, 'in my best voluble bad French', the man said, 'Moi je suis Derain.' For Grierson it was a moment to savour.

Paris, London, Africa

Grierson accepted an invitation to open the first International Festival of Documentary Films, held in Edinburgh from 31 August to 7 September 1947. It was an exciting occasion for world documentary, with Rossellini's *Paisa*, Rouquier's *Farrebique*, Rotha's *The World is Rich* and *The Cumberland Story* by Humphrey Jennings from Britain, Norman McLaren's *Fiddle-de-Dee* and *La Poulette Grise*, and Arne Sucksdorff making a first appearance with *Manniskor i Stad* (*Rhythm of a City*). Grierson paid tribute to the initiative of the organisers, the Edinburgh Film Guild, in launching so ambitious an undertaking so soon after the war. 'Here you are doing a great work', he said. 'It is good that Scotland is making herself known, and on the higher levels of human relations. That is the only true publicity for one nation in its speech to another.'

'I am charged by the Director-General of UNESCO to thank you most cordially for the association of UNESCO with this Festival', said Grierson at the opening ceremony. 'UNESCO has much to do, but it cannot do it itself. It must for ever look to just such organisations as this if its needs are to be served. Its many tasks are concerned in general with the increase of international understanding everywhere. It is concerned with the mobilisation of all the forces of education and of creative workers to that end. . . . In the last resort, the end of UNESCO is concerned with the exchange of men and ideas, with all the arts, and with the cultural heritages of the people.'

Grierson walked to one of the Festival performances with Bernard Sendall who had been Brendan Bracken's principal private secretary at the British Ministry of Information and who, in the rapid changes after V–E Day, found himself a controller of a range of home activities, including government film production. There was much uneasiness about the lack of imaginative direction in government film-making in Britain, which had found forceful expression in an article by Grierson published in the Festival's programme. When Grierson said to Sendall 'You know, I think I would like to come back into Government documentary', the remark—whether casual or deliberate Sendall did not know—stuck in his mind and on his return to London he reported it to Robert Fraser, the director-general. Some months were to pass before action was taken on it.[3]

It was not an empty comment by Grierson. On his return to Paris, after a short visit to the Venice Film Festival, he prepared a letter to Julian Huxley, reminding him that he had agreed to remain in his UNESCO post only until December to help the director-general to get the organisation under way and saying that he must soon be up and

166

about his business again. He had found there was much to be done in Britain of an urgent nature in which he thought his experience would be of help. He believed there was more pressing, more expansive and more creative work to be done 'than the present constipation of the international scene and UNESCO's starved and frightened little budget allow'. He thought he could leave UNESCO with good heart: the programme was strong, departmental teams were shaping up and concrete results were beginning to show. 'My stuff is where things are beginning and expanding and taking chances and in general trying to make two and two make five and you have no idea how tempting Britain is at the moment.'[4]

There was a lot of hard work to be done before Grierson could yield to his temptation. A budget for Mass Communications had to be prepared for submission to UNESCO's second General Conference in Mexico. It was not a task which appealed greatly to Grierson. Moreover the amount seemed pitifully small in comparison with the sum he had at his disposal in Canada. Grierson sailed to New York, *en route* to Mexico, on the *Queen Elizabeth*. On board were the members of the United Kingdom delegation. It was led by David Hardman and included Sir Ronald Adam, Sir Henry French, J. B. Priestley, Sir John Maud, Ritchie Calder and Jacquetta Hawkes. On the voyage there was a difference of opinion between Grierson and Priestley ('They had a flaming row'—William Farr). According to Ritchie Calder, Sir John Maud, half way across the Atlantic, opened a sealed envelope with instructions for the British delegation—instructions which made Priestley so furious that he wanted to go straight back from New York until persuaded to continue by Jacquetta Hawkes. In Mexico Priestley was unwell for part of the duration of the conference. According to Farr, Grierson remained in his room and set up through Farr a chain of instructions, leaving Farr to do much of the speaking.

In the midst of such troubled personal relationships, it is surprising that the conference, and in particular the working party on mass communications, accomplished as much as it did. In his opening speech David Hardman referred to the problem of making UNESCO live excitingly in the minds of ordinary men. The greatest service which UNESCO could do for the common people, he said, was to use these vast new instruments of mass communication to revive hope, temper pessimism and restore faith in the ordinary decencies and common values. 'We must light up the imagination of people with a belief in themselves and in each other. To light up men's minds we need illuminating ideas.' He went on to recommend the setting up of an

Paris, London, Africa

Order of World Citizenship—the conferring of the Freedom of the World on men and women who had made major contributions to welfare and enlightenment—Einstein, Toscanini, Helen Keller, Bernard Shaw. It seemed an exciting idea but it was to be abandoned on advice from the British Foreign Office.

The working party on mass communications devoted much time to discussion of the free flow of information and to the removal of obstacles hampering that flow. Here the difference of opinion between Priestley and Grierson became apparent. Priestley thought the obstacles to the free flow of information stemmed directly from political and economic factors and that the problems were beyond the powers of UNESCO to solve effectively. Grierson believed that UNESCO could become a truly world movement only when the ordinary people took an active interest and shared its work. He supported the creation of an International Ideas Bureau to promote special programmes, documentary and feature films, news stories, articles and books to get across to the world the ideas UNESCO stood for and thus encourage a greater sense of cultural solidarity among the peoples. The debate, in which Grierson did not take part directly, ended in compromise, the two points of view being regarded as complementary rather than incompatible. Meanwhile, elsewhere, Grierson was fascinated by the bullfighting and invited Manolete and his party for cocktails in his apartment.

Back in Paris Grierson was involved in preparations for the conference on 'Freedom of Information and the Press', held in Geneva in March. He drafted the speech made by Julian Huxley and incorporated in it themes to which he held fast. Freedom was an active force or it was nothing. To be free was to be free to do something. Forces of action drew their strength from their relationship with the actual and patent needs of people as they were felt in common, appreciated in common and realised in common. Freedom of information was a necessity if the native and natural frustrations they saw in the world were not to blow up in their faces. There was a warning about the danger of monopolies of information, whether instituted for political purposes or purposes of private gain and a plea for a sense of responsibility on the part of those who used the media of modern communications. Liberty was not to be confused with the forces of privilege or with the forces of anarchy. This must be done away with, 'for only then can man look at the true face of freedom and know, once and for all, that the only begetter of freedom is the spirit of fraternity itself'.

Grierson was nearing the end of his short period of service as director of Mass Communications and Public Information at UNESCO. He had arrived at a traumatic moment in his life and putting aside what he called his 'not uncomplicated affairs', he had helped Julian Huxley in the launching of the organisation. He had never intended to settle there, to become a bureaucrat, pushing around, as he saw others were already doing, an infinitude of paper. He told Huxley he would like to have stayed 'if only to help you swat them, for I am long and professionally practised in the art and enjoy it. You must watch them, or they will have you believing that nothing done is something done if only nothing is done busily and that the chatter of the scullery is high policy.'[5]

To some who saw him in Paris during that year he seemed like a caged lion. His evangelistic zeal was in conflict with international bureaucracy. He was a source of ideas and stimulus, not only in Mass Communications. Those with whom he came in contact recognised that they always drew some inspiration from him.

W. E. Williams came over from London to have lunch with Grierson and Farr. Grierson was hoping to persuade Williams to work for UNESCO in Paris. Williams was hoping to entice Grierson to return to England and lead British documentary again. It was a fascinating encounter. They began using foils and ended by wielding sabres. Grierson was saying to Williams, 'Your experience is exactly what we need. Come over here and do a real job.' Williams was saying to Grierson 'You know UNESCO is baloney. You are achieving nothing here. You are needed in Britain to revive and lead the documentary film thing.' Lunch lasted for four hours.[6]

On 19 February 1948, the Central Office of Information announced in London that Grierson had been appointed controller of the C.O.I.'s film operations to co-ordinate the work of the Films Division and the Crown Film Unit and to take overall charge of the planning, production and distribution of government films. There had been correspondence between Robert Fraser, the C.O.I.'s director-general, and Grierson. When he wrote on 17 February, Grierson said he was concerned deeply with the vitality of the film thing as it could be affected by the C.O.I. and its associates. 'My hopes in this matter are liable to be boundless: not for my own part in it but, if I may say so simply, because of the film stuff it can create and the influence it can have on our time. Not least among these hopes is the hope of finding and developing new talents if only because of the enlivening company it secures.' He emphasised the need for access to and participation in discussions of policy on the highest levels, so that there could be reality and authority in the guidance given to film producers. He referred to Fraser's personal disappointment with the film operation and to his belief in the need for a new and bold approach but he warned that he had no power of personal miracle suddenly to give the existing structure a new power and authority.[7]

As he was preparing to move to London—he left UNESCO on 4 April—Grierson no doubt had another look at the analysis he had prepared about a year before. In effect the British Government was saying, as Grierson had once said peremptorily to Paul Thériault in Ottawa, 'Implement your recommendations.' It is worth looking at several of them more closely because they hold the explanation of the gradual decline of British documentary as a force in the nation's life.

Grievous things, he said, had been happening to the Crown Film Unit, inheritor of the tradition of the E.M.B. and G.P.O. film units. It did not feel part and parcel of the public purpose. It should have taken the lead in information relating to such urgent questions as housing and health, nutrition, labour relations, international affairs and international trade and it was not doing so. He thought it had lost its way because it had assumed the lesser vanities that belong to the craftsman and lost the larger vanities that belong to the public service. Mental and long-sighted leadership had been lacking. He acknowledged the Crown Film Unit's lead in technical skill and, in fairness, recognised that the solution of its problems depended on liaison between the unit on the one hand and on the other the departments requiring film services and those responsible for financial disciplines. Grierson was thinking of Crown as having a central position comparable to the units he had led in the 1930s and to the National Film Board in Canada. When one adds the overhead burdens deriving from Crown's use of Beaconsfield Studios, his diagnosis was accurate but the remedies were never to be applied.

Grierson was equally uncompromising in his comments on the shortcomings of the liaison system between the commissioning departments and the production control officers at the C.O.I. The liaison officer should be in a position to take a film through at least to its penultimate stage without all the amateurism and frigging around which otherwise attended its confused and painful progress. To do this he needed to know his stuff, not to be overburdened with too many films and to have a requisite measure of status and authority. Grierson saw they were seeking a new breed of cat: people at once good public servants and creative leaders in the particular medium of film. Ideally they should be academically equipped as well. He believed that the job of discovering them must be attempted if Britain were to keep, or regain, its lead in the documentary field.

In his long paper he also dealt trenchantly with distribution and the need for a redefinition of the part all the government film organisations were expected to play in a common national plan of work. His analysis was on the right lines; but what he discovered when he arrived at the Films Division was the difference made by the changed status of the Government's information organisation. The Ministry of Information had had the power to formulate policy and to initiate. The Central Office of Information had no minister. It provided a common service to all departments. The films were financed out of departmental budgets and were made at the request of departments who were unwilling to yield to the C.O.I. the kind of general direction of a film policy which Grierson envisaged and desired. Departments made the policy and the films had to be produced to their order and to their liking.

For someone with a creative urge like Grierson the restriction was frustrating. His job, it seemed, called for more administrative skill than creative imagination. He was not greatly interested in the cramping detail of the day-to-day running of an office whose purpose was to provide a service for a dozen different departments, often making competing demands which had to be patiently resolved. The Treasury was firmly in control. Approval for expenditure took much longer to obtain and there was much reference back. He arrived at a time when heavy cuts had been made in the estimates for expenditure on film production, with inevitable conflict between departments when the C.O.I. attempted to implement them. It was not the kind of atmosphere in which Grierson's wide-ranging ideas flourished. He was not prepared to be a dog's-body.

Grierson could still add a brilliant creative touch here and there, when a film was being conceived or completed. When he was offered a long memorandum by someone who wanted a film made he would push it aside and say 'Tell me about it' and one could judge by the look in his eyes if the project was going to prosper. It was a test, as I remember, not merely of articulation but also of confidence. At a rough-cut viewing of a film he could see more sharply than anyone else what was wrong with it and if the film-maker was wise he would act on it. But these were small satisfactions. It soon became clear to him that the C.O.I. machine was not going to allow him to do the bigger, all-embracing things he had planned.[8] This was not wartime Canada. He had no direct access to Attlee, as he had had to Mackenzie King,

171

although many years later, looking back on his experience at the C.O.I., he claimed that he had had the backing of Sir Stafford Cripps and the sympathy of Aneurin Bevan for his ideas. It seems a matter for regret that there could not have been a meeting of minds between ministers planning major changes in the structure of British society and the founder of the British documentary movement committed to social reform.

Frustration was a cumulative process; and there were exceptions, such as Grierson's fruitful relationship with the Scottish Office which produced *Harnessing the Hills* on Tom Johnston's hydro-electric development and a refreshingly original film on Edinburgh, *Waverley Steps*. There were isolated films of quality like *Daybreak in Udi* and *The Undefeated*. Through Helen de Mouilpied (Lady Forman) there was a productive collaboration with the Ministry of Education. There was constructive help also from Niven MacNicoll, Charles Dand, Donald Taylor, Denis Forman, Philip Mackie and John Maddison.

But as early as the summer of 1949, in the review of documentary he wrote annually for the Edinburgh Film Festival journal, Grierson was admitting that he had 'not been able to see easily where the light now leads for the situation economic affects us all and the inspirational side, for reasons economic and other, is dust in the throat'. He mentioned having seen films from France and the Netherlands that returned the eye to the old excitement, 'while we are retiring from behind the camera and shooting from the deck chair, or something'. Even *Daybreak in Udi*, good film though it was, was 'so busy being simple for the ordinary—the last error of authenticity—that it misses time and again the poetic or other far-reaching note which a work of art is nothing without'. In a first reference to television he said that if it inherited, as it surely would, the great B.B.C. tradition, at least half of what they had wanted in documentary was secure.

Two years later, in his review for 1951 (when he had left the C.O.I.), there were no more of the encouraging words which he had used, to his chagrin, 'to support a goodly number of dull wits and fat backsides in complacent and now utterly ugly mediocrity'. Grierson felt free to speak plainly, and did: 'By and large, the men who run documentary to-day—and I mean the people who sponsor its ultimate shapes and qualities—do not care a damn for the purposes it once professed and the ends which gave it its larger life. And how could they care any more for its aesthetic possibilities when, with rare exception, they don't know aesthetic form from a hole in the ground? No, I think the time has come to say plainly that documentary as an art, documentary as a power of persuasion, documentary as a valuable instrument of national projection, is being allowed to go by default and a generation of film-makers ruined and lost to the State by a fumbling regime of sponsors unworthy of their predecessors and their origins. Comfortable as they may be in their all too vulgarly sought bureaucratic security, they are stifling a great public asset and serving their country ill.' Again, and characteristically, he did not spare the film-makers: 'I think a lot of people came into documentary who had no conception whatever of its larger reaches; and a great number still have no inkling of the difference between artist and technician.'

The hope Grierson had brought back into British documentary had died. It was not to be revived and British documentary was not again to have the political-social-aesthetic drive it had had in the 1930s. The reasons were complicated and criss-crossed with many factors, including a lack of political will, timidity in the civil service, the indifference of the new generation of film-makers, and awareness that television with its immediate contact with a large audience could assume the purposes of social documentary.

In his frustration Grierson found other things to do and he was happiest when they took him as far away as possible from the confines of the Central Office of Information in London. First, while he was still charged with enthusiasm for the work he had undertaken, there was a visit to Glasgow on 23 June, 1948, to receive the honorary degree of LL.D. from his old university. The Lord Rector was his old friend, Walter Elliot. The Chancellor was Sir John Boyd Orr who, associated with Edgar Anstey in making *Enough to Eat?*, had a healthy respect for the purpose and achievement of the documentary film movement and, as head of the Food and Agricultural Organisation, was aware of Grierson's international film ambitions. It gave Grierson particular pleasure to receive this first academic recognition from men he greatly respected and who knew his work.

One day in 1948 Grierson received from the Foreign Office a letter concerning the treaty signed in Brussels with France and Benelux and referring to the implementation of Article III by which the signatories undertook to co-operate culturally. It was proposed to include films and the C.O.I. was invited to put forward ideas. Grierson called in John Maddison, whose bilingualism allied with his practical experience of film production and distribution equipped him to represent Britain at international film conferences. Grierson thought that here was an opportunity to do in one area and on a limited scale some of the things he had been advocating at UNESCO. Out of the exploratory talks

173

with Maddison came a memorandum covering the whole field with that combination of high philosophy, practical detail and informed experience which stamped the many such analytical and forward-looking papers Grierson prepared. Its main recommendation was that Britain should propose the setting up of an inter-governmental working group to study European co-operation in films. The memorandum was passed to the headquarters of the Brussels Treaty Organisation, then in London, and the recommendations were accepted.[9]

Two committees were formed, a short-lived one for news-reels and the main cultural committee, to which was attached a working party for educational films. The first meetings were in The Hague. From the beginning Grierson stamped his personality on the proceedings. He had earned the respect of his colleagues in documentary. He showed in his memorandum the breadth of his conception. There were proposals for the co-production of films on European themes, for creative technicians to work in different countries, for the effective exchange and distribution of cultural and educational films, for film schools, film archives and film catalogues, for participation in film festivals, for awards to encourage production.

As out of the Brussels Treaty grew Western European Union and later the Council of Europe, so did the Film Committee expand. It was the agreeable practice from the outset for it to meet in rotation in the capitals of the member countries. Grierson insisted that in addition to the formal sessions the delegations should meet informally documentary film-makers in the various countries. These meetings, and the regular showings of new films, formed an invaluable complement to the business sessions. In countries like Turkey and Cyprus, where the documentary idea was little known, they helped significantly to spread understanding and raise standards.

I was a member of the Film Committee as it passed from one parent organisation to another and saw at first hand an international body grow from an idea on paper to something which, for a time, had real force and influence. Grierson had Maddison, Charles Dand and John Harrison of the Educational Foundation for Visual Aids as other members of the British delegation but he was always the dominating presence, even when he occasionally disappeared, as he did once from Luxembourg, for a weekend visit to Chartres with Pearl Mesta, the American Ambassador. The friendships formed or strengthened were among the intangibles which do not find their place in the records but form the real basis for action.

I think of Dr. Vroom and Jan Hulsker of the Netherlands, Roger

Paris, London, Africa

Seydoux and Robert Lefranc of France, Franz Rowas and Fridolin Schmid of Germany, Henri Storck in Belgium, Roberto Rossellini in Italy. The first co-operatively made film to emerge was *The Open Window*, directed by Henri Storck, on European landscape painting. Later there was a series of fine teaching films, on philosophers like Rousseau, physicists like Rutherford, Einstein and Volta, biologists like Leeuwenhoek, Simpson and Calmette. It took patience and determination to achieve such international co-operation. It took inspiration and leadership to launch the effort and these came in large degree from Grierson.

One less well-known venture by Grierson was the Saturday morning film society he started with John Maddison for young trainee film-makers in London from Europe and the Commonwealth. For him it was a means of finding what younger film-makers were thinking.

Grierson reacted apprehensively to another international documentary occasion. In July 1948 Basil Wright and Donald Alexander represented the United Kingdom at the first congress of the World Union of Documentary, held at Marianske Lazne in Czechoslovakia. The other countries represented included Hungary, Yugoslavia and Poland, with Joris Ivens from the Netherlands and Jean Painlevé and Henri Langlois for France. It adopted its own definition of documentary, prepared a constitution and appointed an International Court of Honour. Grierson did not like it. The dislike was expressed in a letter to the editor of the *Kinematograph Weekly* in which he took pointed exception to a report by Wright and Alexander criticising the operation of documentary in Britain. He reminded them that the only imaginative work for which they were noted had been derived from the government sponsorship they were snidely comparing with the Czechoslovakian wonderwork. He said he was hungry to hear about imaginative dream-children unnaturally cut off. Grierson was understandably sensitive about any attempt which might be made by Communism to capture documentary.

Grierson found himself in difficulties over another kind of European involvement. Lothar Wolff was in London in the summer of 1949 on behalf of the European Co-operation Administration with a proposal for a series of films on communications, housing, health, education and agriculture, showing the contribution of Marshall Aid. Wolff discussed it with Grierson who brought in Stuart Legg, now back in Britain and a producer for the Crown Film Unit. All appeared to be going well when Wolff was suddenly summoned to the U.S. Embassy to attend a meeting at the Treasury in Whitehall. S. C. Leslie was in the chair and

Grierson was present. According to Wolff, 'Leslie read the riot act. He said the Americans never understood how the British Empire worked. There could be no involvement in Europe. Britain would have nothing to do with the idea. The Crown Film Unit was an arm of the British Government.' Wolff withdrew in some discomfiture. He recalled the experience to me as an example of Grierson's positive thinking. 'I have always thought of John as a man of vision.'[10]

On 21 August 1949 Grierson was back at the Edinburgh Film Festival, taking part with Sir Stephen Tallents and Robert Flaherty in the opening ceremony—the only occasion on which three of the founder figures of documentary appeared together in public. Tallents spoke eloquently of the pioneers who had been convinced 'that cinema, moving in a borderland between the sciences and the arts, could provide an incomparable medium for exploring the world and presenting the fruits of exploration in a form which would touch not only the minds but also the imaginations of men'. Grierson spoke with his characteristic pungency and zeal.

Then Flaherty rose to speak, a now somewhat bowed but still splendid figure, with his shock of white hair and explorer's eye yet sharp. The packed audience of over two thousand, who had warm in their memory Flaherty's *Louisiana Story*, given its world première in the same cinema a year before, applauded, and applauded, and applauded. Flaherty, sensing that this was not the time for a speech and that he could never have matched the words of Tallents and Grierson, bowed three times to the audience, 'Thank you, thank you, thank you', and sat down. The applause continued unabated. It was a moving tribute to one of the great men of the cinema, a moment to remember. It was one of Flaherty's last public appearances. He died in July 1951.

Grierson had kept in mind the possibility of completing his work for the Imperial Relations Trust by visiting South Africa. Towards the end of 1949 he had an opportunity to do so, in a visit he paid with Margaret. They arrived in Cape Town by sea on 1 November and went on next day to Johannesburg, visited Pretoria and returned to Cape Town by way of Kimberley on 11 November. Stellenbosch, Port Elizabeth and East London were also visited before Grierson moved on to Zanzibar, Nairobi and, on the return journey, Khartoum on 8 January 1950.

His main purpose was 'to inquire into the existing national film facilities and to recommend a scheme best calculated to give the Government a film service which would do justice to the presentation of South Africa at home and abroad'. An intensive schedule was prepared for him by Charles te Water and he consulted department heads, certain men of science, some representatives of the academic and arts worlds and certain members of industry.

Although the visit was comparatively short, both his general knowledge and his particular experience in Canada, Australia and New Zealand enabled him to prepare a comprehensive report and to reach conclusions. Within the terms of reference the job was done with Grierson's usual surgical efficiency. What was needed, he said, was conviction in high quarters that the film could and ought to be developed as an instrument of national policy; an objective appreciation—free from mere film interest and film enthusiasm—of the relationship of the film to the larger and deeper processes of public information; and a plan of action, which he proceeded to set out in detail.

On the broad issues he offered no sensational solutions: 'No one in his senses will expect, by simple formula, to liquidate the host of misunderstandings and prejudices which, coming from the deeps of 19th century political philosophy and error, now surround the consideration of South African problems.' South Africa, he suggested, should approach the task with confidence and even in a spirit of assertion. He had found the quality of *audace* striking and refreshing in South African political discussions.

Read some thirty years after it was written, the report seems studiously discreet. Grierson had an insatiable appetite for travel and new experience and for some two months this appetite was adequately satisfied. He had seen the country, learned something about Africa and met a number of people who held decision-making positions. Some years later, relieved of any need for polite circumvention, he drew on his experiences when reviewing Alexander Campbell's *The Heart of Africa*. One of the wisest contributions one can make to any understanding of Africa, he wrote, is not to expect the normal, and not to apply normal measures of judgement. 'The commanding and abnormal fact is that a black wave of insurgence is sweeping over the white man in Africa, and from sources so little understood and with an eagerness so uncomprehended, that all reactions can be fitted with difficulty into any Western European pattern of thought.'

He recalled a conversation he had had in South Africa. 'How long do you think it will take before they break through?' one Nationalist asked him. Grierson said, 'How should I know? Perhaps twenty-five years or more [i.e. 1975].' 'No', the Nationalist said, 'seventy-five years or more. And because of that longer period of painful maturing, it will not be so bad, and thanks to us.' Grierson said he was surprised at the admission of the inevitability. 'Of course', said the Nationalist. The African would not be denied, Grierson concluded, because in a world where economic considerations would prevail, he held the whip-hand of his labour. He had seen the African rise in America. 'Perhaps it will be a more painful and bloody affair than it ever was in America, but the African will command the tools and that will be the end of it.'[11]

On New Year's Day Grierson was in Nairobi. He was invited to the Governor's party but declined because he thought the Governor would like to spend New Year with his intimate friends. Instead he went on a fishing trip with a young Kikuyu. The boy asked him: 'Would you like to come and visit my people? We are going to have a sports day to celebrate the New Year.' Grierson said he would be delighted and went with him to a mass gathering of the Kikuyu where there were several friends he had met in England, including Jomo Kenyatta. Between each event there was a speech. Grierson was asked if he would address the gathering of some ten thousand people and agreed, provided Kenyatta would translate for him. Keeping off political matters, Grierson gave them a description of his impressions of the countryside, the costumes and, especially, the beauty of the women. His remarks were punctuated with trumpets and impressive rolls on the drums from the bands on either side of the platform. The crowd went wild with pleasure and he sat down to the best hand he'd ever had.[12]

While he was with Kenyatta he heard Peter Mbyu, the son of Konange, the Kikuyu chief, give an account of nine months he had spent in India. It was to be some years before Grierson could himself visit the subcontinent.

Grierson's responsibilities at the C.O.I. included not only the Crown and the Colonial Film Units but also film activities in the British Zone in Germany, where Arthur Elton was Film Adviser to Information Services Control. He was in Berlin on 5 January 1949 and in Dusseldorf and Hamburg in April. His longest visit was in May 1950, with John Maddison. Gregory Buckland-Smith, in charge of film production for the Central Commission, met them at Dusseldorf airport on 8 May and that evening had the odd pleasure of introducing Grierson to the other John Grierson, the flier: each knew of the other's fame and they had corresponded but never met. According to Buckland-Smith, 'they got on famously with each other. It was a splendid evening.' At

Paris, London, Africa

Wahnerheide Grierson met Sir Ivone Kirkpatrick, the High Commissioner, and on 10 May was in Hamburg.

Grierson's reception by the film people in Hamburg was as exciting as had been Flaherty's a couple of months earlier. He was known and respected, and knew himself to be, especially among the German documentary producers and directors who looked to Britain for guidance and help. A German translation of the book I edited, *Grierson on Documentary*, had been published in 1947. Grierson was familiar with the work being done by Buckland-Smith and his staff: he had seen *Asylrecht* on the refugee problem, short-listed for an Academy Award, and *Rosinenbomber*, on the Berlin airlift. While in Hamburg he saw *Die ersten Europaer* on the work of the DEEC and *Des Kaisers Hafen* about the reconstruction of Wilhelmshaven.

'I won't forget', Buckland-Smith told me, 'how moved he was to see the ruins of Hamburg, mile after mile of devastation, the encouragement he gave to us in the Film Section, or the inspiration he was to our German documentary colleagues.'[13] At one of the press conferences held for him an earnest young woman journalist asked: 'Mr. Grierson, what are the ingredients of a successful documentary film?' He said, 'Sex, violence and sin.' She said 'Please?' He twinkled at her.[14]

At the C.O.I. the Crown Film Unit was a focus of many of the production problems which beset the organisation. The Unit was housed at Beaconsfield Studios, opened in 1949 by Herbert Morrison and Grierson, whose brother-in-law, Donald Taylor, was in charge. The studios were expensive to operate and the films made by Crown had to carry heavy overheads. Robert Fraser believed that the way to reduce the overheads was to have more and more of the C.O.I.'s films made by Crown. The independent producers argued that they could make the Government's information films much more cheaply— as they could. Charles Dand believed that the solution was to reserve Crown for very special films and to accept a reduction of its output.[15] Films like *The Dancing Fleece* were made, not out of conviction that telling a story in ballet would help the export of wool but in part at least because the studios would be used. In Parliament the Conservative Opposition maintained that the films were Labour Party propaganda.

These were among the factors which added intractable complications to Grierson's campaign to restore social purpose and imaginative craftsmanship to British documentary. When the Conservatives won the 1951 general election and the Crown Film Unit was disbanded as one of the cuts in the new Government's information services, Grierson had gone. It was a defeat for documentary and he knew it.

12 Group 3: 'The Brave Don't Cry'

At the end of 1950 Grierson was offered the position of executive producer for Group 3, one of the co-operative film production enterprises receiving loans of government money through the National Film Finance Corporation. For the first time he was involved in the making of story films for the public cinemas. It seemed to run counter to much that he had been saying and writing for twenty years. Why did he accept?

There were, I think, four main reasons. One was negative: he could see little hope of the documentary idea for which he had striven prospering under government/Whitehall auspices. The others were positive. The Government, in the person of Harold Wilson, President of the Board of Trade, was trying to help British feature film-making and thought there was a place for him in the effort. There was the never-failing appeal of a challenge, something new to be attempted. And there was the prospect of discovering and encouraging, perhaps even inspiring, talented young people.

James H. Lawrie, a fellow Scot, was managing director of Group 3. The chairman was Sir Michael Balcon, of Ealing Studios and the Rank Organisation, and together they considered who should be given responsibility for an experiment of some importance to the Government and British film-making. Grierson's achievement was on record and they were well aware of his reputation for finding and leading talented young people. They also knew that he had no experience of making feature films in studios. Lawrie met Grierson, for the first time, in the lounge of the New Norfolk Hotel in Bloomsbury. As they talked he jotted ideas down on the back of an envelope and when that was full he used the other side and even the area round the stamp. 'It was all crazy, but wildly stimulating. I knew at once that this was the man most likely to inspire the young film-makers and to exploit their chance.'[1]

Balcon and Lawrie were mindful of the risks they were running in appointing Grierson. They thought they might minimise these by appointing as production controller John Baxter who had had experience of studio film-making in such films as *Love on the Dole*, *The Common Touch* and *Let the People Sing*, whose first film *Doss House* (1933) had shown some awareness of the drama on the doorstep and who in *The Shipbuilders* had attempted with some success to combine realist and fictional elements. Baxter, a gentle, soft-voiced man, would never have claimed that his work was in the forefront of imaginative film-making; but it seemed that his solid experience would usefully complement Grierson's fire and flair. Moreover he had helped, on behalf of the independent film producers, to formulate the case for the National Film Finance Corporation.

The first films were made at Southall Studios. Later Group 3 was to move to Beaconsfield Studios, after they had been evacuated by the Crown Film Unit. With the ownership (or in this case leasing) of studios inevitably come problems of overheads: the labour and other costs which continue whether or not a film is being produced. A maximum volume of production must be maintained if the overheads are not to become crippling. It takes time to organise a production programme, even a modest one. Group 3 was not given much time. Approval for the financing of the project was given in January 1951. Group 3 was registered as a private company on 31 March 1951. Early in June it was announced that Group 3 would make five films. It would have been wiser if a production programme could have been prepared with more time and thought—more time to find the people to make the films, more thought about their content and style; but the longer these preparations took, the greater the burden of retrospective overheads the films would carry. The NFFC expected the films to recoup their costs, if not to make a profit.

From the beginning, therefore, the directors of Group 3, and especially Grierson and Baxter, were in a dilemma. There had to be films in the studios. There had been insufficient time to search for subjects and prepare scripts. Baxter had a script ready for a simple thriller, *Judgement Deferred*, which it was agreed he should direct. Although it did have a Dorset coastal setting and introduced Joan Collins, it was not the kind of film expected from Group 3. James Lawrie thought of it as 'a stopgap so that we wouldn't have the studios idle at the very start'.[2]

The next three films gave a clearer indication of a distinctive style: a capacity to find humour, a slightly quizzical humour, in everyday situations and an enterprising use of natural locations. *Brandy for the Parson*, a smuggling comedy based on a short story by Geoffrey Household, was filmed on the Devon coast and the Devon Downs. It was directed by John Eldridge, whose promising work was known to

Group 3: 'The Brave Don't Cry'

Grierson through *Waverley Steps*, and photographed by Martin Curtis, the cameraman on the Edinburgh film. It introduced Kenneth More and James Donald. The comedy was a little more relaxed than in the Ealing films and its positive virtues included a fresh feeling for characterisation and the unforced use of the natural scene. It had its feet in reality and its head in a cloud of laughter.

You're Only Young Twice, similarly light in mood, was based on a comedy, *What Say They?* by James Bridie. The setting was Glasgow University and exteriors were shot at Gilmorehill. Terry Bishop, the director, had, like Eldridge, begun in documentary and showed less confidence in handling such diverse elements as Bridie's use of the biblical story of Esther as a parallel and student effervescence at Rectorial elections. The players included Duncan Macrae, Charles Hawtry, Patrick Barr and Robert Urquhart and there was a small part for Ronnie Corbett. Production problems included the realisation after the film was shot that the leading lady's plummy accent was unsuitable. Molly Weir's voice was substituted. The film had a rough reception critically in London, unsympathetic to anything with a strong Scottish flavour. Grierson persuaded Bridie's friend, Walter Elliot, to write to *The Times*, defending the film as being 'fundamentally about the funny side of the immense seriousness of youth'.

Time, Gentlemen, Please was from a short novel, *Nothing to Lose*, by R. J. Minney: again a satirical comedy, taking a sly dig at Whitehall bureaucracy and making a kind of a hero of a lovable old tramp in a village with a 99·9 per cent employment rate. Grierson said it was 'based on the simple but civilised idea that someone somewhere shouldn't work as hard as they keep on telling us to do'. Lewis Gilbert directed and gave more than a hint of the qualities which were to emerge in *Reach for the Sky*, *Sink the Bismarck* and *Alfie*. Eddie Byrne headed a cast which included Raymond Lovell, Hermione Baddeley and Dora Bryan. It was well received in London and, overseas, in points as far apart as Broadway and Wellington.

These films, among their other properties, reflected Grierson's love of fun which was so often overlain by more serious concerns. The next film was expressive of something central in his life. Since his boyhood in Cambusbarron the life of the miner had had a particular meaning for him. He had lived through grey days of depression and had seen his parents help to sustain a stricken community by running a soup kitchen. Now he had an opportunity to make a film which would present the miner's life. He found the theme in a disaster drawn from actuality: the threatened entombment of over a hundred miners at the

182

Group 3: 'The Brave Don't Cry'

Knockshinnoch pit in Ayrshire. Montagu Slater, who had worked with Grierson in documentary, and Lindsay Galloway, the Scottish writer, worked on a treatment.

The Brave Don't Cry was directed by Philip Leacock who had shown promise in the dramatised documentary, *Out of True*, and was later to make *The Kidnappers*. The drama had a threefold nature: resistance below ground, the resource of the rescue teams, and the reaction of the mining community. For his actors Grierson drew heavily on the Glasgow Citizens Theatre, then at the height of its achievement. He brought to London such players as Andrew Keir, Fulton Mackay, Archie Duncan, Jameson Clark, Meg Buchanan and Jean Anderson— 'the best gang I ever worked with'. They stood close to the story in a way that seldom happens in British films: if they were not acting themselves they were acting their next door neighbours.

When the film was completed Grierson arranged a private showing for Norman Wilson, chairman of the Edinburgh Film Festival, and me. We had no hesitation in choosing it to open the 1952 Festival. When the selection was announced there was an immediate reaction from Wardour Street. The Rank Organisation did not want *The Brave Don't Cry* to receive this kind of recognition. Other films were offered, among them *The Importance of Being Earnest*, whose glossy entertainment had nothing to do with the purposes of the Edinburgh occasion. The pressure, firmly applied, was one indication to me of the opposition Grierson was experiencing from the film trade in London. They did not want Group 3 to succeed: it represented government participation in film production for the cinemas and was therefore to be resisted. When Group 3's films were released in London the critics were often not given an opportunity of seeing them. They went into programmes under the derisive heading of 'support', with a consequential effect on their earning potential.

This attitude, which made ultimate success for Group 3 in the cinemas impossible, was only beginning to register with Grierson in the summer of 1952. At the Edinburgh première *The Brave Don't Cry* had a triumphant reception, echoed in tribute from every critic in the country. Hugh MacDiarmid was one of those in the audience which cheered it. Grierson was proud when he said: 'You would think it was about your relations.' When it was shown in the United States later in the year, Bosley Crowther in the *New York Times* praised it highly. 'The varying moods of the trapped miners, the stoicism of their loved ones above ground, the creeping surrender to frustration and the final lift of heroism in the rescue—these things are beautifully articu-

183

lated in the imagery and idioms of the screen.'[3] Its appeal could not be suppressed and it was to become the most widely shown of all the Group 3 films, with the exception of *The Conquest of Everest*. Behind it, as is so often the case with outstanding films, there stood the production courage of one man.

The next few films were closer in style to *Brandy for the Parson*. *Laxdale Hall* (*Scotch on the Rocks* in the United States) was developed by Alfred Shaughnessy from a story by Eric Linklater about the refusal of Hebridean islanders to pay a road tax when they had no roads. It was filmed at Applecross in Wester Ross. John Eldridge directed. A Scottish/English cast included Andrew Keir, Fulton Mackay, Nell Ballantyne and Roddy Macmillan and, for the Sassenachs, Ronald Squire, Kathleen Ryan, Raymond Huntley and Sebastian Shaw. Largely ignored in London it was an immediate and outstanding success in Scotland where exhibitors needing box-office uplift continued to show it for years.

Of *The Oracle*, directed by Pennington Richards, *The Times* wrote: 'Group 3 specialise in films which do not entirely neglect the intelligence', and said it was of more interest than the film it was 'supporting' at the Empire in London.[4] Based on the premise that the successful prediction of future events would spoil things for everyone, it had the voice of Gilbert Harding and the emerging talents of Virginia McKenna and Michael Medwin. Grierson saw it as being about truth, involving comedy but also contemporary satire.

Miss Robin Hood was produced by Donald Wilson (later to be responsible for the B.B.C. series *The Forsyte Saga*) and directed by John Guillermin (whose films were to include *The Towering Inferno*). Margaret Rutherford appeared as an eccentric old lady seeking the recovery of a stolen formula for whisky.

At the end of September 1952 there was a change in the control of production at Group 3. John Baxter became managing director and it was announced that Grierson would concentrate on two or three personal productions while continuing to contribute ideas and advice over the whole range of Group 3's work. Colin Lesslie, Sidney Cole, Herbert Mason and Donald Taylor emerged as producers. Grierson urged that the work of producer and director was complementary and suggested to Baxter that care should be taken in considering their respective qualities.

Grierson's health was giving cause for concern, his frequent bouts of severe coughing alarming his friends. In May 1953 tests confirmed that he had tuberculosis in both lungs. On 14 May he went into

Brompton Hospital for treatment for what he described to Stuart Legg as 'only a pettifogging shadow on the lung and the barest beginning of something which, if you please, is reacting already to the arse injections so that I won't be able to make anything of it after all'. He refused to have visitors. 'If there's a *reductio ad absurdum* of human acquaintance it's surely the tiresome promiscuity of a hospital bed in visiting hours. I was having none of it and none of it I assure you is a pleasure.'[5]

When he left on 29 May he wrote to the secretary of the Brompton saying that he had never been in a hospital before. 'I am astonished that the medical disciplines should be so combined with vitality and good humour and this, I am sure, is in itself some contribution to medical skill.' He had one criticism which he made with gusto. 'Your food is boring. It is even pathetically boring in so far as there is no excuse for such a dreary use of the infinite variety of raw materials which the London markets provide.'[6] Whatever the doctors thought of his health, in spirit he was as buoyant as ever.

Grierson was to spend about a year convalescing at home. In 1948 he and Margaret had signed a lease of Tog Hill, a small seventeenth-century house on the Marquis of Lansdowne's land at Calstone, two miles south-east of Calne in Wiltshire. It was something of a ruin and in return for a peppercorn rent it was arranged that Grierson should more or less rebuild the house. While this was being done he and Margaret lodged in a local farmhouse. They were joined by Golightly who had himself recovered from tuberculosis: a man who knew the countryside deeply and the motives and satisfactions of people who make things grow. They started work on the garden and when they moved into the house in 1950 it was already yielding produce.

The house was found by Dr. Anthony Grierson who had a practice in Calne. It stands on the river Marden. Grierson started stocking the river with fish but it didn't work out that way. He found so much pleasure just looking at them and looking into the water generally that he forgot about catching anything. He enjoyed living in his isolated house, shining down the valley in the western sun. He liked the country. He even liked the foxes which lived around him and once decapitated his ducks in dozens. 'They cross my path contemptuously in broad daylight: they cry out their loves on my doorstep in the dark hours of the night, but it's wonderful to have wild things living around you. It is eminently salutory for human vanity to have wild things about you who don't care a hoot for you human beings and don't like you in the least anyway.'[7]

Group 3: 'The Brave Don't Cry'

Convalescence meant no diminution in Grierson's activity. He received all the Group 3 papers, commented in detail on scripts and story ideas, wrote regularly to his fellow directors, kept in close touch with the units in the studios or on location and answered fully the flow of letters he received from friends. 'From the mass of material you turn out it is hard to realise that you are temporarily out of circulation', wrote Sir Michael Balcon.[8] He drafted his memoranda in bed. He also kept by him in bed a shotgun which he would fire through the open window to scare away the pigeons, making a meal of his cabbages. He accepted his enforced convalescence reluctantly but, as in Florida in 1942, it was not to be an unproductive period.

Of the films in production Grierson had an immediate interest in two. One was a film about a boy jockey, ultimately titled *Devil on Horseback*. Grierson was attracted by skill wherever he found it and while gambling held little interest for him, horse-racing did. He greatly admired Lester Piggott. Out of this admiration came the story of a lad from Wigan with a genius for handling horses who learned the hard way that winning races wasn't everything. Neil Paterson, Montagu Slater and Cyril Frankel, the director, worked on the writing of the story and shooting-script. With Jeremy Spencer as the jockey and Googie Withers and John McCallum in the main horseless parts, the film went into production at the end of June. Grierson had regular reports on its progress from Isobel Pargitor. The reports were promising and the film had a particularly warm reception from the critics when it was shown at the London Pavilion in March 1954. 'The whole film', wrote Dilys Powell in the *Sunday Times*, 'has a freshness and a like-ableness which promises well for its young director, Cyril Frankel.'[9]

Frankel was also the director of the other film in which Grierson was taking the closest personal interest. *Man of Africa* had its origin in Grierson's period at the Central Office of Information where *Daybreak in Udi* had shown there were exciting themes waiting for film-makers in the Colonies. Filmed in Uganda, the story by Montagu Slater was of a tribe forced by soil erosion to move into a new territory inhabited by pygmies whom the Negroes despised; of the slow breaking-down of prejudice and the beginning of a friendly relationship between the two peoples.

The film was at an advanced editing stage when Grierson went into hospital and there were troublous times for the production while he was convalescing. Sir Michael Balcon, who had himself been ill, had strong reservations about the film and was supported in his detailed criticisms by John Baxter and James Lawrie. They thought it full of lovely things but unclear in its story line. In contrast Stuart Legg wrote to Grierson: 'It knocked me flat—the most beautiful thing for years, and politically in the sharpest taste. Certain minor points of clarity in the first half were all I could point to—and for the rest, for God's sake leave it alone. *What* a piece of production! And *what* editing!'[10]

It was not until August 1954 that *Man of Africa* had its première at the Edinburgh Film Festival. The narrative inadequacies were still there and they limited the response to the film. Cyril Frankel's direction was praised for having given freshness and emotional meaning to his theme. Its potential appeal in cinemas was never put to the test: it had only one showing. *Man of Africa* was probably ahead of its time. The wind of change had only begun to blow in the dark continent and the world outside was still indifferent and disinterested.

Tog Hill may be among the most isolated houses in Wiltshire but during Grierson's convalescence it was a-buzz with activity. There were as many visitors as Margaret thought wise. Among them were Basil Wright and Paul Rotha, discussing their film *World Without End*, which was to break new ground by having a première at the Edinburgh Film Festival and a simultaneous showing on television.

On another occasion John Taylor showed him, on the domestic wall, an assembly of *The Conquest of Everest*, a Countryman Films production in which Group 3 had, by happy chance, invested and taken under its wing. Had the Hillary–Tenzing expedition failed so also would the investment. The film Tom Stobart photographed, given a Royal Première in October 1953, was by far the most successful of all the Group 3 productions at the box-office.

At the same time Grierson was commenting on story ideas and treatments. One project which greatly appealed to him but which was never to reach the screen was Naomi Mitchison's play about the herring fishermen, *Spindrift*, on which Lindsay Galloway was working. Others included *The Golden Legend of Schultz* which he had discussed with Eric Linklater and *The Confessions of a Justified Sinner* by James Hogg —exciting film ideas by any reckoning. There was talk of a film to be directed by Joseph Losey and a production project by Thorold Dickinson.

As a director of Group 3 Grierson was also involved in a major policy decision, the transference of the distribution of the company's films from Associated British Film Distributors to British Lion. It was hoped that in this way both wider distribution and more favourable terms would be obtained. There had been no circuit releases for even the best of the early films, *The Brave Don't Cry* and *Brandy for the*

Group 3: 'The Brave Don't Cry'

Parson, and without this returns were slow and uncertain. Group 3 was expected to experiment and to give encouragement to talented young people. Sir Michael Balcon himself said: 'To compete in the ordinary feature field is something I would have little interest in.'[11] But box-office success was the measure being applied. The NFFC expected its investment to produce a return. A report prepared after 1956 showed a total cost of £1,100,972 for the twenty-two feature films made and a total revenue, at that date, of £670,700. Most of the films made went over their budgets, which averaged £50,000. The films in profit in 1956 were *The Conquest of Everest*, *The Brave Don't Cry*, *The Love Match* and *John and Julie*.

Grierson had recovered sufficiently to take *Man of Africa* to the Cannes Film Festival in April 1954. Neil Paterson was there for the Festival showing of *The Kidnappers*. As was often to happen later, Grierson was sought out by the documentary film-makers who wanted an analysis of their films. I was with him when he met Arne Sucksdorff who was showing his first feature length film, *The Great Adventure*. Bert Haanstra and Herman van der Horst were there from the Netherlands and Albert Lamorisse of *Crin Blanc* represented the French documentary film-makers. Grierson relished the encounters and accepted the homage.

Group 3 was an experiment, an experiment made in a climate which at best was only tolerant and at times was actively hostile. 'I think the whole idea of Group 3 was brave and exciting and enormously worth while, but from the start we were fighting heavy odds and there is no doubt that it was something of a gamble', said James Lawrie to me.[12] 'I think we all knew what we were up against but thought the risk worth taking.' Given the whole-hearted support of the industry it could have been of long-term value to British film-making. Bernard Coote, who became managing director of Group 3, said that 'in retrospect we can now see the value of what Group 3 had. There is no doubt that it was a worth-while experiment and had we developed Group 3 it could have grown into something bigger like a national film entity.'[13] Sir Michael Balcon's conclusion was that in a growth industry (as the cinema was then) too little was spent on research and that Group 3 was a modest research laboratory, to be judged not by the immediate results but by what happened to the results.[14]

Grierson told me much later that had he given more effort to finding and encouraging writers Group 3 would have had a more lasting impact as an experimental group. For someone who found delight in the clowns of the screen he was pleased to have noted the talents of

Group 3: 'The Brave Don't Cry'

Tony Hancock, Peter Sellers, Eric Sykes and Ronnie Corbett. James Lawrie thought his particular value lay in being able to convey excitement to the directors who were working on the group's films—Lewis Gilbert, John Eldridge, John Guillermin, Philip Leacock, Wolf Rilla, David Paltenghi, Pennington Richards, Cyril Frankel.

Frankel summed up his experience for me: 'He projected his belief in me to me—and it was because he believed in me that I was impelled to endeavour to bring out the best in myself. . . . Grierson led me through many avenues of self-discovery. Now I understand people are born at different levels of being; he was of a very high level of being, which is why his personality is so riveting—and why he was so often misunderstood. His ideas were of a different and higher level than those of the majority of people he had to deal with and this, of course, was a source of artistic frustration.' In a tribute Frankel wrote for the 1954 Edinburgh Film Festival, he described Grierson as a true teacher who neither demanded nor desired imitation. 'He leads you to the threshold of your own mind, and then when you enter on the adventure, of discovering something for yourself, his joy is to share the adventure with you, lending his advice and criticism.'[15] The truth of that observation is something everyone who worked with Grierson will recognise.

Many who had worked with him assembled to do him honour at a dinner to celebrate twenty-five years of documentary, held during the 1954 Edinburgh Film Festival. Sir Stephen Tallents was there, with Basil Wright, Sir Arthur Elton, Edgar Anstey, Paul Rotha, Alberto Cavalcanti, Stuart Legg and J. P. R. Golightly from the E.M.B. and G.P.O. Film Units. James Beveridge represented Canada, Helen Grayson the United States, John Ferno and Herman van der Horst the Netherlands, Theodor Christiansen Denmark, Fedor Hanjekovic Yugoslavia, and Oxley Hughan New Zealand. Others who spoke during a long and lively evening included Alexander Wolcough, Dilys Powell, Paul Dehn, Denis Forman, John Maddison, C. A. Oakley and Norman Wilson, who was in the chair.

Tallents said he thought television would give the new generation of documentary film-makers the most marvellous opportunity of the century. Grierson himself also had television in mind. 'I think there is a lot of scope before us, but we have to catch up with the original idea, to secure the imaginative nature of public information, whether it is in terms of Government propaganda, or industry, or television.'

Sir Michael Balcon resigned as chairman of Group 3 in July 1954 and was succeeded by David Kingsley, the new managing director of the NFFC. Balcon admitted to me that, as head of Ealing, a director of the Rank Organisation and honorary adviser to the NFFC, he had tried to do too much. If this were so it was only one of the reasons why Group 3 disappeared.

When David Kingsley announced in July 1955 that Group 3 had abandoned its policy of continuous production, he said: 'It is now apparent that the type of middle budget picture which is most appropriate for the training of new directors is not suited to the present pattern of exhibition', i.e. the films would need to be shown as first or co-features on the circuits to recover cost.[16] This did not happen. An idea launched with high promise could not survive in the cold climate of the commercial cinema.

13 The Heart is Highland

Free of even the small measure of administrative routine involved in his work for Group 3, Grierson could turn to other interests and choose what he wanted to do. It was not surprising that one of the first calls on his services came from Scotland: he had always returned to his native country whenever he had the opportunity and from the beginning his films had been of Scotland whenever that was possible.

'I like to produce Scottish films', he said in a B.B.C. talk early in 1954, 'because after a lot of years wandering about I know the Scottish speech is the only one I really understand. I have never understood much more than fifty per cent of what English people said to me. I prefer the Scottish pattern of behaviour because I grew up with it. I like the style of Scottish humour. I like the complicated Scottish approach to the emotions. But all that is simply because I grew up with it. I like the thought that in Scottish films one is making movies about one's own people.' Answering the question: Which films of Scotland would he most like to make? Grierson said: 'The film I ought logically to make is, probably, *Sunset Song*, because it is about the Scotland I know best. But this is not the one I most want to make. I would give my eye teeth to make a Scots film that celebrated for all the world to see the Scottish genius for proletarian comedy.'

The call came from the Scottish Office. With the end of government film-making, a modest flow of worthwhile Scottish films had been cut off. Without independent control of expenditure, the Scottish Office could not resume it on its own account. And so it was forced to adopt the subterfuge of reconstituting the Films of Scotland Committee, under the umbrella of the privately-financed Scottish Council—Development and Industry.

The Secretary of State for Scotland, James Stuart (later Viscount Stuart of Findhorn), gave the enterprise his blessing but no money: 'a remit but no remittance' as the chairman, Sir Alexander King, said. The money, a gift of £10,000, came from Sir Alex's friend, Hugh Fraser (Lord Fraser of Allander), whom he promptly persuaded to be honorary treasurer of the organisation. The Government's welcome for the

The Heart is Highland

idea of projecting Scotland by film was expressed at a luncheon by the Earl of Home, then Minister of State at the Scottish Office.

Grierson was joined on the Committee by several old friends, including C. A. Oakley, Neil Paterson, George Singleton and Norman Wilson. The main pressure for the revival of the Committee had come from W. M. Ballantine, director of the Scottish Information Office at St. Andrew's House in Edinburgh who, in February 1955, arranged for me to be seconded to serve as the Committee's director.

There was nothing nominal or half-hearted about Grierson's service to Films of Scotland. The monies the Committee had for film production were always picayune in comparison with those at his disposal in Canada and London but at the outset at least he accepted the scale of the operation and the fact that finance came in the main from sponsors. He brought to the Committee's counsels not only all his knowledge of films and film-making but also the stimulus of his imagination and enlivening wit. His contributions to the discussions were forceful and constructive. Later he was to say that the Films of Scotland Committee was the happiest and most selfless body he had encountered since he was in Canada. Certainly the members enjoyed having him as a colleague. I have the best of reasons for knowing how much we gained.

In production Grierson's help was of greatest practical value when subjects were being scripted and when an assembly was being shown. He could see how a subject could be lifted out of self-evident sponsorship and given a wider national or occasionally international reference. When rough-cuts were shown he would be sharp in his analysis but would invariably find something encouraging to say to the young film-makers. The Scottish units in the fifties lacked experience. They needed guidance and encouragement and this he gave them generously. On several films Grierson's help went further. He wrote and spoke the commentary for a film on hydro-electric development in the Highlands, produced by Gregory Buckland-Smith. As sometimes happened, we could not find an acceptable title: the obvious ones had been used for earlier films. At two o'clock one morning there was a call from Calne. Grierson said 'I've got your title.' Rubbing sleep from my eyes I asked what it was. 'Scotland be Dammed', he replied, and put down the phone.

Grierson's greatest personal service to the Committee was the writing of the treatment for the film on Clyde shipbuilding, *Seawards the Great Ships*. We had been asked by the Clyde Shipbuilders' Association to make a film on the craft of shipbuilding in which the Foreign

192

The Heart is Highland

Office was interested for distribution overseas. Grierson did a thorough job of research and his treatment had strength and lucidity. He won the respect of the shipbuilding men, especially John Rannie, the big, bluff chief of John Brown's yard, who had seen the two Queens go safely down the slipway at Clydebank.

At the Brussels Experimental Film Festival in May 1958 he had been attracted by the work of a young American director, Hilary Harris, whose *Highway* won a prize. Grierson thought that his obvious feeling for moving shapes was what a film on shipbuilding needed and recommended him as director. There were problems about a work permit but these were overcome. Harris spent about a year in the shipyards before the film was put into production by a Scottish unit, Templar Film Productions. When it was completed, with a commentary by Clifford Hanley and a fine score by Iain Hamilton, we again had difficulty over a title. I noted the word 'seawards' in a Masefield poem and, using it in the sense of 'moving towards the sea', added 'the Great Ships'. Grierson approved, commenting 'It'll be known as *Seawards*.'

Seawards the Great Ships received premier awards at film festivals all over the world and in 1961, when Charles Dand was in New York to nurse the preliminaries of selection, it was awarded an Oscar by the Academy of Motion Picture Arts and Sciences in Hollywood. For Films of Scotland to have reached Oscar standard in five years was a satisfying achievement. Lord Home, then at the Foreign Office, was present to see the Oscar handed to Sir Alexander King by the Ambassador at the U.S. Embassy in London.

Not all the production projects in which Grierson had a personal interest ended so triumphantly. Because of his family connection with lighthouses he wanted to make a film to be called *The Northern Lights*. First he wrote a treatment which was full of visual ideas and, as we expected, deeply informed. It was to have a shooting schedule of twelve months. John Taylor, who had the experience of *Man of Aran* behind him and who had made some superb films of natural life, was to be director-cameraman. By Films of Scotland reckoning it was to be an expensive film. Hugh Fraser agreed to contribute substantially. The National Film Finance Corporation agreed to make an advance, as did the distributors. Unhappily when all seemed set there was disagreement over the division of revenue and the project had to be abandoned. If anyone wished fittingly to commemorate John Grierson's achievement in the cinema this would be the film to make. 'Essentially, the film is intended to be a visual one', his treatment concluded. 'One hopes spectacular. One hopes exciting. One hopes a fresh and rare experience of a world apart but still with a demonstration of courage and character at the heart of it.' Courage and character.

With one other Films of Scotland production Grierson was most closely engaged. It was *The Heart of Scotland*, on his native Stirlingshire. Before he wrote his treatment he sent me a memorandum. 'There are some questions to which I want answers', he said and listed about a hundred. Did Cromwell come this far north? Did Paul Jones ever drop anchor in the Firth? It was a pleasure to know, he said, that Pierre de Ronsard strutted the battlements of Stirling Castle in his new hose and cloak of Spanish frieze and that Mary Stuart strolled across the bowling green, reading his sonnets. Other such associations, he thought, might come to light with a little digging! What brilliancies ever shone in Stirlingshire, he wanted to know. He had a note on a stabiliser for ships, designed in Stirlingshire in the 1890s and tested on the Forth. Were there any other inventors? Even eccentrics might have their relevance. Such insistence on detail was part of his thoroughness. When added to his deep attachment to the area it helped to make a memorable film. Laurence Henson directed it and Edward McConnell was the cameraman.

After the end of Group 3 Grierson began to spend more of his time in Scotland. Since 1949 he had written occasional book reviews for *Scotland*, the monthly magazine published by the Scottish Council—Development and Industry and edited by Willie Ballantine. At the beginning of 1955 it was announced in the magazine that he would write regularly. His essays had the eloquence and authority characteristic of all his writing. Through them he commented on contemporary Scotland, her customs and economy, her writers and her scientists. He wrote about subjects on which he could throw the personal light of his own experience—immigration in the United States, the Canada of Mackenzie King, bullfighting in Mexico. In all the essays there would be passages of revelation or judgement to make them of more than passing interest.

Grierson on James Bridie, for example. He had known him since his years at Glasgow University and was comprehensively familiar with his plays. The great trick with Bridie, he wrote, was that he reversed the normal artist role of justifying God's ways to man. 'He justifies man's ways to God and sometimes with a ribaldry that could easily be misjudged by the staid and the simple. In this, of course, he followed Shaw, but with a difference. Shaw out-argued the gods and brilliantly and sometimes Bridie could do that too but he had also a quality of poetry in him to help him recommend his odder characters to their Maker. It could even be that there are higher moments in Bridie than in Shaw, many of them.' He gave examples of such moments and concluded that however the moment came, it was the sign manual of a wonderful artist and often a very moving one.[1]

On another occasion he wrote wittily about James Boswell: 'Day in, day out, there he is at his Diary, with a fat head almost invariably and dripping with disease most of the time, but busy as a bee and out on the tiles again in a trice, "renewing" with . . . or . . . like any alley cat.' But he argued for a re-assessment. 'There are the epic persistence and colossal industry; there is the conception of a work to be carried through to the bitter end over a lifetime; and lightweight talents do not notably so engage themselves. Whose picture of the times is it anyway? It is not Johnson's but his. If there is no Johnson's journey to Wales or to France, it is possible to suspect there was no Boswell there to give the old man reality. Indeed, what image we give to Johnson is his, only his.'[2]

Very occasionally there was a reminder of the documentary man writing about books. Commenting on John Prebble's account of the Tay Bridge disaster, Grierson noted that he brought to his task a style of documentation and description which was essentially North American. It was highly visual, as if written for transfer to the screen: 'a hard, factual manner, driving on with a nice appreciation of the human images that make it dramatic'. He thought Prebble's account of the disaster was 'based on as thorough a study of the documents relating to it as it has been my privilege in a long life of documentary to enjoy'.[3]

Grierson had the greatest respect for scholarship in research—the study of facts with patience and persistence. A failure in contemporary research and an actual avoidance of fact were at the root, he thought, of the ailing documentary. 'The old picture was of men getting gladly about the country, poking their noses into factory, field and research station and, in a way that was novel, sticking around with people. The new picture was of film-makers propped up on stools in the West End, taking in each other's mental washing. For whatever reason the creative force went in the process.'[4]

Francis Jeffrey, Compton Mackenzie, Eric Linklater, Moray McLaren, Ivor Brown, John R. Allan, Fraser Darling, Wilfred Taylor: Grierson had his say on these and many other writers in Scotland and outside it. It was a fruitful collaboration between an enterprising editor and a responsive contributor prepared to give of his best.

Grierson could be vitriolic. In one piece he savagely attacked the B.B.C. programme, *The Critics*. 'You know the programme which takes the sunlight out of the morning, the chlorophyll from earth's green finger-tips and the sweet song from the bellies of birds, regularly of 12.10 hours of the Sabbath Day', he wrote. 'They are turning criticism into a dereliction of non-feeling, non-appreciation—into conversazione—because they are caught, like so many, without native sap or sense of the stuff that makes for feeling: and without which the will to form and the necessary hungry appreciation of it are impossible. No hope or hunger indeed—no appreciation. They lack in the deepest sense a habitation and a place.'[5]

Before *The Critics* emerged in London there was already a B.B.C. programme, *Arts Review*, in Scotland. Its producer was George Bruce, a poet from Fraserburgh, who set, and insisted on sustaining, a high standard of criticism. Norman MacCaig, Alexander Scott, Ronald Mavor (Bridie's son), David Daiches, Christopher Grier and David Baxendall, Director of the National Galleries of Scotland, were regular contributors to it. Grierson took part on a number of occasions in the critical sessions. There was no lack of feeling in *his* performances. I remember him on Scots comedians, on a film of Picasso at work, and on the film of Ernest Hemingway's novel, *The Old Man and the Sea*— where he found concentration on the mere action of a man catching a fish wasn't enough to give lift to a theme essentially poetic. Often in these sessions he was deliberately provocative: he enjoyed being challenged and the younger the critic disagreeing with him the more he relished it.

When Grierson was in Edinburgh at this time, the later 1950s, he was staying at 87a the West Bow, an upper floor of an old building near the Grassmarket. I called on him one afternoon there to discuss a film commentary and found him cooking—an Irish stew simmering in a pot and a joint roasting in the oven. I asked if this wasn't too much food for one man. It wasn't for him, he explained, but for the neighbours (who probably included some in need of a good meal). Unhappily, he insisted on me sampling the Irish stew which, however exquisite an example it was of his cooking, had little appeal as a mid-afternoon snack after an adequate lunch. He loved cooking, at all times and in any place, and it added greatly to his pleasure when there were appetites to satisfy.

He was once asked what was the strangest meal he had ever had. 'I was invited to a festival in a village not far from Mexico City with some American film men. The first course was cooked white worms. The second course was fried caterpillars. The main course was a goat dug out of a pit of mud where it had been cooked whole. The Americans got whiter and whiter with each course. Me? I found the meal strange —but delicious.'[6] While in Edinburgh Grierson invariably bought fish as he was on the way to the airport for the flight south. It was his practice to ask where his selected haddock had been caught. 'Three miles nor'nor'east of Eyemouth, sir.' A month passed, another visit, another purchase and the same question. 'Three miles nor'nor'east of Eyemouth, sir.' Another month, etc., etc., I waited apprehensively for the answer. 'Three miles nor'nor'east of Eyemouth, sir.' Grierson did not ask again.

During his convalescence Grierson had become very restive. A spell of six months at the horizontal had been hard to take. He was anxious to be up and away. After the visits to the Cannes and Edinburgh Film Festivals, he accepted an invitation by Jan de Vaal, director of the Film Museum in Amsterdam, to talk to groups of film enthusiasts in the Netherlands. He felt a strong affinity with the Dutch documentary film-makers. It had begun in the days of Joris Ivens and John Ferno and continued with Bert Haanstra and Herman van der Horst. With his Group 3 experience fresh in his mind he wanted to see how the Dutch Government was helping to finance the production of both documentary and feature films.

He visited Mary Losey (Field) in Geneva where she had become film and photo officer of the World Health Organisation. She invited him on one occasion to talk to Dr. Brock Chisholm, the director-general, who had known Grierson in Canada and was familiar with the work of the Film Board. Grierson was to advise on how to set up a film programme for W.H.O. which would have some reach and power. But Grierson offended Dr. Chisholm and no programme was set up, although one film, *People Like Maria*, directed by Harry Watt, was to emerge.[7] Grierson was later to describe Dr. Chisholm as 'one of my favourite people . . . one of the greatest schoolmasters born in my time'. He recalled with admiration the contribution he made to education in the Canadian Army. 'His contribution to the United Nations was in similar vein—he saw to the heart of the matter and saw it simply and said it well.'[8] It was unfortunate that at the time of their meeting in Geneva they were not more quickly in accord.

In August 1956 Grierson was again in Edinburgh for the Film Festival and went directly to Venice where he was president of the Festival's jury. For the next ten years he was to be seen regularly at many film festivals. He was jury president at Cork in 1958 and was a familiar figure at Oberhausen. As regular an attender at the film festivals was Molly Plowright, film critic of the *Glasgow Herald*, who gave me her impressions of sharing the festival circuit with Grierson:

' "Don't worry, my dear", said John Grierson, "God always takes care of the innocent." And He did.

'No film festival that John Grierson ever attended proceeded along the lines the organisers had originally planned. He would collide with it, create his own dynamic scene within it, and bring everyone, from the director himself to the floor waiter, within his particular sphere of influence.

'This time it was Venice, 1956, at which he was president. He had been invited to take over this, the oldest festival of all, because in recent years it had been slipping alarmingly into commercialism and away from its original purposes. A return to the purity of the Grierson concept was the idea, and under his disciplines he wouldn't allow the Golden Lion to be awarded that year—he said the jury's majority vote was too small to be truly decisive.

'We were on our way to the very grand reception being given by the festival committee itself, in the Doges' Palace. But there was this little problem. We were on the Lido, the boats to Venice itself had all gone and we'd only one ticket—John's—between us.

'We also looked a little odd. He'd kindly decided to take me along with him (I was the only journalist there from a Scottish newspaper) and sent me a last minute message to say so. I'd been film viewing all day, as he had, and I'd had no time to change. Being a bit short on summer clothes that year I'd borrowed an elderly, grey, pseudo-linen suit from a friend, just for film viewing. She's a lot taller and slimmer than me. This was what I was stuck with, and thinking with loving regret of the new evening dress hanging in my hotel wardrobe, and bought especially in case such an opportunity might occur. John never wore elegant clothes on principle, preferring the cloth cap image, so there we were, two small, crushed, grey people, standing at the quayside and looking over a completely empty expanse of water.

'But even as John spoke the sound of an approaching launch was heard. He was dead right about the Almighty. The launch was on its way to the Doges' Palace.

'Yet there were just one or two more difficulties to overcome. It was full of French film stars in exquisite French evening gowns, and it wasn't stopping. Suddenly I found myself doing a parabola through the air. John had put his hand under my elbow and shoved. I landed—ker-lonk—and if you ever want to know what poisonous hatred is really like it's the look a French film star gives a small, crushed grey person who has just landed on the hem of her most exquisite evening gown. James Quinn, director of the British Film Institute at that time, who also happened to be in the same launch, gave me a gentle, steadying smile, John didn't seem to notice anything, and we crossed the lagoon in silence.

'But when we landed, more trouble. A big crowd had gathered round the Palace entrance to watch the glittering arrivals and when they saw us they booed. Literally they booed. Clinging, rather basely, to the only ticket, I burrowed through the sidelines, got seized by a very feathery carabineri and bundled in.

'Then I turned, tremulously, to see how our highly distinguished president was getting on. By now the crowd was undulating, like the waves of the sea, and every time the central wave reached its peak John's head would appear shouting "I am Grierson", whereupon he was dragged down and disappeared again. But the natural movement of a wave is towards the shore and at last he was automatically washed up at the feet of the carabineri. Once in he forgot all about me and spent the rest of the time in animated discussion with the top brains present, while I retired behind a pillar and shivered for a long, long while. Later I was unearthed by a kindly American couple.

'If you met after being at a festival he would always ask "Who did you see?" Never "What did you see?" It was the talent behind the movie that attracted him most and he had this unerring instinct—an educationist's instinct—for creative spirits and wise minds. In his roamings around the world he'd amassed a great bank of them, and when at festivals himself he'd be the focal point of a marvellously disparate group, ceaselessly forming and re-forming around him.

'Social distinction would be met with a hoot of derision but head waiters loved him, which was fortunate as he had this way of taking over a strategically placed table in their dining rooms. Any time during the day—and evenings into night—he could be found there, or at least there would be news of his whereabouts. Sometimes he would home in on a café or trattoria instead, the tougher the better, and hugely enjoy the turbulence. "Real rififi stuff" as he said beamingly to me on the Venice Lido, while the rest of us were gingerly picking our way to the (hopeful) security of his table.

'He liked good food and would sometimes enthrall us with snippets of cookery advice. Once in Oberhausen he shot into the middle of the dining room to watch a waiter complete a trolley dish. He came back to tell us just how it was done—"and then he added the cream," John said with shining satisfaction.

'If the festival was anywhere near the sea there was always the risk of losing him for hours. He would go out with the local fishermen, or some colleague who also had salt in his blood, like Bert Haanstra or Harry Watt. The sea was the great, life-giving force and he had a relationship with it that was very private. But it didn't help if the festival happened to be landlocked and some of the dark days came upon him. Then one man would find himself the messenger and the rest of us would keep out of the way until the world became incandescent again. And it always did.'

Of film festivals near the sea Grierson had a marked affection for Cork. It is close to Kinsale where he kept a boat, the *Able Seaman*, built under his close supervision in a Cardiff yard after, to his surprise and regret, he failed to find a Scottish boat built by a Scottish hand on a Scottish waterfront at a reasonable price. He enjoyed enticing visitors away from film viewing at Cork for a day's fishing. I remember his delight in acting as host for the Council of Europe Film Committee when they made their awards in Cork in 1968.

Grierson had never lost touch with Canada. He had correspondents, George Ferguson, Charles Cowan and John Bird among them, well placed to keep him advised about what was happening in the country in general and at the Film Board in particular. But he was not satisfied. He wanted to see for himself. Ten years had passed since he had been in North America. It was time to return. Sydney Newman, who had been in charge of production at the N.F.B. since 1947 and had joined the Canadian Broadcasting Corporation in 1953 as television director of features and outside broadcasts, invited Grierson to visit Canada in the spring of 1957 and to be interviewed in Vancouver and Toronto. He also had invitations to lecture at the universities of British Columbia and Alberta. There were other commissions to occupy his time.

He flew in February 1957 to Vancouver and went on by the Alaska boat to Kitimat, then a town of fifteen thousand people which did not exist when he left Canada. He found it no shanty town but beautifully planned and built, with a community centre of theatres, municipal halls, super-markets, landscape avenues, and ambitiously architectured modern houses in wood and aluminium and all the colours of the rainbow. Behind it lay the dam, giving a drop sixteen times the height of Niagara, and the aluminium smelter over two miles in length. Grierson was fascinated—a community industrial development that had everything but seemed too good to be true. He spent two days inspecting the dream town, talking to everybody, asking endless questions. At the end of the short visit some of the local Scots, dressed in tartan jackets, foregathered and sang the twenty-third psalm for him. And 'Scotland the Brave':

> Far off in sunlight [they sang], sad are the Scottish faces,
> Yearning to feel the kiss of sweet Scottish rain.
> Where tropic skies are beaming, love sets the heart a-dreaming,
> Longing and dreaming for the homeland again.

The sad Scottish faces, he thought, looked as if they were all doing fine.

Vancouver he found wonderful with growth—skyscrapers up and going up and the new houses in wood, wide-windowed to the mountains and the sea, the best he had seen anywhere. He found a certain diffidence about the pursuit of culture, an inferiority complex the worse for not having an English derivation. He could not find a bar in which he could see to read a paper and supposed it was a sort of guilt to be drinking in daylight, or even at all. The food had become so civilised he couldn't taste anything but he had only to step down to the Chinese quarter to get everything he could dream of. He had the impression that British Columbia, in spite of being pat at world centre because of the Polar route, the Alaska route, in spite of Kitimat and the new plans for opening up the north, was still self-consciously over the mountains and hankering for the seats of power in the east. He gave fifteen talks of one kind or another in ten days, ending with an hour on television.[9]

He flew to Edmonton and on to Toronto where he was met by Julian Roffman and Ralph Foster. It was an emotional moment, especially for Roffman. They had been in touch by letter since the end of The World Today. Grierson had indeed invited Roffman to join him at Group 3. Roffman had 'deserted the chrome-plated nit-witteries of New York and points south for the more rugged inanities' and set up Communications of Canada in Toronto. He and his partner Foster threw an enormous party for Grierson with some three hundred people present. It went on for a day and Grierson was left in no doubt about the warmth of the welcome he was being given. Sydney Newman and many members of the Board were present.

Grierson spent the last part of his three month visit in Montreal. The Film Board had moved from Ottawa during the spring and summer of 1956 and was now established in a large building on the Côte de Liesse Road in the suburb of St. Laurient. Albert Truman was the retiring commissioner. Guy Roberge, the lawyer and politician from Quebec City, had just been appointed. Pierre Juneau, the secretary of the Film Board, gave a dinner to mark Truman's appointment as director of the Canada Council. Grierson arrived rather late, after convivialities elsewhere. Across the dinner table he said to Truman: 'How could you give up the influence and cultural possibilities of this power-house here for a measly little administrative job at the Canada Council?' Truman, understandably, was much offended. Grant McLean tried to restrain Grierson. He recognised, as his other friends did, that Grierson's directness and outspokenness could cause rufflement, even when there was truth in so much of it.

Grierson was a week at the new N.F.B. headquarters and before leaving Canada at the end of May wrote a long report covering every aspect of the Film Board's operation.[10] He was aghast at the top-heavy bureaucratic hierarchy—enough to run a colony he thought. Instead of the management serving the creative force, the creative force was serving the management. The Film Board was about Canada and about movie and about movie today and not yesterday, with television opening up new roads with a thousand and one bulldozers, and to hell with personnel problems and administrative problems.

Above all it was about talent and who was young and new and rich and just possibly great, to make the two and two make five. He noted the danger of concentrating on the studio because it was there and had to be justified and the consequential danger of withdrawal from the far horizons. As for the films, he recognised that Government departments would themselves decide which films they specifically required—but could be guided. He urged that the Board should make a splendid picture of Canada, extend its imagination, fortify its will. Referring to the Board's preoccupation with psychiatric films, he said he had found it odd to be asked in the far places of the world why so young and great a country was going nuts.

Grierson thought that the U.N. agencies were ready-made instruments for the carrying of Canada's national achievement throughout the world. He recommended the immediate preparation of a film on Canada's handling of Indian affairs to help Lester Pearson at the United Nations. Looking more closely at the Board he didn't think the boys got around enough. Some of them talked too much about techniques and about art and too little about Canada. He recommended that the provincial governments and the great industrial companies should be brought progressively to understand the creative part they had to play in the total national effort.

The Heart is Highland

He thought the Film Board's interest did not altogether coincide with that of the C.B.C. and that there was still much to be done in the film way. To him television was a cheap way of distributing a great part of the Board's programme. Television tended to keep close to the big cities and to subjects that could be done in the big cities. The Film Board had a larger duty to the frontiers of effort. He could not think of the N.F.B. and C.B.C. being other than very close partners. They had the common task of building up the imagination and will of Canadians as well as of entertaining.

It was shrewd analysis and sound advice. If an understanding could have been reached between the film and television operations it would have been greatly to the national benefit and Canada again could have led the world. But there was no understanding and Grierson was to meet the problems again on his return to Canada. He left at the end of May, having restored most if not all of the links with Canada and having demonstrated his unshaken devotion to the country.

14 'This Wonderful World'

Grierson made one or two fleeting appearances on television in the late forties and early fifties. One was the outcome of a visit paid to him in Paris by the B.B.C. producer, Robert Barr. The subject was UNESCO and it was transmitted live on 8 April 1948. He had Ritchie Calder, Jacquetta Hawkes and Julian Trevelyan taking part in it with him, under J. B. Priestley's chairmanship. Films from which excerpts were shown included *Hungry Minds* from Canada, *Here is the Gold Coast* and Paul Rotha's *The World is Rich*. Grierson regarded himself as the merest tyro but the B.B.C. *Yearbook* for 1949 put on record that the programme had broken new ground. More new ground was broken when Grierson took part, with Jean Painlevé and John Maddison, in a programme where the microscope was linked to the television camera and viewers could see the beating heart of the water flea. 'Marvellous thing, television', said Grierson afterwards. Transmitted on 4 October 1948, it marked the opening in London of the second International Scientific Film Congress.

He did not forget that example of what the microscope and television could do in combination. He was fascinated by the capacity of the medium for the instantaneous linking of live and still material, for the freedom to edit on transmission, to use microscope and telescope, to introduce maps and animated drawings, to draw illustration from the vast archive of the moving picture. In 1949 he predicted that the illustrated lecture would one day put a premium on characters who could do it with flash, flair and friendliness.[1] The importance of friendliness he did not forget: to him television was much like going round to the local, meeting people casually and listening to gossip on a person-to-person basis.

While he was in Canada Grierson had been nurturing these thoughts about television. On his return he felt it was time to put his ideas to the test. Again there was the favourable combination of circumstances which Grierson had experienced several times in his life. Roy Thomson, the Scots-Canadian newspaper proprietor and owner of the *Scotsman*, had just been awarded the franchise for Scottish Television. He was looking for a cultural programme, preferably one which would be accepted by the other regions and help him to retain the concession. Grierson was looking for an opportunity to mount the kind of programme he had been advocating and to do so with maximum independence. A meeting was arranged. Grierson held that the initiative was taken by Thomson. Thomson knew of Grierson's reputation in Canada 'and when I realised that he could be available to us at Scottish Television I lost no time in signing him up.'[2]

Grierson believed, however, only in short-term arrangements for the production of a limited number of programmes. He never signed a long-term contract. He preferred freedom and flexibility. The original intention was that he should only produce the programme but he was unhappy with the writers and compères and, in the end, did everything himself: the selection and editing of the film excerpts and the writing and speaking of the linking passages of commentary. In content the programmes had a unity and a kind of continuity; but what from the beginning gave them an immediate impact was the strength of the personality of the seemingly stern man, his eyes glittering with enthusiasm behind his spectacles, who opened each programme with the words, 'I welcome you from the Theatre Royal in Glasgow to our programme *This Wonderful World.* We bring you some of the rich and strange things, the wonderful things, the camera has seen', and who closed it by saying: 'I bid you all in the Highlands and Lowlands, and over the Border, a very good night.' Spoken with warmth and sincerity, the words never became an empty rigmarole.

The first *This Wonderful World* programme went out on 11 October 1957. The property requirements included '1 Chair (swivel) (non-squeaking)' and not much more. The pattern set at the beginning was to be followed for the next ten years although no one who worked on the programme then—Rai Purdy, the producer, Jimmy Sutherland, the director and Grierson himself—could have foretold it would run so long. There were excerpts from four films. The first, which I had myself recommended to Grierson, was from *The Culbin Sands* and showed how the Forestry Commission had successfully replanted six thousand acres of wild sand which in the seventeenth century had blown in from the mouth of the Findhorn in the Moray Firth and covered a fertile estate. The second was from a French record of King penguins in the Antarctic. The third was a burst of jazz from Norman McLaren's *Boogie Doodle*, 'with the great Albert Ammons himself on piano'. The fourth and longest item was on Leonardo da Vinci by Grierson's former UNESCO colleague, Enrico Fulchignoni.

From the beginning Grierson set a demanding standard and he was never to lower it. He found that the harder he made his programme the more popular it became. Nothing was barred—genetics, aesthetics, mathematics he confessed he didn't understand himself. In the second programme he began with a film about the street songs of Edinburgh: he said he had heard the children singing in the tenement closes from his doorstep at the back of the Castle. He moved on to Bert Haanstra's film of Rembrandt of whom he said 'It is not that he shows the saints in the image of his neighbours, but that he shows his neighbours in the image of saints. For my part I am always moved and grateful when I look at Rembrandt. He has gilded my father and mother in splendour, and that may be as you will think of him too.'[3] With communication of this order he was reaching an audience which grew steadily. He would be stopped by people in the street who would say: 'Christ doctor, I liked you on Leonardo.' The programme exploded a myth as to what is popular and what is not.

In the third programme Grierson showed decisively that he would follow no easy paths to popularity.[4] He moved to science with a French film on experiments on the reproductive cells of plants and animals. He spoke about such matters as the nature of the young human embryo and the push towards maleness or femaleness given by the male and female sex hormones—subject matter for a lecture to medical students but here made understandable by the concern and conviction he brought to the exposition. He regarded a subject first as a test of his own comprehension and then as a challenge in communication. 'Everybody appreciates the romantic and the appeal of the far horizon. You don't often change people's interests by teaching them. You do it by interesting them in new interests.'

The new interests were inevitably a reflection of his own enthusiasms. When he showed the first of many films on bullfighting he said he was not going to conceal his affection for it but conceded that many people objected to it on principle. To him bullfighting meant timing *in excelsis*: you have it or you get killed. He thought of bullfighters as a sort of priesthood of human courage. 'You've got to understand that to know why it is that the moment a man fails in courage, the crowd—his worshippers—rise up and destroy him utterly. The passions of our own football fans are just a lot of Sunday school meanderings compared with, say, the passions of the crowd in the Mexico City bull ring when one of their idols lets them down.'[5] He went on to tell the story of Luis Procuna who, charged with being yellow in the Mexican press, went back to the ring and conquered not only a bull but also himself.

Manolete he regarded as the greatest of the great among bullfighters. He paid his tribute by showing *The Day Manolete Died.*

Jazz was another of Grierson's enthusiasms to which he gave recurring expression in his programmes. Big Bill Broonzy, Louis Armstrong, Ella Fitzgerald, Bessie Smith, Mahalia Jackson: he said he had heard most of them when they were coming up in the 1920s and 1930s. To him it was a vivid memory, not of great halls and huge audiences, but of little out-of-the-way dives in Chicago, New York and Los Angeles. Broonzy had a special place among the singers. Grierson believed that you got from him a sense of the sadness from which the folk songs of the poor and enslaved Negroes first came: the heart cry of his people. Grierson introduced *Jazz on a Summer's Day* to Britain. He had heard about it through Kenneth Tynan in the *Observer* and Bosley Crowther in the *New York Times* and did not rest until he had it for his programme. Mahalia Jackson repeating The Lord's Prayer, 'as you have never heard it before or ever will again', in the film became for him a favourite excerpt.

Grierson was fishing a loch at Drummond Castle in Perthshire with Neil Paterson whose twelve-year-old son was rowing the boat. It was a glorious evening. The water was like a mirror. There wasn't a fish within a million miles. They spoke about the beauty of their surroundings and somehow came to the definition of beauty. 'Listen to this, boy', said Grierson to Paterson's son. 'I was sitting in the Spades Club in New York with Hot Lips Page [the jazz trumpeter] and Hot Lips said to me: "Doctor," he said "how do you define beauty?" and I said "Well, Hot Lips," I said, "I always stick with an old guy called Michelangelo, and he said if you can roll it down a hill and nothing breaks off—that's beauty." And Hot Lips said, "Yeah, yeah, I see, Doctor. If you kin blow it dry." '

Grierson admired skill in movement. He thought there was nothing to compare with association football when it came to the skills and the pattern of skill: space, patterns in space, beautiful individual movements, twisting and turning, changing and interchanging to bring one single green rectangle dramatically alive—it was precisely, he maintained, what the great painters tried to do. He thought the most exciting fighter he had ever seen was Hammering Henry Armstrong, the only man who ever held three world championships at one time (Feather, Light and Welter, at 9, 9.9, and 10.7). To present him Grierson sought out an old 1939 news-reel. More than once he told the story of Benny Lynch's triumph at Bellevue in Manchester in 1935 and the sad sequel.

'This Wonderful World'

He loved the circus: the acrobats, the aerialists, the rope walkers and, among the clowns, Popov, who he thought had a tender, almost feminine delicacy he hadn't seen since Harry Langdon. Skill and beauty he found in the mass movement of gymnasts and in the Olympic records, especially Leni Riefenstahl's film of the 1936 Olympics in Berlin. His first item on ballet—Ulanova dancing in the film of *Romeo and Juliet*—was an instant success and he daringly followed it with ancient operatic ballets from China, Japan and Java.

There were many other frontiers of human observation on which he drew for his programmes. The natural world provided him with a rich range of revelation. A film about the ibex, the mountain goat of the Himalayas and Central Asia, jumping miraculously from cliff to cliff, became the top animal act in *This Wonderful World*. He showed war being waged on the locusts in *The Rival World* and quoted Exodus X, verse 15. He introduced a film about bees by recalling how in his native village the lorries came round to take the bees to the heather and how the bee-keepers went off laughing with their legs swinging over the side and bottles of whisky as an antidote to the bites they might possibly get. Inevitably there were many films about fishing, with measured tales to accompany them.

In medicine the films ranged from simple first-aid to the world-wide fight against malaria, leprosy and trachoma. He showed films about some of the strange rites connected with childbirth, a subject which fascinated him. When doing so one night he recalled a film made by Pare Lorentz, *The Fight for Life*, in which the director decided to make childbirth dramatic and rhetorical by having the heartbeat booming away, boom, boom, boom, while the girl was having her baby. A frightening time was had by all, especially Grierson. He was asked to show it at the White House to Eleanor Roosevelt who, when it was over, turned to him and said: 'Pare, you know I always thought that having a baby had something to do with happiness.' He had many requests to repeat another film, *The Biography of the Unborn*, about the nine months' ante-natal growth of the child.

'I have spent most of my life *seeing* things and working at the craft of *seeing* things', he said one night. In *This Wonderful World* the craft embraced inducing a reaction of wonder, fear, delight or pity. By analysing, isolating, spot-lighting, personalising, he persuaded his television audience in their twos and threes to look, to think and to feel.

Grierson thought of himself as having, not an audience, but a congregation. Some of his earlier programmes had the character of sermons. In one he replied directly, and at length, to a Glasgow minister

36. **Man of Africa** (1954) Produced by John Grierson for Group 3.
Directed by Cyril Frankel
37. **The Brave Don't Cry** (1952) Produced by John Grierson for Group 3.
Directed by Philip Leacock

38. John Grierson with Jean Painlevé and John Maddison in a B.B.C. television programme to mark the opening of the International Scientific Film Congress in London in October 1948
39. John Grierson at the Theatre Royal, Glasgow, for the Scottish Television programme **This Wonderful World**

40. Tog Hill, Calstone, near Calne. John Grierson in Wiltshire

41. John Grierson, Margaret Grierson and J. P. R. Golightly with a friend at Tog Hill

42. Dr. John Grierson with Dr. Leonard J. Russell, Professor of Philosophy, University of Birmingham after the honorary graduation ceremony at Glasgow University, 23 June 1948

43. John Grierson
addresses staff of the
National Film Board of
Canada during the Board's
25th Anniversary in 1964

44. After speaking, John
Grierson is applauded by
Guy Roberge, Film
Commissioner

45. John Grierson, Claude Jutra, Pauline Kael and Eric Gee at the 1962
Vancouver Film Festival
46. John Grierson's visit to the India Films Division, 1971. Left to right:
Shri G. P. Asthana, John Grierson, Mushir Ahmad, Len Chatwin, Pramod Pati

47. Left to right: Reta Kilpatrick, Secretary to the National Film Board of Canada; Sydney Newman, Film Commissioner 1970–5; John Grierson; André Lamy, Film Commissioner

48. Edgar Anstey handing Sir Charles Chaplin his Honorary Membership of the Association of Cine and Television Technicians at Shepperton Studios in 1956

49. Basil Wright

50. Alberto Cavalcanti

51. John Grierson, Hyderabad, 1971

who had posed the question 'Is Scotland's Soul in Peril?' and had attacked Scottish Television as 'commercialised corruption'. He was in excellent form. 'I have only one instruction from Scottish Television', he said, 'and that is to go as high as I like and as deep as I can take it— that, reverend sir, is commercialised corruption's only instruction to me.' The old Bible-thumping dictatorial ways had no bearing in a world in which you had communication from everywhere—education and inspiration from everywhere—and you took your pick of more things than ever were offered to the working man before. The Church had once had an exclusive duty to look after the mind, the imagination and the spiritual welfare of a relatively primitive society. 'But there are many, many of us engaged in that task to-day', he said, 'and the artists are not the least among us in brightening lives and giving zest and spirit to the people.'[6]

Grierson felt he knew the members of his congregation. There was a reaction everywhere he went to 'Mr. Wonderful World' and there was a steady flow of correspondence. Some letters he answered in the programme. A correspondent who wanted to know why *This Wonderful World* was not transmitted south of the border (it was to be later) was told that the programme had an audience of three quarters of a million and going up. It was a Scots audience. 'We communicate in Scotland across all the differences because we have only one *mental* language in Scotland. Shove me in the south and it won't be the same at all.' He enjoyed the freedom of his programme. He would often mention his friends. I once had a flyting for an admitted failure to share his enthusiasm for puppet films.

He reported an encounter he had had in Edinburgh with Lionel Daiches, the Q.C. They were talking about television commercials and Daiches said: 'You count your blessings, my lad. There you go, you and *This Wonderful World*, lifted up on the foam of the Detergents of Life.' Chuckling and wondering how he could express his sense of obligation, Grierson started muttering 'Latin *Detergere*—to scour or purge—Purgation—Greek Catharsis—Realisation—sublimination— salvation. *Detergatus*—to be scoured—Pocahontas' body lovely as a poplar—sweet as a Paw Paw in May—*Detergatus*—to be purged— white as a lily—Pure as the driven snow. O magic casement opening on the foam—O Scottish Television.'[7] What did they make of that in the pubs when they listened to *This Wonderful World*? Grierson had the flair to carry it off.

To find the films for his programme Grierson travelled far and wide. Visits in May 1958 to Paris and to Brussels for the Experimental Film

Festival were followed by a trip in June to South America where, in
Montevideo, he was president of the South American Film Festival. In
addition to Uruguay he was in the Argentine, Brazil, Bolivia, Chile and
Paraguay. To him it was a great journey and in a way, he thought, the
most beautiful he had ever made. It left him with a score of vivid
memories.

One night at a Festival dinner a millionaire got up and said he would
like to offer Grierson a present. He wanted to help to finance the
documentary film-makers of the world and to that end he proposed to
hand over to Grierson a large slab of territory on the Amazon to
which he held title. Grierson asked how big it was and was told it was
perhaps as big as Scotland. Grierson was duly impressed but as a Scot
he thought he had better be practical about it and asked how he got
there. He was told that that was the difficulty: it was doubtful if anybody ever got there. It was in fact a large slab of jungle in the Mattogrosso. Later Grierson flew over the Mattogrosso and had a distant
glimpse of the great estate. 'I swear I never saw anything so impen-
etrable or forbidding in my life.'[8]

The high point of the visit in every way was the trip he went up into
the Andes—to Bolivia and La Paz and Peru—twelve thousand feet into
the mountains. He came up on the railway from Lima on the Pacific,
passing from the jungle through the temperate climates, to Lake
Titicaca. From there it was a night's voyage to get to La Paz. The
steamers he found were mostly Clyde built, the earliest of them transported up into the mountains in bits on mules and put together on the
spot. He saw the splendid ruins of the Inca fortresses and palaces. He
saw too the heirs of the Incas and the Aymaras, desperately poor
people tending their haggard flocks of llamas and sheep and tilling
their thin soil. He remembered it was the original potato country and
brought back twelve different species which he later planted and ate.
He went another thousand feet up to the vast plateau of the Alto
Plano and thought it was like being on the moon. High up were the
mines of silver and gold—he saw a Spanish chamber-pot in solid gold—
and in Potosi remembered the line from the Burns poem, 'My Father
was a Farmer': 'Had you the wealth Potosi boasts.'[9]

The mines were not what they were and Grierson was told of the
plans to resettle the people of the high plateau in the richer valleys
below. 'In the transfer something is bound to get lost', he said. 'These
people of the Alto Plano, however poor, have created in their fiestas
such spectaculars of mask and dance that I doubt if there has been the
like at any time, anywhere, from a peasant people. I don't suppose that

will disappear, but what will certainly disappear, and perhaps better so, is the bitter irony of one of the poorest and saddest peoples of the world, putting up for compensation the very richest and most joyous demonstration of their innate pride.'[10]

Grierson was in La Paz during the Festival of St. Juan and the coldest night of the year when every household lit a fire before its doorstep so that the smoke would rise to the heavens and warm the gods. Round the fires the townsmen and villagers from all around danced to a hundred and one bands that appeared from nowhere in the flickering light of the fires and formed and re-formed all night long, every man alive it seemed capable of playing something. He brought back a film of the Bolivian dances by 'one of the most wonderful young film-makers I know', Jorge Ruiz of La Paz. It seemed a miracle to him that a young man isolated and remote in the upper Andes and working on a shoe-string should know so surely what the cinema was all about.[11] In another film, *Sebastiana*, he sensed that Ruiz was saying of the people: 'Poor as we may be, there is a source of nobility in our poverty.'

Oddly, Grierson became better known in South America as an expert on football than on films. The circumstances were unusual and in character. At a press conference in Montevideo Grierson was asked what he knew about Uruguay. Grierson replied that he knew only two things. 'I too come from a modest country, Scotland, and know what it is like to live under the shadow of a great and mighty neighbour.' To this he got a good response and he continued: 'I come from the greatest football country in the world, the one that taught you all. I'm sure that tears will come into your eyes at the thought that Scotland will not be represented this year in the World Cup final. And why? It was eliminated by no other country than Uruguay and it was a greater loss to my country than the loss of India.'

Next day the newspapers carried a story: ' "Greater than the loss of India" says President of the Scottish Football Association.' Thereafter he was known, not as the president of the film festival but as the President of the Scottish Football Association. Curious to know how he combined this expertise in football with his knowledge of cinema and the arts, another newspaper invited him to write an article about the combination. In response Grierson wrote 'one of the funniest things I've ever tried, an essay on ball control, with sexual overtones and undertones. It was translated into Spanish and Portuguese and syndicated all through South America and it was a great success.' The reputation followed him from country to country. On his return to

Scotland Grierson apologised to Sir George Graham for having temporarily borrowed his title.

For the next three years Grierson was constantly on the move. In September 1958 he was president of the jury at the Cork Film Festival and in October was in Brussels for the Festival of 'The Best Films of All Time'. In the spring of 1959 he was in Amsterdam and Oberhausen and went on to Berlin which he found 'still in a great mess'. Prague he found almost untouched by the war and 'still one of the half-dozen most beautiful cities I ever saw'. In Warsaw in July he saw over a hundred films and selected twenty-five which he thought was a good haul. In 1960 he was in Glasgow to share in the pleasure at the successful completion of *Seawards the Great Ships* ('I think it is going to do a lot of good for Glasgow across the world') but was soon off on his travels in Eastern Europe, including Czechoslovakia and Hungary.

Yugoslavia was one of Grierson's favourite countries, 'full of Mediterranean sunshine and a very friendly down-to-earth people'. He liked the streets of Belgrade and Zagreb especially, finding them like Paris without the pretension, and certainly without the commercialism. Everywhere he felt the people were still rooted in the land and that the peasant villages of Serbia and Croatia were just around the corner. At the beginning of March 1961 Grierson was in Belgrade for the eighth Festival of Yugoslav Documentary, Scientific and Short Films. He met everyone and was the most prominent and honoured guest.

Among those he met for the first time was Dusan Makavejev from whose early short film, *The Feast of the Damned*, Grierson had shown a sequence of snails crawling across the carved faces of stone effigies in a graveyard. Grierson did not at first remember having shown the film and did not connect it with the name of the director—the director who was later to make *WR—Mysteries of the Organism*. Makavejev was disappointed. Mid-way through the talk Grierson was giving to the Belgrade union of film-makers he suddenly stopped in mid-sentence, snapped his fingers, looked at Makavejev, said 'Snails!' and stepped down into the audience to shake him warmly by the hand.[12] They were to meet again in Montreal and to become close friends.

With him in Belgrade was Olwen Vaughan who was his research assistant for *This Wonderful World*. Her father, the Rev. Frank Hemming Vaughan, Grierson once described as 'one of the goodest men I have ever known. He lived like a flame. . . . I have never seen so much loving kindness in any man.'[13] He was a leading spirit in the Merseyside Film Society in Liverpool and Olwen, sharing her father's deep interest in the cinema, went as secretary to the British Film

Institute, and after the war, founded the New London Film Society. She also ran the French Club where everyone in documentary fore-gathered in London. Olwen Vaughan was not only familiar with the kind of film Grierson wanted, she also knew how to obtain them. When a television programme was being prepared to Alexandra Palace to mark Chaplin's sixtieth birthday in April 1949 he asked her to get, at two days' notice, some reels of film from the Cinémathèque in Paris. When, after great travail, she eventually appeared with them in time, Grierson barely noticed. He was to show the same complete confidence in her during their ten years' working partnership.

Grierson had an office in Thomson House in Cardiff, within reasonable distance of his Wiltshire home, but the programme was always produced in Glasgow. Lord Thomson said that 'he was an inspiration to all who came in contact with him; not only his immediate programme associates—although they would readily agree that their lives were permanently enhanced through knowing him—but everyone from the mail-room junior to the commissionaire. He would burst through the front door spreading good-humoured insults over all and sundry, demonstrating to the staff that he was no more in awe of the Chairman than he was of them, and instantly the station was a more exciting place to work.'[14] Jimmy Sutherland survived longest as his director, while Laurence Henson and Harley Jones had long runs as his assistant. James Coltart and later William Brown were the understanding chief executives with whom he had dealings.

Despite Grierson's reservations, *This Wonderful World* had been transmitted regularly in English regions from as early as February 1959. It was warmly welcomed by the critics. Maurice Richardson in the *Observer* said 'Grierson makes an excellent commentator, pleasing, stimulating and very quick. He entices you up to his screen, then vanishes like a grey wizard. His editing is inspired.'[15] In the *Sunday Times* Maurice Wiggin wrote of the programme: 'It is here, if anywhere in television, that you are likely to encounter, one quiet night without a word of warning, the burning eyes of the proud beast Truth, ambling solitary and disdainful through the jungle of the ready-made.'[16] Tom Driberg in the *New Statesman* wrote that 'Viewers who like a magazine programme of exceptional quality and originality should not be put off by the name of this one.'[17] Many of the critics noted that the content of the programme was unpredictable and that Grierson refused to compromise.

Grierson welcomed the comments of the critics in England: 'the evaluation of the timing, the evaluation of the impact, the estimate of what I was trying to do, with here and there, of course, my come-uppance about going too far—better still, not far enough'. He was not running the programme, he added, simply because he knew where there were some wonderful pieces of film. There was, for him, a special point in indicating an attitude to what he thought, one way or another, was beautiful or brave, or inventive or illuminating, or great. 'I haven't the vaguest intention of teaching anybody or anything. The mere indication of what you believe to be beautiful or brave or inventive or illuminating or great may be enough to start in others a chain reaction of their own. Perhaps the penny you insert to-day in a small boy's head will one day drop and give him, not your jack-pot, but his.'[18]

There were many jack-pots during the ten years the programme was on the air. In both correspondence and conversation Grierson learned of the impact the programme was making. 'I have a constant picture before me of families arguing out the goods and the bads of a programme and all with different choices and different voices. I am pleased to think that if I haven't enlightened anyone they are all, nonetheless, enlightening each other. The audience relationship in television is to me the most fascinating thing about it.'[19] Wherever he went in Britain he was recognised and enjoyed talking to people who felt they knew him through his programme. 'You never know what subjects will be exciting to people till they light up the target, as they say in the Navy.'[20]

This Wonderful World was among the Top Ten programmes for the week ended 17 January 1960. Grierson said he was not impressed by ratings but the success must have given him some satisfaction. It represented a fight back from the days of ill-health and depression after the demise of Group 3. It was a personal achievement, even though—and characteristically—he always warmly acknowledged the help he was given by everyone, from Lord Thomson to the members of the studio crew in Glasgow.

John Grierson in
This Wonderful World
A cartoon by Emilio Coia

15 Awards and Rewards

Grierson was appointed a Commander of the Order of the British Empire in the Queen's Birthday Honours in June 1961. The Empire that had all but disappeared. The Empire to which he had devoted most of his working life. To his friends it was all too modest a recognition of his public service. He had never been an Establishment figure, either in Canada or in Britain; had never, in the obnoxious phrase, played his cards carefully. The opportunity to honour adequately a man who had unselfishly given so much of himself was not taken. It seemed a sad commentary on the system. If this was the reaction of his friends, who placed a different valuation on Grierson's service to nation and Empire, he himself gave no hint of reservation. He had been ill during the summer but was sufficiently recovered to attend the investiture on 18 October and enjoyed it. Writing in congratulation some years later to Edgar Anstey he said: 'Be prepared to be surprised at the efficiency of the showmanship, including especially the performance of H.M. It's a trick but it is also a dazzler.'[1] The long corridor of the wearisome approach, he added, had some bad pictures—unnecessary, he thought, considering the good ones in other parts of the building—but there was the odd one that was very interesting. It was the reaction of a man who had worked all his life with visual images: there was no mention, for example, of the murmuring music in the background.

Early in 1962 approaches were made to Grierson to visit the United States. They came from the Carolina Symposium of the University of North Carolina, the Museum of Modern Art in New York and the Washington Film Council. It was a journey he needed to make. The circumstances in which he had left the country fifteen years before had been unhappy and had left their mark. It was time to try to erase it. Before much could be done there was the matter of a visa. When he wrote to George Ferguson in Montreal advising him of the visit he said: 'I got a letter from the State Department the other day saying what was all the fuss and I was as pure as the driven snow as far as they were concerned.'[2] Grierson thought it a little strange but did not argue. The arrangements went happily ahead.

Awards and Rewards

In film circles in the United States and Canada there was considerable excitement. Invitations to be entertained in private and appear in public came flooding in. Universities, film councils, television, radio, film societies, film schools. Frances Flaherty, Guy Roberge, Beth Bertram, Nick Read and Guy Glover were among those who wanted to see him. Grierson resisted as many as he could on the ground that, because of commitments to Scottish Television, his visit had to be very brief. He arrived in Raleigh on 30 March and left from New York on 12 April.

The subject of the symposium, a five-day programme of addresses, debates, panel and classroom discussions, exhibits and seminars, was 'Today's Revolutions'. Grierson and Gilbert Seldes, author of *The Seven Lively Arts*, shared the session on 'Revolution and the Arts'. Grierson began with what he had learned in Chicago in the 1920s and ended with the assertion that, 'Fashions of expression will change as they must do but the arts must continue to be rooted finally in the traditional absolutes of human destiny.' There was an audience of over fifteen hundred, mainly students. As he wrote later to the chairman of the Symposium, Joe L. Oppenheimer, he had not only enjoyed the occasion very much but had also found it a vital experience. He had got a great deal out of the students. 'I feel all renewed in my youth.'

The Carolina invitation had been stimulated by Maggie Dent, a film enthusiast Grierson had known for many years. She was chairman of the university film society and was later to run a specialised cinema, the Rialto, in Raleigh. She made an appointment for Grierson to have breakfast with the governor of North Carolina, Terry Sanford. Before the meal was over, and with the help of one or two telephone calls, the foundation had been laid for what, in some three months' time, became the North Carolina Film Board.

The governor, a man of resource and energy, responded enthusiastically to Grierson's ideas. 'If we can make our films meaningful in the lives and thoughts of our people, in the ways they work and see themselves and live, in the value they place on their resources, potentials, and heritage, then we will have hit a high mark, and will have sent a challenge to other states and productions units which cannot be ignored', he wrote to Grierson.[3] In September the governor announced the appointment of James Beveridge as director and Ben Mast of A.B.C. as assistant director. Grierson accepted an invitation to become a member of the Board, in return for his expenses and a few days' fishing a year. Fishing was his main relaxation but, try as he might, he never got very much of it.

Awards and Rewards

Grierson had two speaking engagements in New York. One was an informal meeting of students at Columbia University, arranged by Stephen Sharff, where Grierson, as at North Carolina, found a vital campus. 'I had the impression of a hungry lot', he said afterwards. The other engagement, at the Museum of Modern Art, was arranged by Richard Griffith, the curator, who in introducing Grierson said: 'Out of a thousand random developments in the early days of the movies, he extrapolated and formulated not only the idea and word "documentary" but also the basic concept that the film, in order to succeed as communication for social purpose, must develop its poetic and dramatic elements equally with its expository and didactic possibilities.'[4] He paid tribute to Grierson as having been the first to see that television would give the single greatest impulse to the development of documentary.

As he admitted to Griffith later, Grierson was overtired by the time he reached the Museum. A battery of communications had poured into the Warwick Hotel where he was staying—he counted something like a hundred and fifty messages at one point. With only forty-eight hours to work in, it was inevitable that he failed to keep some appointments. His appearance at the Museum was less than magnetic. As he sometimes did in such moods, he took up an anti-art, anti-aesthetic position which puzzled some in his audience and angered others. One of the latter, Willard van Dyke, said, 'It seems to me, Grierson, you spoke at one point about making poetry about problems.' Grierson hesitated—he could not see the audience because of the lights on the stage—and said 'That must be van Dyke. He made a film at one time where he forgot the smell of fish and chips'—a reference, recognised by the audience, to a review Grierson had written of van Dyke's film, *The City*.[5] In another mood Grierson might well have recalled that, in the same review, he commended *The City* as ' . . . an important film. It is one of the first directive social documentaries done in the United States.'

Grierson asked Richard Griffith to explain his dilemma to some of his older friends. 'If you have a complaint from one or another, please do your best to say that I did not mean discourtesy and hope to make amends soon.' For those, like Bosley Crowther, who were prepared to make allowances, it was 'a wonderful occasion'.[6] For Grierson it was 'a journey I needed to make and I didn't realise how much until I got there. I hadn't remembered well of America and there were reasons for that, but I am certainly glad now to have got such miserable little ill-feelings out of my system.'[7]

Awards and Rewards

Grierson kept his promise to return to America and was there again in July. He accepted an invitation to be a member of the jury at the Vancouver Film Festival, with Pauline Kael and Claude Jutra. For the film critic of the *New Yorker* it was a first festival jury experience and it gave her a marvellously reassuring sense of group-judging she was rarely to experience again: there was not more than a fraction separating their marks for the films. It seemed to her that Grierson 'stood for some of the best traditions of Scottish empiricism which he had applied to films, and merged with his own romanticism about working men and nature. Having come out of the Philosophy Department at Berkeley with similar empirical traditions ingrained in me, I responded to the way his mind worked because we saw many things so similarly. And Jutra, who had been trained as a doctor, revered Grierson as a father figure—the father of Canadian film and the man of good sense who also has a streak of poetry. Both Jutra and I made speeches honouring Grierson at the close of the proceedings and there wasn't a trace of cant in the affection and admiration we expressed.'[8]

Grierson gave the festival organisers some practical notions to ponder over. A film festival, he said, did not depend altogether on its films. 'Venice is great because it is Venice anyway. Cannes is exciting because it has the Mediterranean. Edinburgh is good because it has the scenic splendours of a beautiful town and a beautiful country to fall back on—and everyone is made to know it. Cork is warm and happy because of Ireland and the Irish people. Here in Vancouver you have everything—but everything. And the best thing about this festival for me is Vancouver itself. So I think you should get your festival mixed up a lot more with getting to the lakes and the woods and the sea.'

It was during this visit that Grierson was presented with the Royal Canadian Academy of Arts Medal, 'in recognition of his contribution to the Visual Arts in Canada'. On his return he was invited by B.B.C.–Scotland to give the St. Andrew's Day lecture on 30 November—a radio occasion in public and regarded as an honour for distinguished Scots and the nearest anyone came to giving a State of the Nation speech. Grierson called his 'A Mind for the Future' and began by saying, 'The declaration of one's loyalties is always a very proper and agreeable duty.' He declared his affections, for his parents, his village, his schoolmaster, his work and his work mates. Mellow in tone though the speech was he had some sharp words for the mass media: 'I don't think it is a living culture we are seeing reflected: a living culture out and about, like old Adam Smith in his day, in the living present, forging a mind for our to-morrows: rather a culture, all too often, of the cultural conceits and the culturally conceited.' He ended by saying that what Scotland needed was 'A will to the future and no piking—with all of us who have power in one way or another over the images of the future dedicated to a more dashing account of our stewardship.'

The pattern of Grierson's life continued during 1963, with *This Wonderful World*, overseas film festivals (Belgrade and Venice among them) and Films of Scotland making the main demands on his time.

Early in the year Grierson received an invitation to visit Montreal in August for the twenty-fifth anniversary of the National Film Board. It would have been impossible to hold this birthday party without him! He was happy to be able to accept. All the other commissioners—Ross McLean, Arthur Irwin, Albert Truman and Guy Roberge—were present but it was inevitable that Grierson, founder of the Board, should be at the centre of the celebration. There were informal reunions with so many who had worked with him in building up the Board and who were still there: Tom Daly, Stanley Jackson, Norman McLaren, Guy Glover, Ralph Foster, Leslie MacFarlane; and with former colleagues, including Sydney Newman, head of drama at the B.B.C., James Beveridge, director of the North Carolina Film Board, and Nick Read of Potomac Films in Washington, D.C. Those to whom Grierson was no more than a technical ancestor, a colourful legend in the background of their craft, had at last an opportunity of meeting him.

When Grierson entered the large studio with the other commissioners a great roar went up. According to Sydney Newman, 'Grierson was in the middle—this wee guy and these other bigger Canadians, supporting him. It was a magnificent moment which none of us will ever forget. He looked like the errant boy being hauled before the headmaster. He was so appalled at being dragged in—but loving it.'[9]

Guy Roberge quoted a tribute by René Clair: 'The National Film Board for which you are working is something absolutely unique in the world. And this is not a mere compliment, it is simply the truth.' The primary significance of the occasion, he continued, was the opportunity it offered to express gratitude to all who had made the National Film Board. There was a symposium on 'The Future of the Film in Canada' and Maurice Lamontagne, the minister responsible for the Board, was cheered when he announced the intention of the Federal Government to set up a loan fund to help the financing by private film companies of feature productions.

Grierson was as jaunty and outspoken as ever. He remarked that the *Montreal Star* had said that morning that the taxpayers had received good value for money spent on the N.F.B. 'That I should have lived to see the day . . . '—the rest was lost in laughter. He might also have quoted, but didn't, from the *Montreal Star* which paid a personal tribute and said that the ideals behind his films, the extraordinary rationalism of his approach, his fundamental belief in the film as a means of education, could be of value to any generation.[10] His speech produced one characteristic Grierson aphorism: 'The first principle of documentary—and it must be the first principle because I wrote it—is that you forget about yesterday. The only good film is the one you are going to make to-morrow.'

It was typical of Grierson that he should hunger for a quiet moment, away from the fuss and the noise of the big studio, with one or two of those with whom he had worked most closely in the tough early days. He spent an hour with Tom Daly in his room, talking mainly about the British documentary movement in the 1930s and his conviction that, rather than try to give the films being made then a stronger social-political direction, it might be more rewarding to begin from scratch in Canada where he could develop the movement in a new way and give it a broader international base. For Daly it was a revealing moment.[11]

Grierson's visit to the twenty-fifth anniversary party was to be much more than sharing in a jollification. His links with the Board and with Canada were remade and strengthened. They were to become much closer. He was increasingly consulted, not only about matters affecting the Board but also about radio and television. Canada again became part of his thinking as it had not been since 1945.

Grierson was patron of the Commonwealth Film Festival, held in Cardiff from 27 September to 2 October 1965. There was an entry of over two hundred films. Canadian participation was particularly strong: the première of *Winter Kept Us Warm*, a feature film made by students at Toronto University, a showing of *Nobody Waved Goodbye*, many short films and a delegation from the N.F.B. Gerald Pratley, C.B.C. film critic, was a member of the jury. Stanley Hawes was there for Australia and brought *Funny Things Happen Down Under*, the first Australia–New Zealand co-production, directed by Roger Mirams. There were also films from Malaysia in which Grierson had a personal interest. In 1950 Grierson had arranged for Hawes to prepare for the Government of the Federation of Malaya—as it was then—a report on the unit which helped its continuance. It was in effect a Grierson festival. His assistant for *This Wonderful World*, Harley Jones, was the festival director and Grierson presented the prizes.

Grierson accepted an invitation from Sir Arthur Elton to give the concluding speech at a three-day conference on the use of film and television in modern society, held in London, 6 to 8 December 1966. Grierson's subject was 'The National Need'. According to Elton, the opening sessions were 'a bit rocky and disjointed' but the last day's session, particularly Grierson's peroration, 'gave the whole thing substance and shape'.[12] John Chittock, who organised the conference, said that Grierson reminded his audience of documentary's origin as a key to the simplification of information.[13] He deplored the arty meaning with which it had been falsely endowed by zealous cineastes over the intervening years. Chittock thought that the strongest idea which emerged from the conference was Grierson's plea for a rediscovery of simplification in film and television communication.

In February 1966 Grierson was invited by Jennie Lee (Baroness Lee), Minister for the Arts in Harold Wilson's Government, to serve as a governor of the British Film Institute. He replied thanking her for the invitation but told her she had the wrong man. 'In the name of Bob Smillie, I can think of nothing more alien to my Hope of Salvation than the pursuit of the past in repertory theatres. Many years ago, when its shape and intention were debatable, I was interested in the B.F.I. and would have been glad to serve. Now it has grown up, the case is different. My own concern has been exclusively with the people who make things and, very specifically, with the purposes they serve. My regard for cultural institutions as such is, I am ashamed to say, both marginal and suspicious: even when my favourite Minister is Minister. But this likewise is to assure you of my lifelong and constant respect.'[14] The respect was real: they both came from similar backgrounds and had been similarly influenced by the Socialist movement in Scotland in the early 1920s. Hence the reference to Bob Smillie.

In May 1966 Grierson received an invitation from George Stevens, Jr., director of the Motion Picture and Television Service of the U.S. Information Agency, to take part in a conference on Film and Government Communication at the Airlie Conference Center, Warrenton, Virginia, from 5 to 9 June. The objective of the conference was to establish tielines, defined as 'shared frames of reference among those engaged in production, dissemination and utilisation of filmed governmental communication' and it was hoped that it would lead to 'the more purposeful and intelligent use of film in the interests of the free society'. Grierson's subject was 'Film and Social Persuasion'. He must have been aware of the paradox of the apparent acceptability of his views in an area of U.S. Government information policy and the suspicions concerning them which had deflected him from his purposes twenty years earlier. Among those Grierson met at the conference was Martin Quigley who had been the first to publish his film articles in the *Motion Picture News* (*Exhibitors Herald*) in 1926.

Later in 1966 Grierson was back in Canada, on this occasion with Margaret. Guy Roberge had resigned as film commissioner on 31 March and Grant McLean was acting commissioner. Grierson accepted his invitation to spend six weeks in Montreal, preparing a report on the future activities of the Board. It emerged on 14 September 1966, not as a public paper but as a letter to McLean. Of all the similar analyses prepared by Grierson it was probably the best: wise, lucid, practical. Into it went not only Grierson's knowledge of Canada and the Film Board but also nearly forty years' experience of film-making in the service of governments. Detailed advice was there but it never swamped the broad principles.

Grierson said he found the morale of the Board healthier than on his two most recent visits. He reminded McLean of the Board's terms of reference: the correlation of public duty with aesthetic ambition; the sometimes difficult (but natively natural and vital) problem of correlating the French and English cultural backgrounds in an all-and-all expression of Canada; and the correlation of the Board's duty to public information in respect of the departments of government and the Board's duty on behalf of the nation to give a dramatic and even poetic image of it to the world. It was a timely reminder.

Much of Grierson's analysis, which took into account the intended establishment of the Canadian Film Development Corporation to help to finance feature film-making, was concerned with the possible need for a training centre. He thought the Film Board as a national information service was a model of its kind which had much to teach about the combination of public duty and aesthetic expression but added that the exploitation of the Board for the pursuit of strictly personal conceits could never have been in the thought of Parliament when it supported it. He had a sharp word of criticism for occasional pictures most beautifully made but without knowledge of the subject, nor even any conscience in the matter of subject. Grierson believed that the first emphasis in any film training centre set up by the Board was to teach what the Board could best teach—that within the framework of public information, you could create films of great aesthetic worth.

There was much more that was wise and relevant. Against a popular tendency, he advised McLean not to get overexcited about feature films except on specific request and guarantee from the C.B.C. or elsewhere. It was inevitably a gamble on long shots. 'As an old public servant I would never ask a Minister to defend a long shot in Parliament. It would be unfair.' He recommended the closest links between the Film Board and the C.B.C. and the private sector of the film industry. He pointed to the number of graduates from the Film Board who had set up other units in Canada. 'If I had a young fellow who had a thing about the cinema in Canada', he wrote, 'there are various experiences I would want him to have besides participation in film-making.' The advice that followed had something of the flavour of Polonius but was none the worse for that.

Grant McLean thanked him warmly for the report and said that the governors of the Board had been highly complimentary. Of Grierson's visit he said: 'It's like having my own batteries re-charged.'[15] Grierson told McLean that he liked to be in on the problems of the Film Board and 'felt sort of professional about it. Although I didn't want to presume and shackled myself accordingly, it was a rejuvenating experience.' Meanwhile Grierson had been in correspondence with members of the Government, including the Prime Minister Lester Pearson, about the succession at the Film Board. His advice was sought and he gave it with informed impartiality. Had it been taken, Grant McLean would not have resigned on 21 September 1967. The Prime Minister told Grierson that he personally would have been happy to confirm McLean's promotion to the commissioner's post.[16] At least the letter of appreciation that Pearson wrote to McLean perhaps was the warmer because of the action taken by Grierson. McLean moved to Toronto where, with Don Wilder, director-cameraman of *Nahanni*, and Gordon Burwash, producer-writer who left the Board at the same time he set up a company, Visual Education Centre, with which Grierson was later to become involved.

Grierson had not met the new film commissioner, Hugo McPherson, who came to the Board from a background of teaching English and drama at Toronto University. Sir Arthur Elton met him while in Montreal to see Expo and told Grierson that he was 'unexpectedly tough, direct and clear-headed, with a determination to see public funds devoted to public purposes. He will have something of a struggle on his hands, and not only with the French Canadians who, all the same, may be more vocal in seeking to maintain their private privileges at the Film Board.'[17] Elton described to Grierson the success of the N.F.B.'s *Labyrinth*. 'I've rarely seen shooting like it and all the polish of the Film Board is winking and flashing in the bright Quebec sun.' He thought McPherson had a splendid future if he could 'harness the unsurpassed powers of technique and observation the Film Board

commands to wider and better purposes than in the recent past. . . .
The Board's command of the medium is now at its finest but the
message has got itself a bit lost.'

Earlier in 1967 Grierson had accepted an invitation to be President
of Honour of the jury at the Oberhausen Film Festival. The festival
director, Hilmar Hoffman, said this meant he would not have to work.
But the ceaseless pressures on Grierson were beginning to wear down
his iron resistance, although to his friends it never seemed possible
that his energy could be drained. 'I must say as I stagger home some
evenings exhausted that I envy your constant vitality', Grant McLean
had written after a Montreal visit.

In the summer of 1967 the point of exhaustion was reached. Grierson
returned from Scotland on 26 August and retired to bed with bronchitis.
He had coped quietly with bouts of bronchitis all his adult life but this
one went on for eight days. Early one morning he had an unusually
severe bout of coughing and was struggling for breath. The bedroom
window was opened but it made no difference to the congestion in his
lungs. Anthony, summoned from Calne, diagnosed emphysema and
gave his brother an injection. Together they sat silently at the kitchen
table while it took effect. To Margaret, waiting anxiously, it seemed a
very long time.

Anthony said he could not accept responsibility for Grierson because
of the strain on his heart if the attack continued. A specialist from Bath
was called in and Grierson was taken to the Manor Hospital. He
returned on 13 September but had another attack a few days later and
again Anthony was called. A cylinder of oxygen was obtained and
Grierson started to recover. He went back to Bath for an X-ray on
27 September.

Grierson was a heavy smoker. He did not feel at ease with himself
without a cigarette, even although it was snuffed out almost as soon as
it was lit. He had often been advised by Anthony to give it up. Now he
decided himself to give up both smoking and drinking. He was dis-
mayed by the commotion he had caused and by the realisation of his
dependence on other people. This, rather than the warning that if he
did not give up smoking and drinking he would be dead within a year,
was the stronger motivation.[18]

The effort involved was superhuman. Smoking was an ingrained
habit. Grierson had always enjoyed drinking in company. When I
knew him first it was whisky. Later he preferred gin. To give up all
drinking suddenly needed inflexible will-power. To be with his friends
who were drinking understandably imposed a strain and it did not help

when, with a meal, they would press him to have a glass of wine. On one such occasion in Glasgow I recall a wine waiter asking me in incomprehension if Dr. Grierson really wanted a glass of Vichy water.

His decision made a difference to his life besides extending it. The mental and physical effort involved in the readjustment was prodigious. 'The lungs are pretty good again', he wrote to Francis Essex at Scottish Television, 'but the agony of giving up the cigarettes, the whisky and the wild wild women is plain awful. Don't you ever try it. Come to think of it, if you ever do a programme on behalf of sin I am your man.'[19] The jauntiness was still there. In a footnote to a letter to Lady Elton he wrote: 'There was a moment when I wasn't breathing very good at all but it seems you don't need the stuff much except to concentrate with. So you don't concentrate and all is O.K.'[20]

Grierson's first public engagement after his illness was in Stirling. He found it impossible to refuse the invitation from the Education Committee of Stirling County Council to open the new primary school at Cambusbarron on 10 October 1967. He motored from Edinburgh with his sister Dorothy (Mrs. Duncan McLaren) and together they visited their old home, the schoolhouse at Cambusbarron, occupied by the headmaster of the new school, James Reid. 'I see you still have the cherry tree', said Grierson, looking from the window of the room he had shared with his brother Anthony. When, from the platform at the opening ceremony, Grierson noticed in the audience John Amess, his former teacher at Stirling High School, he interrupted his speech to refer to him. It was inevitably an emotional occasion. Grierson was still weak from his illness but he met the demands of the day and there were no after effects.

Grierson had been considering during the year a proposal made to him by Sir Alexander King on behalf of the Films of Scotland Committee. It was that Films of Scotland and Scottish Television should collaborate in the production of a film on the contribution Grierson had made to world cinema through the documentary film.[21] Grierson replied expressing his appreciation of the honour but expressing some doubt as to how it would work out. 'You know as well as I do that in this business of ours it is difficult to nail down what we actually contribute. Such minor reputation as we have depends so much on the many people of ability with whom we have been associated and in the film business none of us can claim anything very definite from a personal point of view.'[22] He was always opposed to a personality cult in documentary and it was with reluctance that he agreed to make the film. Jimmy Sutherland and I had talks with him about the form of the production but they were only talks. Grierson took the decisions, selected the excerpts, edited the compilation and wrote and spoke the commentary.

I Remember, I Remember was a personal film in which Grierson told the story of being caught up in a new way of looking at things and of making the cinema an observer of the changing world. He used excerpts from *Drifters*, *Granton Trawler*, *Industrial Britain* and *Night Mail* as well as from the Films of Scotland productions, *Seawards the Great Ships*, *The Heart of Scotland* and *The Big Mill*. 'I have lived and worked in other countries', his commentary concluded, 'but I have never lost sight of the good-looking world I saw when I was young. The documentary film I gave a push to forty years ago was a richer form of art than I ever dreamt of and a hundred other talents than mine have proved it so.' Perhaps there were too many competing forces at work in the film. The Scottish connection, to which Grierson loyally sought to do justice, and the documentary idea did not satisfactorily fuse. Grierson was in better form when he later made another version of the film for Grant McLean in Toronto.

While *I Remember, I Remember* was in production, Grierson was approached by the B.B.C. who were anxious to prepare a programme to be televised at the time of his seventieth birthday in 1968. Grierson explained his prior commitment to Scottish Television and Films of Scotland. The matter was politely pressed by the B.B.C. who obtained the agreement of Francis Essex to Grierson's appearance on the rival channel. Again Grierson declined, showing 'a most civilised scepticism' of his achievements. Stephen Hearst, then head of Arts Features at the B.B.C. wrote a further letter 'as a documentary film-maker who feels he would probably not have made his films but for you, and who is anxious to put at least a flavour of Grierson's work and Grierson himself on to the national network'. He told Grierson that if he did not do the programme, 'there are a great many people, colleagues in our documentary movement, who would very much regret your reticence'.[23] I recall Grierson's appreciation of the courtesy shown to him but he would not be moved.

Grierson had been having talks with Scottish Television about the future form of his programmes. Since the end of 1966 *This Wonderful World* had become *John Grierson Presents*. He had accepted the change with some reluctance, arguing to Francis Essex that his constant pursuit of the *non-showmanship* aspect of television (with profundity suggested rather than asserted) had a very special validity in television and an oddly loyal, long-lasting and various audience to go with it.[24]

Awards and Rewards

He was beginning to talk about turning the programme over to others and he thought that *This Wonderful World*, possibly with the subtitle *Speaking Personally*, was a better television continuity than *John Grierson Presents*. With his contact with Canada re-established and likely to become stronger than ever, Grierson had also in mind a collaboration between Scottish Television and the National Film Board and the production of occasional fifty-minute programmes on the model of *Canadian Vision*—the Canadian way of seeing things as demonstrated in their films. Other programmes would give the American, English, Dutch, etc., way.[25] The motivating forces of The World Today were still at work.

At film festivals in Europe over these years Grierson regularly met his documentary colleagues. In Rome he sat one day with Roberto Rossellini looking at a five-hour film on iron and steel. Rossellini had made it on a low budget and there was much padding with stock shots. Eventually Grierson burst out laughing. 'Roberto, you old bastard.' To Pierre Juneau who was present they behaved like very old and understanding friends.[26] With them also was Vittorio Baldi, a leader of the documentary movement in Italy. Baldi and Henri Storck took the initiative in establishing the International Association of Documentary Film-makers (A.I.D.). Founded in Florence on 24 January 1964, it was juridically recognised by *Arrête Royal* in Belgium on 10 June 1965. Grierson, elected president, made a declaration of purposes at the Leipzig Film Festival in November 1965. Meetings had also been held at film festivals in Mannheim in October 1964, Pesaro in May 1965, Oberhausen in April 1967 and Montreal in August 1967. At the end of 1967 the Association had 154 members, including most of the leading documentary film-makers in Europe and a number in North and South America, Japan and India.

At the invitation of the Algerian Government, a general assembly of the Association was held in Algiers from 26 February to 2 March 1968. It was an occasion of some splendour. The Algerian Government provided a chartered plane from Rome to Algiers, put the Palace of Congresses at the disposal of the Association, took the members on an excursion to the holy town and oasis of Ghardaia in the Sahara desert and arranged receptions where they met Algerian film-makers, journalists and critics and representatives of diplomatic, educational and cultural circles. There were retrospectives of the work of Dziga Vertov, Georges Franju, Casare Zavattini, Jean Rouch and Luc de Heusch, and Joris Ivens, Georges Rouquier and Henri Storck were among those who showed their new films to their colleagues.

Awards and Rewards

As honorary president Grierson opened the assembly with a speech which combined a restatement of principles with practical considerations. 'The documentary idea', he said, 'is an honourable idea: honourable in its duty to the observation of reality, honourable in its dedication to the public service, honourable in its aesthetic ambition. It is good to be associated with it.' He emphasised the total independence of the Association and said that the more independent were their judgements about the cinema, the more honest and the more valuable they were likely to be. He counselled detachment: 'We would be short-sighted to put our enthusiasms into one basket.' To be an artist, he maintained, was to be in a minority. 'I believe there is one simple secret in being a good politician in the creation of the documentary film. It is to make your minority view look valuable to the majority view. For this you have to be an imaginative and ingenious politician.'

Writing after the assembly to Henri Storck, Grierson said he had enjoyed it very much—more than any meeting for many years. 'I wonder why? Perhaps it is better to have a big useless noise than none at all. In other words you were probably right at the very beginning when you said that the best thing about A.I.D. was simply that it would enable people to meet—and not necessarily to do anything.'[27] At Algiers Grierson met Marion Michelle and felt an immediate affinity with her. She was originally from the University of Chicago and had worked with Joris Ivens and Jerzy Toeplitz and other international cineastes. Grierson found she was 'the only one who got things done'. Later she edited from her home in Paris *A.I.D. News*, a bulletin with contributions from leading documentary film-makers. Grierson contributed a 'Letter to Michelle' to the first two issues. The third contained a tribute by Basil Wright, 'Remembering Grierson'.

Grierson was seventy on 26 April 1968. There were many public and private tributes, even from those who knew that Grierson was not one for birthday sentimentalities. Guy Glover wrote a piece for the *Montreal Star* in which, referring to Grierson's service as film commissioner, he said: 'Grierson's very virtues on occasion proved difficult for the Government to stomach and, like the elephant's the public service's memory is long. The Film Board's post-war history has been characterised in part by how it improvised leadership in the absence of a Grierson.'[28] Thanking George Ferguson for having arranged the tribute, Grierson wrote ' . . . seventy is a lot to be quiet about. Saying so you make it so and ghosts go with it.'

At a ceremony in the Grand Hotel, Glasgow, on 5 July, Grierson was made an honorary member of the Association of Cinematograph,

Awards and Rewards

Television and Allied Technicians, joining Chaplin, Hitchcock and Anthony Asquith. In accepting the honour Grierson had insisted to George Elvin, the president, that the ceremony must be in Glasgow— a gesture which made it possible for a large number of his Scottish friends to be present, including Sir Alexander King, most of the members of the Films of Scotland Committee, and Bill Brown and Jimmy Sutherland from Scottish Television.

A.C.T.T. vice-president Ralph Bond who made the presentation recalled his early association with Grierson. 'When I applied for my first job', said Bond, 'John Grierson said: "How much can you live on?" I drew a deep breath and said "£5 a week." "Nonsense", said Grierson. "£4." I took the job. I needed it. He worked us all hours of the day and night. So eventually we joined the union and I was told to go and see him and tell him what was what. Of course he got in first: "You can't tell me anything about trade union procedure", he said. "I'm a member of the Transport and General." '

Their tribute was being paid to Grierson, said Bond, because he had devoted his life to the service of the great communication media of the twentieth century: film and television. To both he had brought vision, faith and affection. In thanking the union Grierson recalled his origins. 'I am', he said, 'a product of the Clydeside school of politics: Maxton, Wheatley, Kirkwood, Gallacher and the rest. But instead of seeking a Parliamentary career I felt I could best use the movies to express on the screen what the Clydesiders were doing by oratory'—words which, understood by all and especially in the Glasgow setting, fell with particular pleasure on his host's ears.

Although Grierson's attendances at meetings of the Films of Scotland Committee had become less frequent, the service he had rendered was valued highly by all the members (and by Films of Scotland's director). I had hundreds of reasons for being grateful to him. His presence was always stimulating and while his criticism of film treatments and assemblies was uncompromising, it was also positive and constructive. He helped to encourage the young film-makers in Scotland and allowed two of them, Laurence Henson and Edward McConnell, to use as the name of their company International Film Associates (Scotland), derived from his New York organisation. He was critical of the comparatively small scale of the Films of Scotland operation and had been a member of a small deputation which was met by the Secretary of State for Scotland, William Ross, at the House of Commons where the case for government assistance was argued. In the first twenty years of its existence Films of Scotland was never in financial difficulties but

Grierson believed that it had earned through its service to the country more than verbal appreciation.

On 25 August 1968, at its annual Edinburgh Festival performance, the Committee thanked Grierson for his work and paid tribute to him for his contribution to world cinema by presenting to him the Golden Thistle Award for Outstanding Achievement in the Art of the Cinema. The award was presented at the public performance where an audience of two thousand saw *I Remember, I Remember* and heard Grierson speak about the documentary idea. At a luncheon preceding the performance, with Sir Alexander King in the chair, the Secretary of State praised Grierson's work for his country. During the lunch Grierson had taken the opportunity of putting his case for financial help and William Ross made what Grierson and the members of the Committee assumed to be a commitment that government aid would be given. When later it was refused, Grierson wrote a letter to the Secretary of State in powerful and punishing terms. I was charged with having 'put Grierson up' to write the letter but that was a misreading both of Grierson's susceptibility to such pressure and of any influence I had over him. He was angry, and I was not alone in thinking he had cause to be. Had there been the response he expected there would have been more contentment in the last few years of his life.

As part of the Edinburgh Festival visit Grierson delivered the Celebrity Lecture. His subject was 'The Motion Picture and the Political Leadership'. His central point was that the power of persuasion and inspiration had passed from the platform, the pulpit and the pamphlet to the film and television and was being operated without any clear-cut relationship with political responsibility. His own practical proposals in the political context had worked best when the political power was actively interested in the long-distance creative intentions of the mass media. He used as illustration the Scottish situation where he said support for the national film-makers barely existed and where the political power did not seem to care a whit whether support existed or not. 'The making of films in Scotland and for Scotland is denied to us on a level which would make our work nationally effective. . . . The case is plain: let it be met.'

But it was not. Grierson in effect turned his back on Scotland, although nothing could extinguish his deep and fierce love for the country. He was to make one further return journey of consequence, to receive the honorary degree of Doctor of Literature from Heriot-Watt University, Edinburgh, on 8 July 1969. It pleased him to have his writing recognised.

Awards and Rewards

During the same visit he fulfilled another engagement which meant more to him—the opening of the Scottish Fisheries Museum at Anstruther—and found much to praise in an admirable, independent undertaking.[29] He spoke about *Drifters* which was shown later in the day in the local cinema to an informed and appreciative audience. It was based, he said, on the proposition that the common things of this earth are noble. 'It was a declaration of faith that there is beauty in the common things, in the common man and in his destiny.'

16 Return to Canada: Indian Summer

One day in August 1968 John and Margaret Grierson had two visitors for lunch at Tog Hill. One was John Kemeny, the director who left his native Hungary after the rising of 1956 and who had joined the Film Board. He had been in Stockholm, arranging for the production of a series of films as a co-operative effort between the N.F.B. and the Swedish Institute of Cultural Relations. He was dispirited about his work and needed philosophical refreshment. Who better to satisfy that need than Grierson? His companion was Bram Chandler, then the N.F.B. representative at Canada House in London. Grierson made light of Kemeny's discomfiture, once calling through to his wife: 'Margaret, did you hear that? It's Alex Korda all over again!'

They had a splendid lunch prepared by Margaret and afterwards walked round the garden where Grierson completed the short course of philosophical refreshment. As his guests prepared to leave, Grierson said that he had been thinking about lecturing on film in a more organised way than he had done in the past. 'I was recently invited to lecture at the University of Belgrade', he said, 'and I found I was enjoying the experience and the audience. I wonder if I couldn't be asked to do a series of lectures at, say, the University of Montreal? I might do a similar series in my home town, at Stirling University.' Chandler and Kemeny said it was a good idea and they would explore the possibilities.[1]

A week later Hugo McPherson, the new film commissioner, telephoned Chandler to say he would be in London at the end of August. A luncheon meeting was arranged with Grierson for 26 August, the day after he received the Golden Thistle at the Edinburgh Festival. Grierson explained his feelings about Canada and about returning to lecture there. McPherson, who found Grierson as 'charming and dynamic' as he had expected, responded to the suggestion and on his return to Montreal wrote to university departments across Canada.

In the following months there was prodding from Chandler in London and pressure from Frank Spiller, head of N.F.B. production, and Tom Daly in Montreal. The University of Montreal was considered

232

unsuitable as Grierson would have been obliged to lecture in French. At McGill University McPherson discussed the proposal with Donald Theall: they had both been students at one time of Marshall McLuhan. Theall was preparing a programme on communications and thought it would be valuable to have Grierson as a visiting lecturer. Just how big an impact he would make at McGill Theall did not then realise.

On 15 December McPherson phoned Grierson at Tog Hill and told him to expect an invitation to lecture from McGill. Two days later Grierson wrote to Chandler thanking him and adding: 'I need a look again at your place to rejuvenate the wilting spirit.' On 18 December Grierson received a cable from Theall with an offer of a half teaching load for one term, to begin on 10 January 1969. Grierson accepted and flew to Montreal on 8 January. At seventy he was off again.

Before he left Grierson had clearly in mind what he wanted to do. He wanted to try to work out a curriculum for studying television in relationship with other disciplines like politics and anthropology and sociology and aesthetics. 'I don't just want to do a lecture, the visiting fireman stuff', he told Magnus Magnusson. 'I want to explore, to study, all the mass media as a phenomenon of our times, as a necessary part of the human sciences.'[2]

These ideas he discussed with Donald Theall as soon as he arrived at McGill. The programme in communications was not to be about making films. It was to be a fairly wide open, interdisciplinary programme: academic and theoretical rather than practical. Grierson believed that it should involve a good knowledge of the history of philosophy, history and perhaps the history of economics, and a lot of good solid information. Planning the programme at the university there was a group of a dozen people from different disciplines: psychologists, sociologists, anthropologists, linguists, economists. There were some real collisions initially but eventually the programme was worked out.

When Grierson arrived in Canada the student revolt was at its height. At one university a million dollars' worth of computers were burnt up. At McGill the students spat at the board of governors as they arrived. They staged riots and broke up meetings. They were strongly activated politically. The bitterness between the French and English elements in Quebec was an additional source of unrest. They hoped to find an ally in Grierson whom they regarded as a Socialist, a left-wing thinker. But the man who came among them was not what they expected.

Grierson met them head on. 'You think you're revolutionaries', he said. 'You know nothing about revolution. If you want to stage a revolution sit down and do your homework. Get your facts straight and then be very tough-minded about what you are doing.' What he found were a lot of individuals protesting about a lot of different things, with no cohesive point of attack, only that all authority was ghastly. The more the students questioned and challenged Grierson the more he relished it. He had always enjoyed intellectual argument and although he thought the students were ill-equipped for the kind of debate he had known in Glasgow, he went into battle with gusto. He was appalled to discover that not a single member of his class had read Plato, not one. They knew of Trotsky's writing only superficially, by reputation. Aristotle was only a name to them. Grierson was not aware that the classics had disappeared from the Canadian school curriculum but at least he expected university students to have a basic education. Trotsky's *Literature and Revolution* was the first text he gave his students to read.

What Grierson regarded as ignorance was accompanied by attempted indiscipline in the lecture room. Grierson would not tolerate familiarity in the relationship between teacher and student. It was normal for a lecturer entering the room to find half of the students reading the *McGill Daily* and the other half lounging about. It was part of the attitude: 'What can you teach me?' Grierson would have none of it. One day he fixed his eye on a student wearing a cap. He remembered a picture he had once seen of Dostoevsky wearing a similar kind of cap. Grierson said to him: 'I have a picture of Dostoevsky wearing a cap like yours. When you can write as well as Dostoevsky wrote, you can wear a cap in my class.' The cap was removed and not worn again.

On another occasion he was interrupted by a lout who interjected that he could not see the use of 'all this mother-fucking stuff about film history'. Grierson fixed his beady eyes on the youth and said that if he wished to exchange gutter language with him he would be challenging a professional whose career began with several years in the Royal Navy, a service which prided itself on its linguistic accomplishments in that field; and further that Grierson had a more intimate knowledge of the subject of incest and fornication in general than the youth would ever learn in a lifetime. 'So, young man, don't try to intimidate an old hand at that game. If you wish to be humiliated in a private session I'm available. If you need to leave now to practise your skill you may be excused.'[3]

In a month Grierson had two hundred students. Enrolment for his class was to grow to about seven hundred. His lectures were given in Leacock 132, the largest lecture room at McGill—vast, like a Roman coliseum, with a very high ceiling. He gave three lectures a week, each of an hour's duration, with an hour more for teaching. He was being overworked but was enjoying it.[4] He realised that with the large classes he was giving a performance but he made determined efforts to make contact with the students. One method he used was to say to the students: 'I want you to write a letter to your mother or your father' about this or that thing. 'Don't hand me in an essay.' When he got five hundred papers he read them—and knew much more about his students than any other professor or lecturer at the university.

Later he carried the process of identification further by having the students write a brief biography to which was attached a passport picture. There was some resistance. 'What goes on here? What sort of identification is this? What difference does it make to you who my parents are?' To which Grierson replied with a lecture on the importance of ancestry and the importance of descent and the importance of culture. He could not associate with this vast number of students unless visually he could picture them. For someone so visually minded a picture was a necessity. His concern and his thoroughness were a new experience at a large university. Few other professors, especially those with large classes, ever bothered to know the students.

Grierson was too intelligent a teacher not to appreciate the educational ineffectuality of classes of this size. He had two smaller classes, each of about fifteen students. With his first teaching assistant, Ron Blumer, he went over the personal papers written by the students and selected his groups. One class was on politics and the other on aesthetics but the selection was random and it was his judgement whether a student was a political or an aesthete. Certainly it had nothing to do with what they thought they were. To the over-politicised to be in the aesthetics class may have had something to do with the achievement of balance in their lives.

The small seminars were held in his apartment at the Crescent Hotel, a small hotel on Crescent Street, just round the corner from the grocery store run by M. Dionne, the French Canadian epicure, whom Grierson came to know well. Here he would prepare food for the students, often Caribbean fresh shrimps cooked in clam juice, and provide liquor for them while he drank his black coffee. According to Ron Blumer these seminars were dynamite.[5] Adam Symansky, another student, found the classes the most exciting educational experience he had ever had, because of the close contact, the give-and-take in discussion, and the constant challenge.[6] A student who had been sitting quietly in a corner would suddenly be asked 'What about you there?'

and, under Grierson's questioning, would begin to expand like a flower. According to Eleanor Beattie, one of his assistants, Grierson 'had an idea that he had this power to help people to grow and expand. He was truly interested in people. . . . I often think he was charged by the adoration and active love which he received.'[7]

Grierson was constantly on the look out for talented students. When he thought he had found them his method was much the same as it had been at the National Film Board: he would challenge them and see if he could disarm them and if a student had any kind of strength he would be put on his mettle. Gary Evans had this experience when, at his suggestion that history should be put on film to teach students, Grierson snorted 'What a ridiculous thing to suggest!' and Evans walked out feeling demolished.[8] When Ron Blumer was interviewing him for the *McGill Daily* Grierson stopped him and said: 'This isn't any good at all. You should be asking me all sorts of other questions.' Blumer said: 'He first broke me and then put me together again, which I found was his technique with other people.' There were inevitably critics of his methods within the university. One fellow professor, a gentle, kindly man, said he thought the methods were insensitive and impossible for any but the most aggressively confident student and that Grierson absolutely squelched the timid and unsure. But some who had been timid and who through his influence lost their timidity would not agree.

At his large classes Grierson showed a number of films: the classic British documentaries of the 1930s, the early Russian films, Leni Riefenstahl's *The Triumph of the Will* and *Olympiade*, Flaherty's *Man of Aran*, Bert Haanstra's *The Human Dutch*; and he analysed these and other films in the light of his experience and related them to the broader basis of his teaching. But he did not think of himself as being at McGill to show films, nor did Donald Theall. 'I suppose the idea was that I should lecture about films', he wrote in his first 'Letter to Michelle', 'and certainly there is a monstrous desire among North American students to learn how to make movies. To be frank I don't like the movement at all. I suspect it. They shout to me that "The day of the cinema has at last arrived." They mean by that that the 8 mm camera now comes so cheap (for North Americans) that every babe in arms can have a go. They mean by that that they have fallen for the old nonsense that the old bad day of writing has gone and the good new day when they will shoot madly any old how and all over the place and be *all seeing* has arrived. They have got their minds addled by reading (note you, "reading") on McLuhan who tells them these things:

forgetting that he, McLuhan, is a writer and not even a good writer and certainly not a visual writer of any quality whatsoever.

'Anyway, it is my privilege nowadays as a full-blown professor to shout back and what I shout back is "Who gives a goddam for the 8 mm revolution if it is going to let loose on us *the 8 mm mind*?" So I am involved in another phase of teaching altogether. I am concerned with the civic, national and international implications of the mass media, all the mass media. And just to make sure everyone is not going crazy about the media and the mystiques of media and the miracles of media, I am quick to declare that far the most important mass medium of all is the medium of education (and in all its aspects: family, church, school, college, field, factory, the lot). And just to make sure we get the priorities right (and I mean the priorities governing the establishment of sentiment, loyalties, powers of appreciation, etc.) I shout loudest of all that the most important function of all is the teaching of teachers, which is to say the creation of standards by which excellencies are measured.

'This, of course, gives the cinema a new position altogether in the academic world. It is not just an incidental consideration in the field of aesthetics, and it is certainly not the handicraft which is included with other handicrafts in those departments which in lesser schools are devoted to *bricolage*. No, it becomes ranked with the other great forces which affect the affections and look after the loyalties. And it happens to be the one medium in which these matters can be most easily demonstrated.'[9]

I have given this quotation at length, partly because the source is not easily accessible but also because it reflects Grierson's thinking at a time when he was writing infrequently for publication. The emphasis on the importance of teaching is significant. All his adult life he had been a teacher and it is possible to see, as Donald Theall has, all his work in documentary film and the establishment of national and international agencies as an extension of teaching, and propaganda as the instrument of the teacher confronted with massive problems at times of crisis. It was Theall's belief that 'while Grierson was always a teacher in his own mode and always an intellectual, the extent of this manifested itself only in his last years when he made a formal commitment of teaching and intellectual work here at McGill.'[10]

At the end of the first year the students gave a party for Grierson. A neat little invitation card in French and English arrived on the desks of the Chancellor of the University, some members of the teaching staff and several members of the National Film Board: 'The students

237

of John Grierson at McGill University invite you to a gathering in his
honour to be held at the University Center, 3480 McTavish Street,
Sunday, April 13, from 8 to 11 p.m.' There was a large gathering, some
people in hippy clothes, others in formal evening dress. According to
George and Mary Ferguson who were present, there was the nicest
possible feeling: the students were obviously delighted to be giving a
party in Grierson's honour. It was a remarkable gesture, especially at a
time when students loathed anyone who looked like a professor or a
parent or an older person. Several of the students spoke and Grierson
replied in a speech full of respect and affection.[11]

In addition to McGill, Grierson was also lecturing once a fortnight
at Carleton University in Ottawa where his old friend Lester Pearson
was chairman. Here the lectures were not part of a course on communication but were linked optionally to a course on journalism. The
number of students attending regularly was very small, fewer than a
dozen, and the lectures did not generate the same excitement as they
did at McGill. It made no difference to Grierson. A chance visitor at
Carleton one day was Bob Anderson who told me that when Grierson
began to speak it was like turning on a light. When Grierson noticed
the stranger he said: 'Do you people know about Anderson? The Film
Board for many years was known abroad for Norman McLaren's stuff
and Bob Anderson's films about nuts'—a reference to Anderson's
notable series of psychiatric films. 'I could never understand it',
Grierson continued, 'but that's the case.'[12]

One of his regular students was Susan Schouten who organised the
class for him and was later his assistant when she took her Ph.D. in
Communications at McGill. Through *Grierson on Documentary* she
was familiar with his work and when he began his first lecture she
thought 'I just want to spend the rest of my life listening to this man
talk.'[13] He talked for three hours. At Carleton he spoke about the
relationship of governments to all forms of creative art and analysed
the nature and function of propaganda. Over the period he was
regularly in Ottawa Grierson formulated a proposal for a communications institute at which visitors from overseas would make recordings
about aspects of life in their countries. Whatever its merit, the project
was to remain unrealised.

Much more fruitful was his contact with the Canadian Radio and
Television Council of which Pierre Juneau was appointed chairman
when it was created in 1968. Grierson had met Juneau, formerly of the
N.F.B., shortly after his appointment and within minutes of meeting
had started telling him what his duty was: Grierson knew the Broad-

casting Act and held strong opinions about what radio could do for Canada. 'You should do this and it's about time you did that' was his manner.[14] When he returned in 1970 he again saw Juneau. After a meeting with André Martin, director of research for C.R.T.C., and Rod Chiasson, his assistant, an arrangement was made whereby Grierson would visit their office whenever he was in Ottawa and make recordings. For Grierson this became one of his most important duties. He continued to make the recordings regularly and was to do so until the last day of his residence in Canada.

Grierson had met André Martin often in Europe, at film festivals in Venice and Cannes, and in Paris where Martin worked with a group of cineastes in the 1950s and 1960s. Grierson was invariably upbraiding him about the lack of responsibility in the French cinema, isolating itself in pity and bourgeois affairs. Martin thought Grierson was haunted by public responsibility, not social responsibility. He recalled seeing a piece of paper on which Grierson had two columns, one headed 'Private' and the other 'Public'. In the private column he had prayer and making love. Everything else was public. Grierson saw television as a very powerful instrument and often quoted Baldwin to Martin: 'Power without responsibility has been the privilege of the harlot throughout the ages.' Martin gave him a book about the Morning Conferences of Dr. Goebbels and when he had read it Grierson said 'It's fantastic how we had them figured out'—a reference to his *World in Action* days at the National Film Board.[15]

Between Grierson and Chiasson there developed a very close and friendly relationship. Shortly after their first meeting Chiasson invited him to dinner. 'I never go to dinner', Grierson said. 'I'll come to breakfast. How is your household on Sunday morning?' Chiasson had four daughters and later a son, born after Grierson's death and named John. When he arrived on the Sunday morning he went with Chiasson's wife into the kitchen where she prepared breakfast. She preferred her coffee weak. When Grierson tasted it he said: 'Madam, that's the worst coffee I've ever drunk in my life.' Chiasson's wife was taken aback; but on her mother's side and her grandfather's side she was of Scottish origin. She put her hands on her hips and said: 'Well, Mr. Grierson, if you can do better, do it yourself.' He became a frequent and always welcome visitor.

Grierson spent many hours with Chiasson, on one occasion at the Château Laurier until five in the morning. 'I was like the student before the great teacher', Chiasson told me in Ottawa. He could not explain the source of Grierson's tremendous energy. 'It was the strength of his mind, his mental power, which kept him alive. I never heard him say "I'm tired."' Chiasson, himself a traveller, was impressed by Grierson's first-hand knowledge of Canada. 'I am certain he was in the Western Arctic; of the Eastern Arctic I am not so sure. He once asked me what I thought of the Eskimos. I said I thought they were polite but not servile and that they were helpful but they didn't want you to lose face. At one time I was trying to fix something, a tent. I wasn't managing and they didn't help me. Once I turned round and asked they came rushing. They wouldn't meddle in your affairs if you didn't ask. Grierson said: "You're right. They're the last British gentlemen I know."' [16]

Grierson's activities in Canada began to multiply in a way that might have been understandable for a man in his forties but was astonishing for someone of seventy whose university work was continuous and demanding. Among Grierson's first visitors was Grant McLean whose Visual Education Centre in Toronto was successfully expanding. Grierson collaborated with McLean in preparing a new version of *I Remember, I Remember* in which, using the same film excerpts as in the earlier production, he linked them with commentary addressed to a world rather than a Scottish audience. McLean introduced him to his American partner, Charles Benton, who had left the Encyclopaedia Britannica organisation to found Public Media Inc. in Chicago and who later invited Grierson to join his board. Grierson declined but agreed to serve as consultant, a position which did not restrict in any way the contributions he made at the board meetings. Benton told me in Chicago that he 'would come out with the most outrageous good sense. No sham, no pretense: it was too late for that. He just got down to the kernel of truth and wisdom.' [17]

Grierson's association with Benton and McLean was close and productive. They planned for American television a series of programmes in the same spirit as *This Wonderful World*, with Benton as narrator. Benton had seen in Paris experimental animated films by Peter Foldes which greatly attracted him and he brought both the director and his films to Chicago where together they made a pilot. It was rejected by the Public Broadcasting System because it contained too much nudity (in animation!). From the detailed comments made by Grierson on the pilot both Benton and Foldes learned a great deal. He lectured them for two hours, pouring out what he had learned in ten years at Scottish Television and repeatedly emphasising that they must not comment but rather evoke. 'The moment you tell the audience, they don't want you.' Happily a tape recording was made. It is as penetrating a piece of constructive critical analysis as I have ever heard.

On another occasion in Chicago Grierson spent a day with Benton's film-makers, seeing films and criticising them. It was another demonstration of his capacity for incisive analysis and positive guidance. Out of the discussion which this 'Day with John Grierson' generated came the title for the television series. It was *They Move, They Move!* the rallying cry used by the barkers to draw crowds to the old time nickelodeons.

Grierson visited the Film Board only when invited: it was part of his attitude that he should not interfere in an area where others carried responsibility. Ross McLean, Tom Daly, Harvey Harnick and Lou Applebaum were among the first to visit him at his apartment and many more were to follow. Sydney Newman had returned to Canada as chairman of the National Film Board. It was for him an especially difficult time. He had been in England for twelve years and had not realised the extent to which the quiet revolution had changed conditions in Montreal and Quebec. The French film-makers at the Board had a cause: there was in their films a passion missing from the work of their English-speaking colleagues. Newman saw Grierson often and was grateful for the help and advice he was readily given.

Almost as acute a problem as the French question was the attitude of the Film Board to television. Few of the Board's films appeared on television, a situation which Newman with his experience at the C.B.C. and the B.B.C. could not accept. The film-makers at the Board would not agree to the commercial interruptions on which the C.B.C. insisted. They had thoroughly indoctrinated the members of the Board. In despair Newman called Grierson, explained his dilemma and asked for help. 'When Grierson came into the room where the Board members were meeting', Newman told me in Ottawa, 'it was as if he had been shot out of a cannon. I introduced him around and one by one he proselytised every member to give up this idiotic nonsense of no commercials, that if you made films they had to be seen. He was taut and pertinent and he convinced the whole Board. With Board approval I won the battle with my staff.' This was only one of the battles in which Newman was involved. In all of them he knew he could have the help of a man who had known and relished battles all his life.[18]

At the first Canadian Inter-University Film Conference, organised by Donald Theall and the N.F.B. in 1969, Grierson and Dusan Makavejev were guests. They had last met in Belgrade. Each gave an evening screening and talk. Later, whenever they were both in

Montreal they met and talked, on one occasion all through the night. Grierson admired Makavejev's ability to make his films inexpensively and thus be free. To Makavejev Grierson was 'the prototype of a man who was always bigger than films. Also bigger than life in some ways, a guru, if you like, of social purpose. Socialist countries abuse films and the idea of social purpose. Grierson stood, not for governments or employers, but for social philosophy. He was one of the great influences on Yugoslavian documentary.' Makavejev observed shrewdly when he said that Grierson 'had direct relationship with you right away. His authority was genuine. Sometimes he played the authoritarian but this came out of his personality and not out of his position.' Grierson asked Makavejev what he was doing in North America and when he replied that he was studying the technicalities of American film-making Grierson was disgusted and said: 'I will tell you what to do. Enjoy the vulgarity of America.' 'I appreciated his advice', Makavejev told me, 'because it was the right advice.'[19]

Grierson had more requests than he could meet to be a jury member at film festivals. He agreed to serve for the Canadian Film Awards of 1970, held at the St. Lawrence Centre in Toronto. His fellow jurors were Miklos Rozsa, Jan Kadar, Louis Bresky and Marc Gervais, who taught film courses in Montreal. To Gervais 'Grierson, in spirit still by far the youngest and most vital of our group, is a man who reacts and who believes in calling a spade at least a spade. Time and again, in stage whispers well calculated to reverberate through the entire theatre, he could be heard revealing his soul state with a muttered, "What monumental trash!" or, "I'm leaving Canada" or, "This is sheer magnificence."' What Grierson did note with pleasure was the English-Canadian cinema's love of the great outdoors and delight in the beauty of nature. The Toronto event, organised by Gerald Pratley, reflected Canada's increasing concern with the production of feature films.[20]

This was a development in which Grierson inevitably became involved, both because of his natural interest and because of his experience at Group 3 in Britain. Among the producers who approached him was Harry Gulkin who believed that the nascent Canadian cinema could be enriched by bringing in directors from overseas. Together they saw Michael Spencer, Grierson's former N.F.B. colleague, at the Canadian Film Development Corporation and put forward their ideas. Jiri Weiss was the first director to be invited and he was followed, among others, by Jan Kadar who directed *Lies My Father Told Me* for Harry Gulkin. Grierson agreed to act as consultant for Gulkin and arranged key meetings with investment sources. He was excited about the possibility of a film on Louis Riel and the Red River Rebellion, seeing in it a story rooted in the reality of Canadian history and Canadian space, and promoted it as the greatest untold story for the Canadian screen. Gulkin thought Grierson's ideas were sound and simply needed someone to transpose them from the documentary terms in which he saw them into a form with dramatic structure.[21]

The commitments continued to multiply. In January 1971 Grierson gave the keynote speech at the opening of the Mid-West Film Conference in Chicago. According to Robert Edmonds, chairman of the motion picture department of Columbia College, he held an audience of five hundred people fascinated. In introducing Grierson Edmonds said he was probably the greatest film teacher who had ever lived because he had provided more environments congenial to the development of film-making than anyone else in the world. Edmonds had invited him to lecture to his class and Grierson, in agreeing, said he would have to charge a fee. He spoke for an hour and a half and answered questions for an hour and a half, without a break. 'At seventy-one that was a long haul', Edmonds said to me in Chicago. 'All he had was a cup of tepid coffee. He made an extraordinary impression on my students. They said to me: "Do you know, he's the youngest visitor you've had." ' As Grierson left he said to Edmonds: 'I'm not charging you a fee. Your kids are better than mine at McGill.'[22]

Another invitation came from Brock University, near Niagara, Ontario, where he was introduced by an old friend, secretary to Mackenzie King during the war period, Brock's president, James Gibson. Maurice Yacowar, chairman of the department of drama at the university, met Grierson at a party in Montreal, 'and somewhat upset him with my graduate student name-dropsy. But when we found ourselves talking about Krazy Kat everything was suddenly smoothed. He told me of his once making a pilgrimage to meet the master, George Herriman. Some time later, when I invited Mr. Grierson to come to Brock University for a public lecture, his reply came in the form of a barely decipherable card: "I surface for Krazy Kat." He came and, of course, was sensational. That was in the spring of 1971. I've never encountered such an alert, probing eye and mind as John Grierson had.'[23] Grierson had been a fan of the cartoon strip, Krazy Kat, from his earliest years in the United States. At that time he made a collection of the cartoons, the only collection of anything I remember him making. There was something surrealistic in them which appealed to him.

Return to Canada: Indian Summer

Grierson spoke at the Lethbridge campus of the University of Alberta. He went twice to York University, Toronto, to talk to James Beveridge's students. 'It was a liberal education to follow his speech, but you had to have a certain amount of equipment to begin. I thought at one point "How the hell are these young souls going to grasp on to any part of what he is saying? Really they can't. I can't. Well, I barely can." Nevertheless, in his audience there was the most attentive silence and respectful, almost painful, concentration. He had something: he had this tremendous intensity of communication . . . the meaning somehow burned through the complexities of his speech and his own knowledge, which was encyclopaedic.'[24]

In Montreal Grierson had countless requests for radio and television interviews. He wasn't an easy subject and was impatient with interviewers who hadn't done their homework. One who survived an initial rebuff was Elspeth Chisholm, film lecturer and researcher, who called on him at his apartment. 'There he was, small, grimly furrowed face, neat, sparse hair brushed smooth, blue cashmere sweater matching the fierce owl-eyes, glaring at you from magnifying glasses. He was a dynamo, a camera, a computer, gathering, challenging. There was Grierson, come from conquering the unruly under-graduates with his intellectual bull-whip, holding them in thrall as he did all of us.'

In the interview he gave Elspeth Chisholm he said many perceptive things, of which one gives a clue to the spirit he brought to his teaching: 'There, at the university, is where a young person has the greatest moment of privilege in his life. Suddenly all the horizons of knowledge are opened up to him. The world is his personal oyster. He doesn't know yet, please, if he is or is not William Shakespeare. Just imagine that absolutely blissful period when you don't know yet that you're not William Shakespeare!' The interview later formed part of an ambitious C.B.C. radio programme, 'The Canadian Indian Summer of John Grierson', prepared by Elspeth Chisholm.[25]

Grierson also made two long recordings for Jim Beveridge in which he set out afresh his version of his Canadian experience. He chose this opportunity to correct Beveridge's description of his manning the Film Board by 'picking all the nuts around'. Said Grierson: 'No, no, I didn't pick nuts. I went after all the people who were talking nationalism in Canada. If you look back on all the youngsters I brought in, including yourself, you had the common bug of being very Canadian and being very aware of it and not putting up with any nonsense any more from the English raj and what it represented. I delighted in doing this because every Scotsman is a suppressed, repressed anti-

244

Englander and is liable to join any anti-English revolution everywhere except in Scotland, and that shows his good sense. You will find one thing in common that you all had and that is you were heirs of this wonderful thing being built up.' The focus was clarifying rather than changing.

One of Grierson's assistants at McGill was Rashmi Sharma, a young Indian girl who had remained in Montreal after helping to plan the Indian pavilion for Expo. She accompanied him to Chicago where the first thing he did was to buy her a copy of Carl Sandburg's poems from which he later read to her. Through her companionship and conversation his latent interest in India was stimulated. 'He had wanted to go to India for a long time', she told me in Montreal, 'but never thought very much about it and he did not have the time to make a journey with no purpose.'[26]

Suddenly and unexpectedly there was a purpose. The special adviser in population and health for the Canadian International Development Agency was Dr. George Brown who was interested in the use of film and film strips in assisting teachers working in the field of family planning in the developing countries. He invited the National Film Board to provide a team to go to India to investigate the possibilities of Canadian assistance to the Indian Government's family planning programme. Included in the team he wanted someone unconnected to either the Canadian Government or the N.F.B. and suggested Jim Beveridge. Beveridge, teaching at York University, was not free to go, although he had worked in India and was interested in the country's problems. He recommended Grierson—a suggestion welcomed with enthusiasm by Dr. Brown and by Robert Verrall, head of English production at the N.F.B., who had responsibility for the project. The other members of the team, Ken McCready and Len Chatwin, were 'stunned and delighted at the prospect of working with Grierson'.[27]

Grierson accepted the invitation. It was the kind of governmental advisory mission which always appealed to him. At the end of March 1971 they flew together from Montreal to London where they waited two days for a flight to New Delhi. On the flight to London Grierson asked McCready what he knew about family planning. McCready replied, 'Enough to get along with', to which Grierson confessed, 'I don't know a damn thing.' While in London McCready noticed a paperback on contraception and thought, 'That's just the thing for Grierson.' On the plane he handed it to him and said, 'Here's something to help you to prepare yourself for India.' It was a long night flight of fourteen hours. Long after the departure and after the cabin lights had been lowered, Grierson was still reading, avidly, about contraception. Suddenly he would burst out in his penetrating voice: 'It says here so-and-so. Is that what you do? Come on, tell me.' McCready answered as well as he could, well aware that the technical details were being relished by an ever-widening radius of now wide awake passengers. The inquisition continued long into the night. 'I think it was a bit of showmanship he couldn't resist', McCready told me in Montreal. 'It was very, very funny.'

Later Grierson was to quote effectively from the book the advice given to a woman who suffered undesirable effects that she should pick up the telephone and speak to her doctor. 'What kind of advice is that?' he said. It was fine for North America with its sophisticated culture but was meaningless in India. The greatest means of communication in India, he found, was word of mouth. When the Americans landed on the moon, everybody in India knew about it in two days, without telephones. Grierson realised early in the research therefore that sophisticated technologies and means of distribution were useless in India because they would not reach the people. Women working in the fields in the rural areas did not have transistor radios with them to hear the broadcasts addressed to them during the day. That was where the growth in population was taking place, although its effects were most apparent in the cities to which the surplus population found its way in the hope of making a living.

Grierson was convinced that word of mouth was the most effective means of communication. He thought this might be stimulated by the strolling groups of entertainers, the puppet shows and the song and dance troupes, who go from village to village and he recommended that they should be asked to incorporate family planning messages in their performances. This led to a concept of decentralising the system of communication. A film on family planning made in the Punjab, for example, made no impact in Southern India where not only the language was different but also were cultural and religious attitudes. The longer Grierson and his colleagues were in India the more they became convinced of the need to establish small, modest production units throughout the country which would produce material of significance for local people. Especially was this true of a very personal kind of subject like family planning.

His experiences in India affected Grierson in different ways. One was his increasing conviction that his support of what he called the festival circuit had been a mistake. Initially he had done so to promote the documentary idea; but the utilitarian aspect of documentary had been lost sight of as the film-makers came to consider the winning of accolades at festivals more important than whether the film had any social significance or was capable of implementing social change. He felt that in India there was an opportunity to recapture the social usefulness of film. One of the reasons why he wanted to put the means of production into the hands of the field-workers and the teachers who were actually doing the job was to avoid the kind of prejudices and the desire for prestige which many professional film-makers would have brought to the same task. Grierson told Ken McCready that he would like to have devoted the rest of his life to realising in India the social use of film in which he had always believed.

The Canadian team was in India for about two months, working fourteen hours a day, seven days a week and going 'just about everywhere'. The day would begin at 8 a.m. when, over breakfast, they discussed the programme. By 9 a.m., if they were in Delhi, they would be in a government office talking to people, or they would be on their way to a small town or village to visit a family planning clinic. Grierson always insisted on talking to the workers as well as the supervisors, learning directly about their hostile reception and the consequences of the inadequate medical facilities for the family planning programme. In Bihar he was told of the tragedies which resulted from imperfectly performed vasectomies and the murder by husbands of wives later found to be pregnant and suspected of adultery.

At breakfast Grierson would always be reading at least two newspapers. He read them very quickly, picked out and clipped items of significance and put them in his pockets. While they were in transit he would read the clippings and when meeting people could discuss with them the news of the day. In this way he was able to establish a rapport quickly while on their part they felt, 'Here's a man who knows us, who knows what's happening.' He tended to shy away from official involvement, although he did have talks with the ministers responsible for family planning, information and broadcasting. When he was introduced to Mrs. Gandhi he said: 'How does it feel, madam, to be the very embodiment of the Goddess Kali [the principle of force and creative energy in Indian mythology] and the embodiment of women's lib. at the same time?' The Prime Minister threw her hands up in the air and said, 'Oh, you're just as terrible as they said you would be!'

The tour began and ended in Delhi and encompassed Amritsar, Bombay, Poona, Madras, Hyderabad, Ootaccamund, Calcutta, Patna, Lucknow and Ahmedabad. Among the Indians in the group was V. B. Chandra, director of the films division of the Ministry of Information and Broadcasting. Grierson urged him to think about making films with the people and not about the people. Communication should come up from the village and not down to the village and there should be collaboration all along the line. Film-makers should take a bicycle and go out to the villages. He was critical of some of the films he was shown. 'I am afraid the films division is falling prey to some of the cheap film festivals of the Western affluent countries. I am definitely not in favour of getting prizes for having caught the sickness of some of the frustrated countries of the West.' In India, films, he urged, must serve as positive catalysts of the social revolution of the country.[28]

Some of the Indian film-makers were given a rough time for what Grierson regarded as their self-indulgent films, using a public purse for private pursuits. He was impatient of hero-worship, as one film critic found. 'Small-built and outwardly very much the dour Scotsman and certainly in his burred speech, Dr. Grierson sticks doggedly to his Scottish woollen cardigan underneath his neat suit and beneath that cardigan beats a heart of pure gold. His youthful non-conformist views, teamed with what I can only describe as a canny Scots instinct about hypocrisy in people and institutions, must have made him a holy terror. But his natural kindliness and generosity shine through his outer fierceness and a puckish sense of humour softens even his most scathing judgments which are so precise that there is really no defence against them.'[29]

Grierson himself summed up his experience at the end of a 'Memo to Michelle' published in *A.I.D. News*. 'In India', he wrote, 'there is a special imperative for decentralising the film-making process. All the mass media together reach to only a hundred million of the population, leaving four hundred and fifty million to word-of-mouth, local educators and itinerant entertainments of native origin. Obviously the biggest role in economic and social progress of all kinds will be with the local educators; making it necessary to add, in every way possible, to their local powers of persuasion. Here, with the local educators, I associate all developments involving the community welfare. The local activist front is complex. In India, too, there are many languages to contend with and areas distinctive in ethnic and cultural background. Film-making at the District level is, I would think, a logical development: and one to which the various Foreign Aid programmes should soon be giving their attention. This means, among other peripatetic entertainments, the appearance of peripatetic teachers of film-making, moving modestly from District to District, teaching the doctor-teachers and other local educationists, how to hold their cameras steady and shoot simply, as their own native powers of exposition direct them. That would be a real 8 mm revolution, anchored in necessity.'[30]

Grierson returned to Montreal and collaborated with McCready and Chatwin in preparing the long detailed reports for the Canadian International Development Agency and the National Film Board. He was in England for only a brief period during the summer and then was back in Canada.

Did Grierson have any notion that this was to be his last visit? If so he gave no hint of it as he took up his work again, and added to it. The National Film Board had approached him about a film on his life and work.[31] When they first put the proposal to him, Roger Blais and David Bairstow found him vehement on one point: he was not interested if the film was to be a memorial to John Grierson. He did not believe in testimonials to the dead, any dead, starting with himself. But he would agree to a film on his ideas and how they had worked out in Canada: a film about documentary principles and the obligations and meaning of communication.[32]

He delegated the day-to-day supervision on his behalf to Jim Beveridge, with final approval reserved to himself. In reply to a formal letter from the Board he wrote a short note saying: 'The gist of what you have said is the gist of what I have understood and I don't want to be bothered any more. Until you need me personally work through Jim Beveridge.' The work began during the autumn and winter of 1971. Contact was made with Grierson's friends and colleagues, in North America, in Europe, Mrs. Gandhi in India, Joris Ivens in China, Bert Haanstra in the Netherlands. This was the plan. But there was to be a basic change in the plan which none concerned had foreseen.

Grierson was back for the new term at McGill where Hugo McPherson was now director of the graduate programme in communications. He was being given considerable help by his young assistants—Ron Blumer, Susan Schouten, Rashmi Sharma and Marjorie Saldhana. Teaching the large class now seemed to demand more effort. The small seminars in his apartment were much more to his liking. He was in Chicago for meetings of the board of Public Media Inc. After what was to be his last meeting he was with Charles Benton and his wife and he gave her a little silver pillbox. He did not say 'This is to remember me by', but the gesture gave them the sense that they might not see him again.[33]

Sydney Newman called him. He had a problem on which he needed advice. Secretary of State Gerard Pelletier had evolved a concept for a new film policy for Canada which would mean absorption of the Canadian Film Board in a larger film structure referred to then as the Canadian Film Commission. Newman felt it would diminish the importance of the Film Board and the film commissioner. He asked if Grierson would help to frame a reply. Grierson agreed at once and took a taxi to Newman's home. He read the document. They spent more than four hours together, first in argument and then in exposition. Grierson's capacity first to disturb and then to lead towards a fresh imaginative view of a subject was as powerful as ever.[34]

There were to be no more meetings with Newman, one of the vital young Canadians he found and brought into film-making. Grierson deputised for Newman at a party given on 17 November by the Film Board to launch the publication of a book of photographs by the N.F.B. photo service, *A Time to Dream*. The photographs taken of Grierson that day are of a man suffering pain but there were few present who were aware of it. Grierson resented any inference that he was not in the best of health.

Rod Chiasson was with Grierson on his last day in Canada. In Montreal with his eight-year-old daughter, he asked if he might call. When he did Grierson asked if he could get some drugs for him which, with his wife's help, Chiasson was able to do. Grierson had a copy of Shakespeare's plays and read to Chiasson's daughter from *Macbeth*. He was familiar with the play and, for an hour, made it live for the little girl. 'It was just enthralling', Chiasson told me. 'She just sat there quietly and took everything in! I think he knew some parts by heart.'

> Three score and ten I can remember well:
> Within the volume of which time, I have seen
> Hours dreadful and things strange.

As the afternoon turned to darkness Grierson did not turn on the lights in his apartment. They went on talking. Eventually Grierson said: 'O.K., Chiasson, it's time to go. Someone's going to take me to the airport.' They shook hands and said goodbye.[35]

Grierson flew to London on 14 December 1971. His intention was to return to India and his air tickets had been purchased. The visit had been delayed, first by C.I.D.A. and then by the December war with Pakistan. On 23 December he wrote from Tog Hill to Lady Elton: 'India was lined up for a largish project but the mess there has delayed the final discussion of a scheme, which the N.F.B. will run for two to five years, of wandering teachers on film technique. I am not sorry about India's delay. I was greatly caught up and would have gone but am now reminded that I am too tired to take easily to their complicated scene. But it is a bother to decide. The country is very, very rich in everyday fairytale but as we see there is diabolism too. . . . I go back [to Canada] around January 10 but expect it will be my last term as a professor. It is a pity because it has gone well and I have been invited by several universities to hang up a hat. But wear and tear goes with it.'[36]

The wear and tear had been greater than he knew. On 2 January 1972 he called Marjorie Saldanha in Montreal and said he was going into hospital for a medical check-up. On 5 January he was admitted to the Forbes Fraser Hospital, Bath. The diagnosis showed cancer in the liver and cancer in his left lung. On 13 January the doctors said he had a month to live. On 9 February he wrote to Grant McLean: 'I am stuck pretty permanently in hospital and will not be back in Canada. . . . You might as well tell the good Charles [Benton] that I don't expect to be around at his inspired, not to say holy, meetings: not any more. This hospital sure thinks it has got me.'

Whatever the weaknesses in his body, Grierson's mental energy was unaffected. His hospital room was full of newspapers, books and electronic equipment: television, radio, tape recorders. Because of reception difficulty in the Bath area, aerials were strung across from wall to wall, compounding the congestion. He dictated letters, attending to such details as the return of borrowed films. Margaret gave him such help in these secretarial matters as he needed. He had written the letters in his mind before dictating them to her and she was as impressed as ever by his careful use of words, his consideration. She was staying at the York Hotel in Bath and spent the days at the hospital. John Taylor and his wife, Barbara Mullen, were with her most weekends. Grierson was unwilling to have visitors. To inquirers Margaret would say quietly: 'John is in his last illness.'

John Taylor was with him a few days before his death. They spoke about the ideas to which he had held firmly throughout his life and the continuity in convictions held. A few years before, when Grierson had been asked: 'If you could live your life over again is there one particular pitfall you would avoid?' he replied: 'Pitfalls are the spice of life. And young folk should know that. But there's never been a pitfall that the human spirit can't dig itself out of. Probably the most dangerous pitfall is the loss of faith in the human spirit and its infinite variety. If that happens, remember—it's you that's at fault.'[37]

Grierson was unconscious on 18 February. Margaret had the impression that he knew he would die within a few hours, as if, having been in charge of his life, he was now in charge of his death. He had discussed with her where the urn containing his ashes would be placed. The last entry in the last of the large black-bound notebooks he invariably used for drafting letters and speeches contained the instructions, set out clearly in capital letters. The urn was to be placed in the sea off the Old Head of Kinsale, beyond the outer turbot mark, so that the fishermen would not bring it up in their nets and curse him for his thoughtlessness. He welcomed Margaret's suggestion that the urn with the ashes of his brother Anthony might be placed in the sea at the same place.

After his brother's funeral in August 1971, Grierson had written out precise instructions and left them in an envelope marked 'if and when':

De minimus non curat lex. But it seems better to specify, so I specify:
1. Cremation.
2. No one to attend except the undertaker.
3. No reading of the burial service. The burial service is the heart of religion and I'll do it myself.
4. No musak.
5. Delay announcement for two or three days. There's nothing like the past to shuffle off fuss.
6. No memorial service.

J.G.

He died on Saturday 19 February 1972. In due course the instructions, negative and positive, were carried out. On a clear, bright day at Kinsale, the *Able Seaman* put to sea, with John Taylor and Garry Culhane on board. Flags in the little port were at half-mast. As a further mark of esteem and affection, the Kinsale boats formed a little flotilla in the wake of the *Able Seaman* and followed it out to the Old Head of Kinsale. As Garry Culhane gently lowered the urns into the sea the fishing boats sounded a last farewell on their sirens.

Was there a gruff voice somewhere muttering: 'Sing no sad songs for me'?

17 The Right of the Prophet

M_y last meeting with Grierson had been at Dorval airport. I was passing through Montreal at the end of a two months' tour of Canada and the United States and he made the long trip out from his downtown hotel to spend two or three hours with me. We had time to talk of many things: of Canada and Scotland; of his students at McGill; of what he hoped might still be accomplished in his native country; and of the wider opportunities for documentary in a changing world. He was as always direct, lucid and forthright. On everything we spoke about he threw a searching light. There was not a hint of receding powers. Here was a man living fully in the present, yet with his eye on the future and his mind actively concerned with the contribution he might make.

I found it difficult therefore, some twelve months later, to accept his death. For some forty years he had been a strong, positive influence in my life. It did not matter very much whether he was four hundred or four thousand miles away. What he stood for, what he taught, remained compulsively with me, influencing action and stimulating effort. It did not need his physical presence for the force to be active.

In this, of course, I was not alone. In all the many talks I had with those who knew him best in Britain, North America and elsewhere in the world, I was struck by the vividness of their recollection, their eagerness to acknowledge the impact he had made on their lives. This was as true of those who had known him first in the 1930s as of the students he taught in his last years in Canada. They had all been conscious of an urgent, compelling presence: a demanding, uncompromising man, his convictions aflame in his eyes; a man who had the gift of making exciting everything he spoke about, who could inspire endeavour above and beyond the normal.

To quote only one of scores of similar tributes. From his home in Prince Edward Island Bram Chandler wrote to me of his appreciation of Grierson's 'very great gifts, of his unique ability to express his vision in memorable words, of his grasp of the intellectual and political history of Western society, and his intuitive understanding of the current significance of that history. And along with all that talent a deep

253

concern for humanity in general and a love for individuals in particular. An exasperating and lovable man who had the gift for life from which we all benefit.'[1]

What made Grierson exasperating? His determination to see things only his way arose for the most part out of strong conviction; but his impatience with opposing opinion (for him the unimaginative) was often understandably resented. He was able to forget his own failures which, in the case of International Film Associates, had hurt other people as well as himself; or, more often than not, he later rationalised his failures so that they tended to be minimised. Others whose eyes were not so firmly on tomorrow did not forget so easily.

Grierson's overriding restlessness was another element in his character which some did not find it easy to understand. One of his students at McGill likened him to a cowboy out of the old Wild West. He'd come in to clean up Dodge City. 'This is the job you wanted me to do and I did it. I hang up my gun and here's my badge.' Then he would ride off, leaving those behind asking 'Who was that man?' As Grierson himself put it, 'My stuff is where things are beginning and expanding and taking chances.' He did not like adventures when they began to look like jobs. He was always on the move. *This Wonderful World* was his longest semi-continuous undertaking. Among other things it gave him an income when he needed it. He had no interest in material possessions and spent everything he earned.

One consequence of his peripatetic existence was that he never had, or could find, time to write a book. He was grateful for *Grierson on Documentary*, the book of his writings which I edited, because of the expression it gave of what he had been driving at over the years. He admitted in the postscript he wrote for it that he had hewn out some theory in his time, affecting the principles of education and affecting the use of the film as a vital instrument in public education. 'But writing, for all of us in the documentary movement, has been incidental to the business of making the word flesh.' Later in his life, when he was recovering from illness in 1953, he began writing a novel about Jan Masaryk and a ballet dancer. 'I always had a suspicion that any Scotsman who remembered *Quentin Durward* and *The Pirate* and had walked over the Pentland Hills and/or the Cuillins would finish up doing John Buchan.'[2] But the more the story came out the more it depressed him and he did not finish it.

It was once said of Grierson that 'The one romantic streak in his nature is a generous sympathy for the bluffer.'[3] Sometimes he allowed a legend to grow around him when he might have cut it down. One such which flourished among the more credulous of his associates in North America was that during the war he had been 'head of M.I.5 [Military Intelligence] in Canada' and that his real mission there was to secure the involvement of the United States in the war. I was told this—with seeming seriousness—so often during my researches that I made formal inquiries, only, as I expected, to have the notion summarily demolished. It was odd to find it being given any credence in Canada.

'Grierson was either a missionary or he was a phoney', said Guy Roberge to me over lunch at the Rideau Club in Ottawa.[4] 'I think he was a missionary', added the former film commissioner who, as a young lawyer, first met Grierson in Quebec early in the war. Grierson latterly described himself not as a missionary but as a medicine man. In one of the last interviews he gave, to his assistant Ron Blumer, in Montreal, he said: 'If you think I do not feel I have been in the business of conditioning the imagination of mankind, you're crazy. But then, every goddam rabbi, every prophet and every priest before me has been in the business of conditioning the imagination of mankind. I derive my authority from Moses. And I won't be pushed aside from this. I deny this miserable modern habit to deride or to deny the right of the prophet or the preacher. Masterminding is a valid activity of the human spirit, and medicine men are worthy of their hire. They all represent controls—all represent imaginative discipline, seeking of the power which will enable them to operate.'[5]

And so we have one, the strongest, continuing element in Grierson's life: the desire to condition the imagination. By the accident of opportunity it emerged first in the form of the documentary film; but, as Grierson often said, documentary was never really an adventure in film-making at all but an adventure in public observation. It might as easily, he maintained, have been a movement in documentary writing, or documentary radio, or documentary painting—to which we would add today documentary television. The basic force behind it, he said, was social not aesthetic. He was not impressed by art movements which did not articulate a message, order their followers and work through some discipline.

The motivation of the documentary film movement was 'a desire to bring the citizen's eye in from the ends of the earth to the story, his own story, of what was happening under his nose'. It was to help people to see themselves and their world, as it was and as it ought to be. From the most insignificant beginnings it became a force big enough to influence social thinking in Britain during the 1930s, to contribute powerfully to the war effort and for a time to give a realistic backbone

The Right of the Prophet

to British story film-making. With Grierson it went overseas, to Canada, Australia and New Zealand, and spread in greater or lesser degree to all the countries of the Commonwealth. Documentary became part of the art of communication in every film-making country in the world. Thousands of film-makers who never knew Grierson were influenced by his teaching and example. He was the acknowledged founder and leader of a movement.

All who worked with him were not influenced at the same depth or in the same way. John Taylor believes that one of the strengths of documentary was the many different interpretations put on the word. Basil Wright appeared to be happiest when he was developing the poetic use of the documentary approach, as was true later also of Humphrey Jennings. Harry Watt's preference was for personalised documentary. Paul Rotha held firmly to social comment, with the rare exception of his story film, *No Resting Place*. With Joris Ivens documentary had a strong political basis. At the end of his life Grierson held that 'the great achievement of documentary to-day is what it has done and is doing in the less privileged countries.' He asserted that the most important force in the contemporary world was the teaching force and that 'if the teaching force begins to arm itself with the serious use of film as a power of expression for democratic purposes then you've got yourself a very very big development indeed, which makes all our developments of the 1930s look like two cents.'[6]

'As I have understood Grierson', said Edgar Anstey to me, 'his purpose was to provide and then to exploit creative opportunities to bring alive in man's consciousness the astonishing nature of his own activity.' He saw this as explaining the difference between pre-war documentary in Britain and wartime documentary in Canada and the required reaction in both countries. In a broader context, Anstey saw Grierson's work as a plea for respect for man as a creative creature and as a contributor to the development of his own society. Grierson, he suggested, thought it was important to celebrate the enormous achievements and the enormous potential of man in his group activity and that because he would not conceive of this in a narrow political sense he was often misunderstood.[7]

Grierson's politics have been the subject of endless argument, both inside and outside the movement. He was once asked plumb by M. J. Caldwell, leader of the Co-operative Commonwealth Federation in Canada, what his politics were. 'I said I stood one inch to the left of the Liberal party in power and would stand one inch to the left of a C.C.F. party in power—which would be easy—and would hope for an

256

inch to the good even if a Progressive Conservative party were in power.'[8] This is the nearest he ever came to a definition of his politics. He was never a member of a political party. His radical inclination was clear from his university days. He said he was a product of the Clyde-side school which in his day was as far left as he could go, short of Communism. He was not a Communist. It may be noted in passing that while he visited nearly every other country in Europe, he was never in the U.S.S.R. He always thought of himself as a public servant; and if he sought to pull the particular administration he was serving more in the direction of progressive thinking than might have been its inclination, that was as much as he was prepared to do within the system. In Britain he was intrigued to find that he had more tractional success with the Conservative than with the Labour party when in power.

Grierson has been charged with unwillingness to recognise that the state imposes rather severe constraints on its servants and that although there may at times be a wide range of flexibility, the service must ultimately be of the social groups which dominate it. During the 1930s Grierson saw film as the most powerful means of mobilising communal loyalties. Behind documentary there was the assumption that the film-maker as public servant could re-create these loyalties, not only on behalf of the state, but also to some extent independently of the state and on behalf of private corporations presenting themselves as public benefactors.

To Alan Adamson this was a delusion but it was a delusion which could be taken for reality twice in Grierson's life—in Britain during the depressed 1930s and in Canada during the war—because he was dealing with states in crisis and to that extent somewhat more susceptible to manipulation. 'His success, his magnificent success, in exploiting and organising these ephemeral advantages must have added irresistibly to the illusion that he and his disciples were creating part of a new world as well as celluloid artefacts. But the balance of political reality reasserted itself after 1945. The indifference with which Grierson was treated by the Canadian bureaucracy when the war was over would confirm this view, as would the rapid decline of docu-mentary in the inhospitable climate of the cold war. It was politics, not technology (i.e. television), that killed documentary, and that left Grierson effectively stranded in the 1950s.'[9]

Documentary was not killed. As I have shown in these pages, the movement lost its cohesion and force, partly because of the post-war situation. This was more true of Britain than of many countries which had adopted and fostered the documentary idea, most notably Canada where, after a period of uncertainty, the National Film Board regained its impetus and influence. In other parts of the Commonwealth and in many European countries documentary flourished. In Britain, as I have shown, the leadership passed from the government information service to other sponsors who saw the value of using documentary to serve their interests or to create loyalties of one kind or another.

More often than not it was one of Grierson's disciples who was behind the drive in those areas. Edgar Anstey at British Transport Films brought the richly varied beauty of the British landscape to the screen in a notable series of films which set and sustained the highest standard in this genre. Several were directed by John Taylor and others by Stewart McAllister, who joined Anstey from the G.P.O. Film Unit. The biggest volume of sponsorship came from Shell, pioneered and developed by Sir Arthur Elton, and later from the wider oil industry. The films of technical exposition made a contribution to the closure of the gap between science and society; and the global surveys of agriculture, medicine and food did much to focus, in the Western world, the problems and needs of the emergent countries. The development stemmed directly from Grierson's teaching and attacked new areas of concern. But the various efforts and achievements, separate and un-co-ordinated, did not add up to a movement as we knew it in the 1930s.

Grierson himself recognised the inadequacy. Noting that there must be a logical relationship between sponsor and documentary, he said: 'The trouble with people to-day is that they don't know how to sell the relationship because they are not tutored as we were in the political and economic relationships of things. The documentary film in Britain has failed for lack of an intelligentsia. It hasn't got an intelligentsia to-day that can really go and tell the people in sugar or the people in some other commodity why logically they are concerned in a particular educational or inspirational purpose.'[10]

Had television been, in 1930, the medium it was some forty years later it would have been logical for documentary to have been a television rather than a film movement. Logical, because of its access to a large audience, its freedom from the cumbersome processes of film production and distribution, its immediate sight of public events and because of its capacity for observation, analysis and comment on current affairs. A month of television in Britain will produce more documentary than came in a year from the movement in its early days: *Panorama, This Week, Weekend World, World in Action, Horizon,* and all the many other programmes on individual subjects.

The point was well put by Angus Macdonald, head of features at

The Right of the Prophet

Granada Television, when he spoke at the opening of the Grierson Archive at Stirling University in October 1977. He claimed that 'the Griersonian ideal of art and entertainment married to social purpose is alive, reasonably well and living in television. . . . I suggest no simple causality and certainly no apostolic succession—but it is worth remembering that you don't have to have documentary on television: a lot of American television manages to get by quite well without them.' He saw the tradition of *Nanook*, *Moana*, and *Song of Ceylon* continuing in such programmes as *The World about Us* and *A Disappearing World*; and he saw what Grierson did to bring the workaday world to the screen re-emerging in series like *Days of Hope* and *The General Strike*, giving expression to previously excluded experience of working-class history and politics. 'I believe that the common people of Britain have now more access to honest information than ever before', said Macdonald. 'More opportunity to participate in their society and change it than ever before.' He suspected that had he been alive, John Grierson, 'Samurai of so many causes but independent to the end', would have been with them in the battle, preferring as ever the excitements of flyting to the quiet life.[11]

Grierson was a close observer of trends in television in Britain and in North America. He noted television's supremacy over the cinema in the immediacy of its news reporting and in the distinction of its journalism-in-depth. As an extension of its excellent journalism it had done much in the way of dramatic social observation and had influenced social reform in such productions as *Cathy Come Home*, produced by Sydney Newman. Lindsay Galloway, one of the writers Grierson had encouraged at Group 3, was responsible for *Sutherland's Law* which gave a dramatic shape to social comment on life in a small town. Television Grierson thought was in a field of its own with intimate theatre—*Coronation Street*, *Dr. Finlay's Casebook*, and the like. 'Nothing in the history of the cinema', he shrewdly observed, 'provides an equivalent for this vicarious satisfaction of a metropolitan society, short on community feeling and community gossip.'[12]

Grierson wanted to see films made not *about* people but *with* people —the presentation of the local story by the local people. Even this, he suggested, was not enough, because you were making films with people and then going away again. He referred to an idea put forward by Zavattini that all the villages in Italy should be armed with cameras so that they could make films by themselves and write film letters to each other. It was supposed to be a great joke. 'I was the person who didn't laugh, because I think that *is* the next stage—not the villagers making

259

film letters and sending them to each other, but the local people making films to state their case politically or otherwise, to state their case whether it's in journalistic or other terms.'[13] He would have welcomed the programmes in which this has precisely happened in Britain, on both the B.B.C. and the independent channels.

To the end of his life, therefore, Grierson was looking ahead, restless and unsatisfied, believing that there were horizons towards which the art and practice of communication could still be pushed, radiating confidence that a better future for all mankind could be fashioned if only there were imagination enough to discern and foster the real growing points in each society and culture. He was still asking 'What's new?' He was a propagandist who believed to the end in social equality and individual freedom and in the possibility of a genuine internationalism. For these beliefs he worked all his stormy, embattled life.

Grierson was a private man. He said the known person was no damn good. He thought this idea was well expressed by Arthur Miller at the end of *View from the Bridge*: 'The tragedy was that he wanted to be fully known.'[14] He considered that appreciation of another man's privacy was something that was very vital to life. He certainly acted on his belief. Yet in this, as in so much else, there was a contradiction that was characteristic of him (although doubtless he would have explained it). 'I talk to everybody I meet', he said; and he did, wherever he was: to taxi-men and chambermaids, cabinet ministers and ambassadors. He could maintain a flow of conversation that was, by sentences, persuasive and commanding, caustic and charming, convincing and alarming. He was unpredictable. As someone said, he could drip contempt while beaming good humour. There was something almost demoniac about the way he could worm his way into your life and make himself an integral part of your being. Once there he remained, like a grumbling conscience. His own privacy was inviolable. He seemed unaware of the paradox, and unbothered by it.

Despite his crusty exterior and caustic wit, Grierson was a lovable man. He inspired loyalty and earned affection wherever he went. When he joined a group there was an immediate acceleration in tempo, a sense of sharpened observation, an expectancy of revealing comment, a sudden burst of laughter as a humorous shaft found its target. The days were brighter when he was around—and certainly longer. One of his friends said that he lived two lives, because he never slept. The source of energy for such double exposure remained a mystery.

Margaret was the quiet centre of his life. She was there waiting for him on his return from the journeying which he found essential if he was to have the stimulus he needed. He was away from his home for longer periods than he was in it, although he enjoyed life in his Wiltshire retreat and the companionship there until his death of Joe Golightly, with whom he and Margaret had a deep, natural understanding. Whenever he had the time he wrote long letters to his friends. Among his most regular and appreciated correspondents were Margaret Ann Elton and Mary Ferguson, wife of George Ferguson, his staunchest supporter in Canada's newspaper world.

Grierson enjoyed the company of women. He counted among his friends Iris Barry, one of the founders of the Film Society in London and later curator of the Museum of Modern Art Film Library in New York; Mary Losey (Field) who worked with him in New York where she helped to prepare the American edition of *Grierson on Documentary*; Lotte Reiniger who joined him at the G.P.O. Film Unit to make her silhouette films, *Tocher* and *The King's Breakfast*; and Leni Riefenstahl from whose shoe he is said to have once drunk champagne at a party at the French Club in London. Not all women found him irresistible. When he was visiting a studio set Gloria Swanson said: 'There's a man here whose eyes are hurting me. Throw him out.'[15]

Of the many who wrote about Grierson after his death I think Irving Jacoby came nearest to expressing the complex character of the man and the contradictions that were part of his personality. 'By temperament he was a Calvinist preacher and he actually spoke from the pulpit in his student days at Glasgow University. By training he was a political scientist and operated within that discipline his entire life. By disposition he was an intellectual elf, with a twinkle in his eye, a joy in mischief and an enormous appetite for bombarding complacency and shocking it out of its easy chair.

'He played at being a film pundit, a political thinker, a social gambler, a tough journalist. He would sometimes think of himself as a show-biz character, or a modern radical philosopher, or a Jew or a member of the Mafia; but behind all the disguises there remained a clever Scotsman who could tie an effective trout fly, dance a reel, tell hilarious stories about the Scottish soldier and his gal. And a man who thought he could make a better world by applying principles of political science to real problems, by changing the pattern of thoughts and feelings of the electorate.

'He was a revolutionary, but his bombs were verbal and visual. He was an innovator, but his inventions were based on his solid knowledge of Greek classical writing. He was an annoying gadfly but his stings were sharpened by the failures of what his victims wanted to do or to be, not by what he wanted them to be. Like other Protestant ministers before him, he enraged his congregation by simply holding a mirror up so that they could see themselves. In their words, he bore witness. In my words, he was one of the few serious men I ever knew, politically mature, generous, full of humour and warmth, and to his dying day a man trying to make this a better world for people to live in.'[16]

In his *Grierson on Documentary* postscript he said the documentary movement had been greatly fortunate in its men and in its friends. 'We have held together as no independent movement in art has done in our generation: across the years and across the distances, physical and psychological, which separate nations. I could say it was the idea that held us, for it has at its core the secret of the co-operative spirit and no consciousness of boundaries to the common interest of mankind; but I have also the best reason to know how unselfish men can be.'

One other memory of Grierson and I will have done. Knowing his deep and continuing interest in painting, I asked him to review a film on Picasso for a radio programme on the arts I was chairing. 'I found it one of the great privileges of my life', he began, 'to be present with Picasso drawing and painting *ad infinitum*. To see a great master at work—to see his mind move—is surely a compensation for all the mediocrity of life—and one's own in particular.' There are many throughout the world who had the privilege of seeing Grierson at work and value the experience highly. If this biography has helped others to understand how his mind moved I feel it will have served its purpose.

Acknowledgements

On a number of occasions during his life, and especially after the publication in 1947 of the first edition of *Grierson on Documentary*, John Grierson would send me copies of speeches he had made or articles he had written. The inference was that I should keep the record and that a biography might emerge, although there was no formal understanding. He declined an invitation to write an autobiography. After his death Margaret Grierson accepted my offer to write a biography and was encouraged to do so by Basil Wright. I am grateful to her for the confidence she placed in me. She made available to me all his surviving papers and gave me information which I could have obtained from no other source. Eventually she read the biography in manuscript and made helpful suggestions. It could not have been written without her understanding and generous assistance.

Apart from his occasional dispatches to me Grierson did not bother to keep what he called his 'stuff' and there were many blanks in the record, some created when he had a bonfire of his papers at Tog Hill. These blanks I sought to fill by interviewing his friends and colleagues, in Britain, North America and France, and by correspondence with those who knew him well in other countries. I am grateful to all who gave me of their time. Their recorded comments and recollections would fill many volumes. I have indicated specific sources by acknowledgement in the text; but no less valuable was the general impression left by conversations with so many whose lives had been affected by him.

In Canada the film commissioner, André Lamy, gave me the informed services at the National Film Board of Roger Blais, producer of their documentary, *Grierson*, who both supplied information from his files and co-ordinated arrangements for interviews in Montreal, Ottawa, Toronto, Chicago and New York. I am grateful to him for his practical assistance and his kindness inside and outside his office. In New York I was able to complete a formidable programme of interview visits largely through the help of Content Cowan, formerly of Time-Life, who transported me confidently through the metropolitan maze, and beyond.

Acknowledgements

In Los Angeles research was undertaken for me by my friend Walter Evans. The librarian at the Margaret Herrick Library of the Academy of Motion Picture Arts and Sciences alerted him about the existence of the Grierson-Strauss correspondence which had been deposited by Mordecai Gorelick in the Humanities Research Center, The University of Texas at Austin. The Center kindly supplied copies of the letters which, by agreement, are now in the Grierson Archive at Stirling University. I am grateful to the Center for permission to quote from the correspondence.

In Britain I was able to have a number of conversations with Grierson's closest colleagues of the 1930s and, in Paris, with Alberto Cavalcanti. Lady Elton kindly made available to me the files on documentary kept at Clevedon Court. John Taylor and Edgar Anstey read the manuscript and Stuart Legg the chapters on Canada and the United States. The early chapters were read by Grierson's sisters, Dorothy McLaren and Marion Taylor, and by Dr. J. R. Peddie, adviser on studies at Glasgow University during Grierson's student years. I am grateful to them for the helpful suggestions they made. In addition to talking to Paul Rotha I have had the benefit of familiarity with his books on documentary, invaluable for anyone writing on the subject.

I wish to record my gratitude to the Scottish Arts Council whose Literature Panel made a grant to assist in my travel. When tapes were removed from my luggage at Mirabel airport in Montreal, British Airways kindly made possible a return visit to make good the loss.

Many of the illustrations have been supplied by Margaret Grierson and these, with all the other Grierson papers, are now in the Grierson Archive at Stirling University.

Notes

Chapter 1: Growing Up by the Gillies Hill (between pages 11 and 17)

1   John Grierson, *This Wonderful World*, 27 December 1957.
2   Letter to John Grierson from J. Brown Strang, President, Oregon Committee, The British War Relief Society Inc. of the United States of America, 19 May 1944.
3   John Grierson, 'Every Man His Own Stevenson', *Scotland*, November 1950.
4   John Grierson, letter to Anthony Grierson from Sarasota, Florida, June 1942.
5   John Grierson, 'When is a Highlandman?', Council of Scottish Clan Societies, 8 September 1962.
6   Ibid.
7   John Grierson, 'Stirling's Heritage', *Scotland*, February 1949.
8   John Grierson, letter to John Amess, 29 November 1967.
9   John Grierson, 'My Father Was a Teacher', *The Land*, Vol. II, No. 3, 1942–3.
10 John Grierson, 'The Film at War', broadcast from Ottawa, 30 November 1940.

Chapter 2: Able Seaman to Clydeside Radical (between pages 18 and 30)

1   John Grierson, 'When is a Highlandman?', Council of Scottish Clan Societies, 8 September 1962.
2   John Grierson, *This Wonderful World*, 29 January 1959.
3   Ministry of Defence, letters to author, 6 December 1976 and 13 January 1977.
4   John Grierson, *This Wonderful World*, 12 October 1960.
5   John Grierson, letter to Frances Strauss, 7 September 1927.
6   John Grierson, 'When is a Highlandman?', Council of Scottish Clan Societies, 8 September 1962.
7   John Grierson, 'Notes for a Film on the Highlands', *Scottish Bookman*, February 1936. Grierson made a tour of the Hebrides in the winter of 1935–6 with Cavalcanti and Basil Wright. 'Cavalcanti was to give an alien's view of all he read. Wright was to keep our academic conscience clear by reading—as he generally does—everything. We went by Glencoe and Ardgour, by Mallaig, by Portree round Skye, by Tarbert and round Harris. If the journey was hurried, it was only, as one must in preparation of any film project, that we might breathe again "the air of the place".' The notes were written for Heloïse Russell-Ferguson.

Notes

8 John Grierson, 'Background for the Use of Films by Rehabilitation Officers', 15 February 1945.
9 John Grierson, *Sunday Post*, 4 December 1966.
10 John Grierson, 'Background for the Use of Films by Rehabilitation Officers, 15 February 1945.
11 Rev. J. C. M. Conn, M.A., Ph.D., letter to author, 10 December 1972.
12 Rt. Hon. Thomas Johnston, *Memories* (Collins, London 1952), pp. 41–2.
13 John Grierson, 'Background for the Use of Films by Rehabilitation Officers', 15 February 1945.
14 Charles H. Dand, letter to Jack C. Ellis, June 1967.
15 Alan Adamson, interview with author, Montreal, 21 June 1976.
16 John Grierson, preface to *Documentary Film* by Paul Rotha, Richard Griffith and Sinclair Road (Faber and Faber, London 1952), pp. 22–3.
17 John Grierson, Postscript, *Grierson on Documentary*, edited by Forsyth Hardy (Faber and Faber, London 1966), p. 395.
18 Charles A. Oakley, interview with author, Edinburgh, October 1976.
19 Rev. J. C. M. Conn, M.A., Ph.D., letter to author, 10 December 1972.
20 Charles H. Dand, letter to author, 24 August 1976.
21 William H. Law, letter to author, 28 May 1947.
22 John Grierson, address at Canadian-Soviet Friendship Congress, Toronto, November 1943.
23 John Grierson, 'Pygmalion', *Glasgow University Magazine*, Vol. 33, No. 4, 14 December 1921.
24 John Grierson, 'Pay Day', *Glasgow University Magazine*, Vol. 36, No. 8, 21 February 1923.
25 Charles H. Dand, letter to author, 24 August 1976.
26 Ibid.
27 James Dickinson, interview with author, July 1977.
28 John Skeaping, R.A., *Drawn from Life* (Collins, London 1977), pp. 67–8.

Chapter 3: Chicago, Hollywood, New York (between pages 31 and 43)

1 John Marshall, interview with author, Wilton, Connecticut, 12 March 1976.
2 John Grierson, *Today's Revolutions in the Arts*, North Carolina, April 1962.
3 Gordon Weisenborn, interview with author, Chicago, 7 March 1976.
4 John Grierson, *Today's Revolutions in the Arts*, North Carolina, April 1962.
5 Ibid.
6 John Grierson, letter to Professor W. L. Renwick, 22 December 1925.
7 John Grierson, 'Propaganda and Education', an address before the Winnipeg Canadian Club, October 1943.
8 Rockefeller Archive Center.
9 John Grierson, 'A Mind for the Future', St. Andrew's Day Address, B.B.C.-Scotland, 30 November 1962.

Notes

10 John Grierson, 'Of Whistler and a Light that Failed', *Chicago Evening Post.*

11 John Grierson, letter to Professor Renwick, 22 December 1925.

12 John Grierson, letter in *The Times*, 21 November 1968.

13 John Grierson, *Motion Picture News*. The articles were published between 20 November and 18 December 1926.

14 John Grierson, address at the 14th Annual Awards Ceremony, Academy of Motion Picture Arts and Sciences, Biltmore Hotel, Hollywood, 26 February 1942.

15 Donald Ogden Stewart, *By a Stroke of Luck!* (Paddington Press, New York 1975), p. 138.

16 Ibid., p. 153.

17 John Grierson, 'Von Sternberg—and Joe', *Everyman*, 14 April 1932.

18 John Grierson, address to Paramount Theatre Managers School, reported in *Exhibitors Herald*, 26 September 1925.

19 John Grierson, '*The Circus*', New York *Sun*.

20 John Grierson, 'Personal Memories of the Early Russian Cinema', D.D.R. Film Archive, 1967.

21 John Grierson, 'Tribute to Eisenstein', London, 2 May 1948.

22 Frances Hubbard Flaherty, *The Odyssey of a Film-maker* (Beta Phi Mu, Urband, Illinois 1960).

23 Ibid.

24 John Grierson, '*Moana*', New York *Sun*, 8 February 1926.

25 John Grierson, 'First Principles of Documentary', *Cinema Quarterly*, Winter 1932.

26 John Grierson, letter to Professor Renwick, 22 December 1925.

Chapter 4: 'Drifters' (between pages 44 and 56)

1 Robert Nichols, 'Why Don't We Get Better Pictures?' *The Times*, 5 September 1925.

2 Sir Stephen Tallents, unpublished manuscript.

3 John Grierson, 'Propaganda', *Sight and Sound*, Vol. II, No. 8.

4 Ibid.

5 John Grierson, letter to Frances Strauss, 10 October 1927.

6 John Grierson, letter to Frances Strauss, 16 October 1927.

7 John Grierson, letter to Frances Strauss, 21 October 1927.

8 Lewis Jacobs, letter to author, 4 August 1977.

9 John Grierson, letter to Frances Strauss, 6 August 1927.

10 John Grierson, letter to Frances Strauss, 2 July 1927.

11 John Grierson, letter to Frances Strauss, 12 July 1927.

12 John Grierson, letter to Frances Strauss, 16 November 1927.

13 Sir Stephen Tallents, unpublished manuscript.

14 John Grierson, letter to Frances Strauss, 21 February 1928.

15 Charles H. Dand, interview with author, Eastbourne, 5 October 1976.

16 John Grierson, letter to Frances Strauss, 21 February 1928.

17 John Grierson, 'Making a Film of the Sea', *World Today*, Vol. 55, March 1930.

18 John Grierson, ibid.

19 John Grierson, ibid.

20 Charles H. Dand, interview with author, Eastbourne, 5 October 1976.
21 J. R. Watson, interview with author, Glasgow, June 1973.
22 Charles H. Dand, interview with author, Eastbourne, 5 October 1976.
23 Margaret Grierson, interview with author, Calstone.
24 John Grierson, 'Personal Memories of the Early Russian Cinema', D.D.R. Film Archive, 1967.
25 Robert Herring, 'The Movies', *Life and Letters Today*, December 1929.
26 Sir Stephen Tallents, unpublished manuscript.

Chapter 5: The Documentary Movement (between pages 57 and 71)

1 Basil Wright, interview with author, Frieth.
2 John Grierson, 'The Story of the Documentary Film', *Fortnightly Review*, August 1939.
3 Sir Stephen Tallents, unpublished manuscript.
4 Caroline Lejeune, *Observer*, 18 March 1945.
5 Warren Nolan, *New York Telegram*, 8 February 1930.
6 Caroline Lejeune, *Observer*, 12 June 1931.
7 Trevor Lloyd, interview with Raleigh Parkin, Montreal, 2 March 1972.
8 John Grierson, letter to Sir Stephen Tallents, 5 February 1931.
9 Sir Stephen Tallents, unpublished manuscript.
10 Basil Wright, interview with author, Frieth.
11 John Taylor, letter to author, 24 October 1977.
12 John Grierson, review of *The Innocent Eye* by Arthur Calder-Marshall (W. H. Allen, London 1963) in *Spectator*, 28 June 1963.
13 John Grierson, 'First Principles of Documentary', *Cinema Quarterly*, Winter 1932.
14 John Grierson, 'Flaherty', *Cinema Quarterly*, Autumn 1932.
15 John Taylor, letter to author, 24 October 1977.
16 John Grierson, review of *The Innocent Eye*, op. cit.
17 John Grierson, letter to author, 2 January 1936.
18 Caroline Lejeune, 'The Documentary Fetish', *Observer*, 11 August 1932.
19 Edgar Anstey, interview with author, 7 October 1976.
20 John Grierson, *This Wonderful World*.
21 John Grierson, 'The Story of the Documentary Film', *Fortnightly Review*, August 1939.
22 Paul Rotha, 'Some Principles of Documentary', *Documentary Film* by Paul Rotha, Sinclair Road and Richard Griffith (Faber and Faber, London 1952).
23 Sir Stephen Tallents, unpublished manuscript.
24 John Grierson, 'The Story of the Documentary Film', op. cit.

Chapter 6: G.P.O. Film Unit (between pages 72 and 91)

1 Paul Rotha, *Documentary Diary* (Secker & Warburg, London 1973), p. 117.
2 Ibid., p. 122.
3 Alberto Cavalcanti, interview with author, Paris, February 1976.

Notes

4 Herbert Read, 'Experiments in Counterpoint', *Cinema Quarterly*, Autumn 1934.

5 Harry Watt, *Don't Look at the Camera*, (Elek, London 1974), pp. 65–6.

6 Paul Rotha, letter from Benjamin Britten, 15 July 1970.

7 George Orwell, *Inside the Whale*, 1940, p. 559.

8 Basil Wright, interview with author, Frieth.

9 Basil Wright, 'Filming in Ceylon', *Cinema Quarterly*, Summer 1934.

10 Arthur Calder-Marshall, *The Mind in Chains*, edited by C. Day Lewis (Muller, London 1937).

11 Arthur Calder-Marshall, *The Changing Scene* (Chapman & Hall, London 1937).

12 John Grierson, 'Films of Fact', *The Times*, 23 November 1935.

13 John Grierson, letter to author, 4 February 1936.

14 J. B. Priestley, *Rain Upon Godshill*, (Heinemann, London 1939).

15 Harry Watt, *Don't Look at the Camera* (Elek, London 1974), p. 101.

16 Alberto Cavalcanti, interview, *Screen* (Society for Education in Film and Television, London), Summer 1972.

17 Paul Rotha, letter to author, 17 June 1938.

18 Sir William Coldstream, 'John Grierson', *Journal of the Society of Film and Television Arts*, Vol. 2, Nos. 4–5, 1972.

19 Norman McLaren, interview with author, Montreal, 29 February 1976.

20 Edgar Anstey, letter to author, 8 November 1977.

21 Harry Watt, *Don't Look at the Camera* (Elek, London 1974), p. 78.

22 Basil Wright, *The Rise and Fall of British Documentary* by Elizabeth Sussex (University of California Press, Berkeley 1975), p. 91.

23 Paul Rotha, ibid., p. 90.

24 Lord Ritchie-Calder, 'Scottish Testament', *World Film News*, November 1938.

25 John Grierson, 'Censorship and the Documentary', *World Film News*, November 1938.

26 Arthur and Phyllis Cain, interview with author, London, 7 December 1976.

27 Lord Ritchie-Calder, 'European Citizen of the World', *Journal of the Society of Film and Television Arts*, Vol. 2, Nos. 4–5, 1972.

28 Brooke Crutchley, manuscript note to *The Times*, March 1973.

29 Lord Ritchie-Calder, 'European Citizen of the World', op. cit.

30 John Grierson, 'Films and the I.L.O.', an address before the International Labour Organisation, Philadelphia, 26 April 1944.

31 Ross McLean, interview with author, Ottawa, 3 March 1976.

32 John Grierson, 'At the Bottom of the Garden', *Scotland*, November 1957.

33 Harry Watt, *Don't Look at the Camera* (Elek, London 1974), p. 96.

Chapter 7: Canada, Australia, New Zealand (between pages 92 and 108)

1 Raleigh Parkin, interview with author, Montreal, 29 February 1976.

2 Mary Ferguson, interview with author, Montreal, 29 February 1976.

3 John Grierson, 'Report on Canadian Government Film Activities', August 1938.

Notes

4 John Grierson, manuscript article.
5 John Grierson, letter to W. D. Euler, Minister of Trade and Commerce.
6 John Grierson, 'Report on Canadian Government Film Activities', August 1938.
7 Herbert Kline, interview with author, Edinburgh, August 1975.
8 Paul Rotha, *Documentary Film* (Faber and Faber, London 1952), p. 324.
9 Jiri Weiss, letter to author, 13 April 1976.
10 John Grierson, letter to Sir Stephen Tallents.
11 John Grierson, address to Academy of Motion Picture Arts and Sciences, Hollywood, 13 September 1939.
12 John Grierson, letter to Sir Stephen Tallents, 10 September 1939.
13 John Grierson, letter to Sir Stephen Tallents, 9 November 1939.
14 George Ferguson, interview with author, Montreal, 29 February 1976.
15 Ross McLean, interview with author, Ottawa, 2 March 1976.
16 John Grierson, letter to Sir Stephen Tallents, 9 November 1939.
17 John Grierson, letter to Raleigh Parkin.
18 John Grierson, letter to Basil Wright, 24 March 1940.
19 John Grierson, report to Tourist Department, New Zealand Government.
20 John Grierson, letter to Basil Wright, 24 March 1940.
21 John Grierson, ibid.
22 John Grierson, letter to Basil Wright, 20 April 1940.
23 John Grierson, ibid.
24 Stanley Hawes, 'Grierson and Australia', *Journal of the Society of Film and Television Arts*, Vol. 2, Nos. 4–5, 1972.
25 Stanley Hawes, ibid.

Chapter 8: By the Ottawa River (between pages 109 and 127)

1 David Copland, interview with author, Toronto, 6 March 1976.
2 Stuart Legg, interview with author, Calstone, 11 August 1976.
3 Janet Scellen (Bull), letter to author, 25 March 1976.
4 John Grierson, letter to James A. Mackinnon, Chairman, National Film Board of Canada, 27 November 1940.
5 L. W. Brockington, memo to Prime Minister, 2 December 1940.
6 John Grierson, letter to Basil Wright, December 1940.
7 *Winnipeg Free Press*, 'Why Lose a Genius?', 18 December 1940.
8 *Le Droit*, 13 December 1940.
9 John Grierson, letter to Basil Wright.
10 Sir Arthur Elton, letter to John Grierson, 4 May 1940.
11 Sir Arthur Elton, letter to John Grierson, 14 July 1940.
12 Paul Rotha, letter to John Grierson, 27 August 1940.
13 *Documentary News Letter*, 'Ruby Grierson', October 1940.
14 John Grierson, letter to John Marshall, 7 October 1940.
15 Walter Turnbull, interview with author, Ottawa, 4 March 1976.
16 Tom Daly, interview with author, Montreal, 25 February 1976.
17 Stanley Jackson, interview with author, Montreal, 25 February 1976.
18 Norman McLaren, interview with author, Montreal, 29 February 1976.

Notes

19 Julian Roffman, interview with author, New York, 13 March 1976.
20 Boris Kaufman, interview with author, New York, 9 March 1976.
21 George L. George, interview with author, New York, 10 March 1976.
22 James Beveridge, 'Grierson and Canada', *Journal of the Society of Film and Television Arts*, Vol. 2, Nos. 4–5, 1972.
23 Sydney Newman, interview with author, Ottawa, 1 March 1976.
24 Graham McInnes, unpublished manuscript, deposited at National Film Board of Canada, Montreal. McInnes was later Canadian representative at UNESCO in Paris with ambassadorial rank. Books on his childhood in Australia include *The Road to Gundegai*.
25 John Grierson, letter to John C. Cairns, Professor of History, University of Toronto, 16 February 1966.
26 Lou Applebaum, interview with author, Montreal, 27 February 1976.
27 Eugene Kash, interview with author, Toronto, 5 March 1976.
28 George Ferguson, interview with author, Montreal, 29 February 1976.
29 Beth Bertram, interview with author, Toronto, 5 March 1976.
30 Lady Elton, interview with author, Clevedon Court.
31 Helen Watson (Gordon), interview with John Grierson, Calcutta, 31 May 1971.
32 Marion Meadows, interview with author, Montreal, 26 February 1976.
33 Alan Adamson, interview with author, Montreal, 21 June 1976.
34 Elspeth Chisholm, interview with John Grierson, Montreal, 1968.
35 Wesley Greene, interview with author, Chicago, 8 March 1976.
36 John Grierson, 'A Film Policy for Canada', *Canadian Affairs*, Vol. 1, No. 11.
37 John Grierson, letter to Basil Wright, 8 October 1941.
38 John Grierson, ibid.
39 Alan Adamson, interview with author, Montreal, 21 June 1976.
40 John Grierson, speech at the fourteenth annual awards banquet of the Academy of Motion Picture Arts and Sciences, Biltmore Hotel, Hollywood, 26 February 1942.
41 Gordon Weisenborn, interview with author, Chicago, 7 March 1976.
42 Julian Roffman, interview with author, New York, 13 March 1976.
43 John Grierson, letter to Sir Stephen Tallents, 5 June 1942.
44 John Grierson, letter to Anthony Grierson, June 1942.
45 John Grierson, 'Eyes of Democracy', unpublished manuscript.
46 John Grierson, letter to Sir Stephen Tallents, 5 June 1942.

Chapter 9: Canadian Summit (between pages 128 and 149)

1 Irving Jacoby, interview with author, Wilton, Connecticut, 12 March 1976.
2 Alan Field, 'The Unsung Hero of Filmland', *Ottawa Citizen*, 8 September 1972.
3 Sir Stephen Tallents, letter to John Grierson, 1 February 1943.
4 John Grierson, letter to Sir Stephen Tallents, 16 February 1943.
5 John Grierson, letter to Sir Stephen Tallents, 14 July 1943.
6 John Grierson, letter to Duncan McLaren, 12 March 1943.
7 Dunton Davidson, interview with author, Ottawa, 2 March 1976.

8 Trevor Lloyd, interview with Raleigh Parkin, Montreal, 2 March 1972.
9 John Grierson, letter to L. R. LaFleche, Chairman of the National Film Board, 10 January 1944.
10 Basil Wright, letter to author, 18 July 1977.
11 James Thomson, letter to John Grierson, 8 October 1943.
12 Ron Dick, interview with author, Montreal, 19 June 1976.
13 Paul Thériault, interview with author, Ottawa, 2 March 1976.
14 Alan Adamson, letter to author, 9 September 1977.
15 John Grierson, C.B.C. talk, 20 August 1944.
16 John Grierson, 'Grierson Asks for a Common Plan', *Documentary News Letter*, Vol. 5, No. 5.
17 John Grierson, letter to George Ferguson, 3 April 1944.
18 John Grierson, letter to J. P. R. Golightly, 27 December 1944.
19 John Grierson, letter to William Lyon Mackenzie King, Prime Minister, 10 August 1945.

Chapter 10: A Dream Crumbles (between pages 150 and 163)

1 John Grierson, letter to Sir Stephen Tallents, 19 September 1945.
2 John Grierson, letter to Charles G. Cowan, Ottawa, October 1945.
3 John Grierson, letter to Brooke Claxton, Chairman of the National Film Board of Canada, 12 November 1945.
4 John Grierson, 'Notes on the Government's Film Activities', 5 January 1946.
5 John Grierson, 'Notes on the National Film Board of Canada,' 12 November 1945.
6 Gordon Weisenborn, interview with author, Chicago, 7 March 1976.
7 John Grierson, letter to author, 27 September 1946.
8 Beth Bertram, interview with author, Toronto, 5 March 1976.
9 Report of the Royal Commission. The extracts are taken from the reports of the Taschereau-Kellock Commission on Espionage in Government Service, Ottawa, 1946.
10 John Grierson. Grierson prepared a note, 'Thoughts on the Causes of the Present Discontent', which appeared to be addressed to the Canadian Government. It is not clear from his papers what happened to it.
11 George Ferguson. George Ferguson was in New York where he took John and Margaret Grierson to see *The Iceman Cometh*. Grierson, who arrived at the interval, told them that 'the State Department was after him'. They did not go back to the show but got drunk instead and talked until two in the morning, trying to figure out what to do next, if anything.
12 Mary Losey (Field), interview with author, New York, 10 March 1976.
13 Raleigh Parkin, recorded conversation between Louise and Raleigh Parkin, Montreal, 29 February 1972.
14 Gordon Weisenborn, interview with author, Chicago, 7 March 1976.
15 Mary Losey (Field), interview with author, New York, 10 March 1976.
16 William Farr, interview with author, Paris, 2 February 1976.
17 *Film Daily*, 17 February 1947. A similar report appeared in the *Daily*

Telegraph on 22 February 1947. It quoted Grierson as saying in Paris: 'I am not a Communist, and any inference of this kind is ridiculous.'
18 Mary Losey (Field), 'Grierson in New York', *Journal of the Society of Film and Television Arts*, Vol. 2, Nos. 4–5, 1972.

Chapter 11: Paris, London, Africa (between pages 164 and 179)

1 William Farr. Much of the information in this chapter is based on interviews with William Farr in Paris in February 1976.
2 Sandy Koffler, interview with author, Paris, February 1976.
3 Bernard Sendall, interview with author, London, 8 December 1976.
4 John Grierson, letter to Sir Julian Huxley, 14 September 1947.
5 John Grierson, ibid.
6 William Farr, interview with author, Paris, February 1976.
7 John Grierson, letter to Sir Robert Fraser, Director-General, Central Office of Information, 17 February 1948.
8 Charles Dand, interview with author, Eastbourne, 5 October 1976.
9 John Maddison, interview with author, Windlesham, 6 October 1976.
10 Lothar Wolff, interview with author, New York, 9 March 1976.
11 John Grierson, review of *The Heart of Africa* by Alexander Campbell (Longmans, London 1955), *Scotland*, February 1955.
12 John Grierson, 'Hogmanay—An Empty Celebration?', *T.V. Times*, 25 December 1959.
13 G. Buckland-Smith, letter to author, 11 October 1976.
14 John Maddison, interview with author, Windlesham, 6 October 1976.
15 Charles Dand, interview with author, Eastbourne, 5 October 1976.

Chapter 12: 'The Brave Don't Cry' (between pages 180 and 190)

1 James H. Lawrie, letter to *The Times*, 7 March 1972.
2 James H. Lawrie, interview with author, London, February 1972.
3 Bosley Crowther, '*The Brave Don't Cry*', *New York Times*, 6 November 1952.
4 *The Times*, '*The Oracle*', 14 May 1953.
5 John Grierson, letter to Stuart Legg, 25 May 1953.
6 John Grierson, letter to Secretary, Brompton Hospital, 29 May 1953.
7 John Grierson, *This Wonderful World*, 24 August 1961.
8 Sir Michael Balcon, letter to John Grierson, 11 August 1953.
9 Dilys Powell, '*Devil on Horseback*', *Sunday Times*, 21 March 1954.
10 Stuart Legg, letter to John Grierson, 23 June 1953.
11 Sir Michael Balcon, interview with author, Hartford, 10 December 1976.
12 James H. Lawrie, interview with author, February 1972.
13 Bernard Coote, interview with author, London, 7 October 1976.
14 Sir Michael Balcon, interview with author, Hartford, 10 December 1976.
15 Cyril Frankel, letter to author, 15 May 1974.
16 David Kingsley, address to A.C.T. annual general meeting, reported in *Films and Filming*, August 1955.

Notes

Chapter 13: The Heart is Highland (between pages 191 and 203)

1   John Grierson, review of *Meeting at Night* by James Bridie (Constable, London 1957), *Scotland*, March 1957.
2   John Grierson, review of *Boswell in Search of a Wife* by James Boswell (Heinemann, London 1957), *Scotland*, September 1957.
3   John Grierson, review of *The High Girders* by John Prebble (Secker and Warburg, London 1956), *Scotland*, February 1957.
4   John Grierson, *Scotland*, May 1957.
5   John Grierson, *Scotland*, December 1949.
6   John Grierson, interview *Sunday Post*, 4 December 1966.
7   Mary Losey (Field), interview with author, New York, 10 March 1976.
8   John Grierson, letter to Dorothy Henderson, 11 March 1966.
9   John Grierson, letter to Lady Elton, 16 March 1957.
10 John Grierson, memorandum on National Film Board of Canada, 27 May 1957.

Chapter 14: 'This Wonderful World' (between pages 204 and 214)

1   John Grierson, *Sunday Mail*, 7 August 1949.
2   Lord Thomson of Fleet, 'Grierson at STV', *Journal of the Society of Film and Television Arts*, Vol. 2, Nos. 4–5, 1972.
3   John Grierson, *This Wonderful World*, 18 October 1957.
4   John Grierson, *This Wonderful World*, 25 October 1957.
5   John Grierson, *This Wonderful World*, 3 November 1958.
6   John Grierson, *This Wonderful World*, 3 January 1958.
7   John Grierson, *This Wonderful World*, 3 April 1958.
8   John Grierson, *This Wonderful World*, 28 September 1961.
9   John Grierson, *This Wonderful World*, 29 January 1959.
10 John Grierson, *This Wonderful World*, 16 December 1966.
11 John Grierson, *This Wonderful World*, 9 February 1959.
12 Dusan Makavejev, interview with author, Paris, February 1976.
13 John Grierson, *This Wonderful World*, 27 November 1958.
14 Lord Thomson of Fleet, 'Grierson at STV', *Journal of the Society of Film and Television Arts*, Vol. 2, Nos. 4–5, 1972.
15 Maurice Richardson, *Observer*, 21 September 1958.
16 Maurice Wiggin, *Sunday Times*, 15 February 1959.
17 Tom Driberg, *New Statesman*, 31 January 1959.
18 John Grierson, *TV Times*, 6 February 1959.
19 John Grierson, *TV Times*, 15 June 1962.
20 John Grierson, *Viewer*, 16 January 1965.

Chapter 15: Awards and Rewards (between pages 215 and 231)

1   John Grierson, letter to Edgar Anstey, O.B.E., 24 January 1969.
2   John Grierson, letter to George Ferguson, 23 February 1962.
3   Terry Sanford, letter from the Governor of North Carolina to John Grierson, 16 August 1962.

Notes

4 Richard Griffith, speech at Museum of Modern Art, New York, in introducing John Grierson, 25 April 1962.
5 Willard van Dyke, interview with author, New York, 13 March 1976.
6 Bosley Crowther, letter to Maggie Dent, 14 June 1962.
7 John Grierson, letter to Maggie Dent, 26 April 1962.
8 Pauline Kael, letter to author, 24 July 1977.
9 Sydney Newman, interview with author, Ottawa, 1 March 1976.
10 *Montreal Star*, 5 August 1964.
11 Tom Daly, interview with author, Montreal, 25 February 1976.
12 Sir Arthur Elton, letter to John Grierson, 12 December 1966.
13 John Chittock, *Financial Times*, 13 December 1966.
14 John Grierson, letter to Baroness Lee, 16 February 1966.
15 Grant McLean, letter to John Grierson, 18 October 1966.
16 Lester Pearson, letter from Prime Minister of Canada to John Grierson, 11 September 1967.
17 Sir Arthur Elton, letter to John Grierson, 29 September 1967.
18 Margaret Grierson, interview with author, Calstone.
19 John Grierson, letter to Francis Essex, 29 November 1967.
20 John Grierson, letter to Lady Elton, 28 September 1967.
21 Sir Alexander B. King, letter from the Chairman of the Films of Scotland Committee to John Grierson.
22 John Grierson, letter to Sir Alexander B. King, 24 May 1967.
23 Stephen Hearst, letter from Head of Arts Features, B.B.C., to John Grierson, 26 March 1968.
24 John Grierson, letter to Francis Essex, 9 August 1967.
25 John Grierson, letter to Francis Essex, 27 August 1968.
26 Pierre Juneau, interview with author, Ottawa, 3 March 1976.
27 John Grierson, letter to Henri Storck, 2 May 1968.
28 Guy Glover, 'Canada's Film-maker', *Montreal Star*, 26 April 1968.
29 John Grierson, opening of the Scottish Fisheries Museum, Anstruther, 4 July 1969.

Chapter 16: Return to Canada: Indian Summer (between pages 232 and 252)

1 Bram Chandler, letter to author, 25 October 1976.
2 Magnus Magnusson, interview with John Grierson, *Scotsman*, 13 January 1969.
3 Bram Chandler, letter to author, 25 October 1976.
4 John Grierson, letter to Lady Elton, 18 February 1969.
5 Ron Blumer, interview with author, Montreal, 24 February 1976.
6 Adam Symansky, interview with author, Montreal, 24 February 1976.
7 Eleanor Beattie, interview with author, Montreal, 24 February 1976.
8 Gary Evans, interview with author, Montreal, 24 February 1976.
9 John Grierson, 'Letter to Michelle', *A.I.D. News*, January 1971.
10 Donald Theall, 'Grierson as Teacher', *Journal of the Society of Film and Television Arts*, Vol. 2, Nos. 4–5, 1972.
11 Mary Ferguson, interview with author, Montreal, 29 February 1976.
12 Bob Anderson, interview with author, Ottawa, 2 March 1976.
13 Susan Schouten, interview with author, Montreal, 24 February 1976.

14 Pierre Juneau, interview with author, Ottawa, 3 March 1976.
15 André Martin, interview with author, Ottawa, 2 March 1976.
16 Rod Chiasson, interview with author, Ottawa, 2 March 1976.
17 Charles Benton, interview with author, Chicago, 8 March 1976.
18 Sydney Newman, interview with author, Ottawa, 1 March 1976.
19 Dusan Makavejev, interview with author, Paris, February 1976.
20 Marc Gervais, *Montreal Star*, 10 October 1970.
21 Harry Gulkin, interview with author, Montreal, 20 June 1976.
22 Bob Edmonds, interview with author, Chicago, 7 March 1976.
23 Maurice Yacowar, letter to author, 15 February 1973.
24 James Beveridge, 'Canadian Indian Summer of John Grierson', C.B.C. radio programme by Elspeth Chisholm, February 1976.
25 Elspeth Chisholm, ibid.
26 Rashmi Sharma, interview with author, Montreal, 28 February 1976.
27 Ken McCready, interview with author, Montreal, 27 February 1976.
28 V. B. Chandra, 'Dr. John Grierson in India', 31 December 1973.
29 'John Grierson: The Reluctant Guru', *Sunday Statesman*, New Delhi, 9 May 1971,
30 John Grierson, 'Memo to Michelle', *A.I.D. News*, November 1971.
31 Roger Blais, interview with author, Montreal, February 1976.
32 David Bairstow, interview with author, Montreal, 17 June 1976.
33 Charles Benton, interview with author, Chicago, 8 March 1976.
34 Sydney Newman, interview with author, Ottawa, 1 March 1976.
35 Rod Chiasson, interview with author, Ottawa, 2 March 1976.
36 John Grierson, letter to Lady Elton, 14 December 1971.
37 John Grierson, *Sunday Post*, 4 December 1966.

Chapter 17: The Right of the Prophet (between pages 253 and 262)

1 Bram Chandler, letter to author, 25 October 1976.
2 John Grierson, letter to Lady Elton, undated but in 1953.
3 Profile of John Grierson, *Observer*, 31 August 1947.
4 Guy Roberge, interview with author, Ottawa, 4 March 1976.
5 John Grierson, interview with Ronald Blumer, *Lower Canada Review of Arts and Politics*, 28 February 1972.
6 John Grierson, interview with Elizabeth Sussex, *Film Quarterly*, Fall 1972.
7 Edgar Anstey, letter to author, 14 November 1976.
8 John Grierson, letter (undated) to George Ferguson.
9 Alan Adamson, letter to author, 15 December 1976.
10 John Grierson, interview with Elizabeth Sussex, *Film Quarterly*, Fall 1972.
11 Angus Macdonald, address at opening of Grierson Archive, University of Stirling, 22 October 1972.
12 John Grierson, 'Why Cinema Still Leads Television', *Scotsman*, 10 June 1968.
13 John Grierson, interview with Elizabeth Sussex, *Film Quarterly*, Fall 1972.

Notes

14 John Grierson, interview with Ronald Blumer, *Lower Canada Review of Arts and Politics*, 28 February 1972.
15 Martin Knelman, *This is Where We Came In* (McClelland and Stewart, Toronto 1977), p. 13. Writing in *Everyman* on 3 March 1932, Grierson said: 'I met Swanson twice in the States: once being intelligent about *Potemkin*, before most people were intelligent about *Potemkin*; and another time when she near-hove me from the Uptown Studio in New York.'
16 Irving Jacoby, 'A Small Packet of Scottish Dynamite', *Sight Lines*, May–June 1972.

Index

Index

Index

Blok, 26
Blumer, Ronald, 235, 236, 249, 255
Blunt & McCormack, 53
Boddam, 11
Boggs, Lawrence S., 19
Bolivia, 210
Bolton, Laura, 119
Bombay, 247
Bond, Ralph, 88, 229
Boogie Doodle, 205
Borneman, Ernst, 138
Borrodaile, Osmond, 69
Bosch, Hieronymus, 133
Boston, 31
Boswell, James, 195
Boyer, Raymond, 155
Bracken, Brendan, 100, 124, 166
Brahms, 33
Brandy for the Parson, 181, 184, 187
Brave Don't Cry, The, 183, 187, 188
Bresky, Louis, 242
Bridie, James, *see* Mavor, O. H.
Brisbane, 106
Britain, 70, 87, 90, 94, 100, 167, 255, 257, 259, 263
British Airways, 264
British-American Bank Note Co., 93
British Broadcasting Corporation (B.B.C.), 18, 172, 184, 191, 196, 204, 218, 219, 226, 241, 260
British Columbia, 141, 142, 201
British Columbia, University of, 200
British Council, 87, 143
British Embassy, Washington, 100
British Empire, 44, 45, 47, 70, 100, 176
British Federation of Film Societies, 67
British Film Institute, 72, 73, 151, 199, 212, 221
British films, 90, 143
British Foreign Office, 173, 178, 192
British Government, 90, 151, 170, 176, 180
British Lion, 187
British Ministry of Agriculture, 68, 91
British Ministry of Education, 161, 172
British Ministry of Labour, 79
British Transport Films, 258
British Treasury, 49, 64, 88, 171, 175
Brittany, 142
Britten, Benjamin (Baron Britten of Aldeburgh in the County of Suffolk), 75, 76, 82, 105
Brockington, Leonard, 110, 146
Brock University, 243

Brompton Hospital, 185
Broonzy, Big Bill, 207
Brown, George, 245
Brown, Ivor, 195
Brown, John, 193
Brown, William, 213
Bruce, George, 196
Brunke, Bette, 119
Brussels, 173
Brussels Film Festival, 78, 80, 193, 209, 212
Brussels Treaty Organisation, 174
Bryan, Dora, 182
Buchan, John, 254
Buchanan, Andrew, 81
Buchanan, Donald, 18
Buchanan, Donald W., 89, 93, 114, 119, 121, 123
Buchanan, Meg, 183
Buckland-Smith, Gregory, 178, 179, 192
Buffalo, 34, 159
Bull fighting, 168, 194, 206
Bunny, John, 37
Burns, Robert, 210
Burwash, Gordon, 223
Bushman, Francis X., 37
Butt, Clara, 18
Byker, the, 29, 30
Byrne Edward, 182
Byron, Lord, 15, 25

Caen, 142
Cagney, James, 123
Cain, Arthur, 87, 88
Cain, Phyllis (Long), 88
Calcutta, 119, 247
Calder, Ritchie (Lord Ritchie-Calder), 87, 88, 161, 167, 204
Calder-Marshall, Arthur, 67, 80
Caldwell, M. J., 256
Calendar of the Year, 75
Calgary, 93, 94, 132
Callaghan, Morley, 115
Calmette, Albert, 175
Calne, 185, 192, 224
Calstone, 185
Calthrop, Donald, 65
Calvinism, 84, 261
Cambridge University, 30, 57, 58, 62, 74
Cambusbarron, 13, 14, 15, 16, 21, 182, 225
Cameo, Broadway, 46
Campbell, Alexander, 177

281

Index

282

Index

Index

Index

Empire Marketing Board, 44, 45, 46, 48, 49, 50, 53, 54, 57, 60, 62, 70, 71, 73, 127, 130, 147
E.M.B. Film Committee, 49, 54, 77
E.M.B. Film Unit, 58, 59, 60, 61, 63, 64, 65, 68, 69, 70, 89, 170, 189
Emporia, 32, 35
Emporia Gazette, 35
Encyclopaedia Britannica, 150, 240
End of St. Petersburg, The, 54
English Canada, 63, 129, 242
English Potter, The, 65
Enough to Eat?, 79, 86, 173
En Rade, 74
Erria, 149, 150
Eskimos, 240
Eskimo Village, 59
Essex, Francis, 225, 226
Euler, W. D., 90, 93, 95, 99, 101, 110
European Co-operation Administration, 175
Evans, Ernestine, 89
Evans, Gary, 236
Evans, Walter, 159, 264
Everyman, 60
Expo, 223, 245
Eyemouth, 197

Fabian Society, Glasgow University, 23, 27
Face of Scotland, The, 87
Fairbanks, Douglas, 36, 40
Falls of Shin, 59
Famous Players, 101, 102
Famous Players–Lasky, 36, 38
Farne Islands, 69
Farr, William, 161, 164, 165, 167, 169
Farrebique, 141, 166
Fauconberg, Lords of, 73
Feast of the Damned, 212
Federal Bureau of Investigation (F.B.I.), 160, 162
Ferguson, George, 93, 101, 115, 118, 158, 200, 215, 228, 238, 261
Ferguson, Howard, 93
Ferguson, Mary, 93, 238, 261
Ferno, John, 116, 189, 197
Feuerbach, Ludwig Andreas von, 138, 139
Fiddle-de-Dee, 166
Field, Alan, 117, 128
Field, Mary, 46, 81, 87
Field (Losey), Mary, 98, 153, 155, 158, 161, 162, 163, 197, 261

Fifth Avenue Playhouse, 46
Fight for Life, The, 208
Film and Its Techniques, 101
Film Centre, 84, 89
Film Society, London, 54, 62, 74, **261**
Film Till Now, The, 58
Films of Scotland Committee, 89, **191**, 192, 193, 194, 219, 225, 226, 229, **230**
Findhorn, 205
Firth of Forth, 70
Fitzgerald, Ella, 207
Fitzgibbons, J. J., 102
Flaherty, Frances, 63, 216
Flaherty, Robert, 41, 42, 63, 64, 65, 66, 67, 85, 124, 151, 163, 176, 179, 236
Flanagan, Aubrey, 55, 61
Flannans, 20
Flavell, Gilbert H., 19
Florence, 227
Florida, 125, 129, 186
Foldes, Peter, 240
Folkestone, 91
Food and Agricultural Organisation, 173
Food—Weapon of Conquest, 120
Football, 207
Forbes Fraser Hospital, 251
Ford, John, 124
Forestry Commission, 205
Forlong, Michael, 105
Forman, Sir Denis, 172, 189
Forster, Ralph, 108, 149, 150, 201, 219
Forsyte Saga, The, 184
Fortnightly, The, 90
Fortress Japan, 143
Fowle, Chick, 58, 76
France, 26, 46, 47, 62, 74, 83, 117, **124**, 142, 172, 173, 195, 263
Franco, General, 83
Franju, Georges, 227
Frankel, Cyril, 186, 189
Fraser, Donald, 93, 101, 109
Fraser, Gordon, 157
Fraser, Hugh (Lord Fraser of Allander), 191, 193
Fraser, Peter, 103
Fraser, Sir Robert, 166, 169, 170, 179
Free and Responsible Press, A, 136
Freedom of the Press, Commission **on**, 136, 148
French Canada, 63, 101, 109, 111, **129**, 130, 139, 223, 233
French Club (Le Petit Club Français), 213, 261
French, Sir Henry, 167

285

Index

French Revolution, 15
Fulchignoni, Enrico, 205
Funny Things Happen Down Under, 220

Gainsborough, 58
Gallacher, William, 229
Galloway, Lindsay, 183, 187, 259
Gandhi, Mrs. Indira, 247, 249
Garbo, Greta, 38, 61
Gas, Light and Coke Company, 79
Gaumont-British, 65, 81
General Post Office (G.P.O.), 71, 72, 80
G.P.O. Film Unit, 72–91, 170, 189, 258, 261
General Strike, The, 259
Geneva, 89, 168, 197
George V, 90
George, David Lloyd, 44, 56, 91
George, George L., 116
Georges V Hotel, 161
Georgia, 159
Germany, 39, 46, 47, 58, 96, 120, 128, 149, 178, 179
Gertler, Maynard, 158
Gervais, Marc, 242
Ghardaia, 227
Gibson, James, 243
Gilbert, Lewis, 182, 189
Gillies Hill, 13
Gilmorehill, 16, 23, 182
Glace Bay, 97
Glasgow, 23, 32, 43, 83, 86, 97, 209, 212, 214, 225, 228, 229, 234
Glasgow Citizens Theatre, 183
Glasgow, Film Society of, 62
Glasgow Herald, 26, 61, 198
Glasgow School of Art, 83
Glasgow University, 16, 21, 28, 29, 44, 53, 173, 182, 261, 264
Glasgow University Magazine, 26
Glenborrodale, 28
Glencoe, 14
Global Air Routes, 120, 143
Glover, Guy, 115, 139, 140, 153, 158, 216, 219, 228
Goebbels, 70, 239
Gold Coast, 57
Golden Legend of Schultz, The, 187
Golden Thistle Award, 230, 232
Golightly, J. P. R., 64, 65, 68, 89, 141, 142, 145, 185, 189, 261
Gorelick, Mordecai, 264
Gorno Marionettes, 53
Gouzenko, Igor, 154, 155

Goya, 133
Graham, Sir George, 212
Grampians, 13
Granada Television, 259
Grand Hotel, Glasgow, 228
Granta, 58
Granton, 69
Granton Trawler, 69, 226
Grass, 36, 46
Grassholm, 69
Grassmarket, 196
Grayson, Helen, 189
Great Adventure, The, 188
Greece, 22, 144
Greene, Lorne, 109
Greene, Wesley, 121
Greig, J. Y. T., 29
Grémillion, Jean, 141
Grier, Christopher, 196
Grierson, 263
Grierson, Agnes, 13, 16
Grierson, Anthony, 13, 28, 125, 185, 224, 225, 252
Grierson Archive, Stirling University, 259, 264
Grierson (McLaren), Dorothy, 13, 225, 264
Grierson (Anthony), Jane, 12, 16, 61, 91
Grierson, Janet, 13, 16
Grierson, John (aviator), 178
Grierson, John, birthplace, 11; parents, 11–12; schooling, 13–17; R.N.V.R., 18–21; University of Glasgow, 19–29; Armstrong College, 29–30; Rockefeller Foundation fellowship, U.S.A., 31–43; film reviewing, 39–41; first use of 'documentary', 42; Empire Marketing Board, 44–7; production of *Drifters*, 44–56; marriage to Margaret Taylor, 60; Robert Flaherty, 64–7; G.P.O. Film Unit, 72–88; Canadian film investigation, 92–6; National Film Act, Canada, 96; outbreak of war, 99; New Zealand visit, 103–5; Australian visit, 105–8; National Film Board of Canada, 112; Oscar for *Churchill's Island*, 123; manager of Wartime Information Board, Canada, 129; French Canada, 139–41; Brittany visit, 142; resignation as film commissioner, 147; The World Today, Inc., 152–62; Royal Commission on Espionage, 154–8; General Conference of UNESCO, Paris, 161; director

Index

287

Index

289

Index

Index

Manniskor i Stad, 166
Man of Africa, 186, 187, 188
Man of Aran, 193, 236
Manolete, 168, 207
Manor Hospital, Bath, 224
Maoris, 104
March, Fredric, 159
March of Time, The, 81, 86, 98, 101, 102, 120, 121, 161
Marden river, 185
Margaret Herrick Library, 264
Marianske Lazne, 175
Marine Biological Research Station, 52
Mariposa, 103, 108
Marsh, Jane, 119
Marshall Aid, 125
Marshall, John, 31, 113
Martin, André, 239
Marx Brothers, 53
Marx, Karl, 139, 156
Masaryk, Jan, 254
Masefield, John, 193
Mason, Herbert, 184
Mason, Richard, 85
Massey, Vincent, 89, 90, 92, 95
Massingham, Richard, 82
Mast, Ben, 216
Matisse, Henri, 35
Matson Line, 103
Mattogrosso, 210
Maud, Sir John (Lord Redcliffe Maud), 167
Mavor, O. H. (James Bridie), 27, 159, 182, 194, 195
Mavor, Ronald, 196
Maxton, James, 24, 29, 229
Mayakovsky, 26
Mayer, Peter, 96
Mbyu, Peter, 178
Meadows, Marion, 119
Medwin, Michael, 184
Méliès, George, 66
Merriam, Charles E., 31, 34, 136
Merrick Square, 60, 65, 91
Merseyside Film Society, 212
Mesta, Pearl, 174
Metro-Goldwyn-Mayer, 116
Mexico, 111, 194
Mexico City, 111, 167, 196, 206
Meyer, Arthur, 158
Michelangelo, 207
Michelle, Marion, 228
Midsummer Night's Dream, A, 15
Mid-West Conference, 243

Military Intelligence (M.I.5), 255
Miller, Arthur, 260
Ministry of Information, London, 100, 112, 113, 120, 122, 126, 136, 143, 152, 166, 171
Minney, R. J., 182
Mirabel Airport, 264
Miramar Studios, 104
Mirans, Roger, 220
Miss Robin Hood, 184
Mitchison, Naomi, 187
Mix, Tom, 53
Moana, 36, 42, 46, 47, 63, 259
Moe, Henry, 98
Moholy-Nagy, 84
Monachs, 20
Monet, 90
Montagu, Ivor, 54, 83
Monterey, 105
Montevideo, 210, 211
Montreal, 92, 111, 141, 155, 201, 215, 219, 222, 223, 224, 244, 245, 246, 249, 250, 253, 263
Montreal Film Festival, 227
Montreal Standard, 92, 132
Montreal Star, 158, 219, 220, 228
Montreal University, 232
Mont St. Michel, 143
Mony a Pickle, 83
Moray Firth, 205
More, Kenneth, 182
Morison, Sir Theodore, 30
Moscow, 40, 88, 155
Moses, 255
Mother, 54
Motion Picture News, 36, 40, 222
Mouilpied, Helen de (Lady Forman), 161, 172
Mousehole, 82
Movietone, 94
Moyna, E. P., 152
Moyne, Lord, 90
Mullen, Barbara, 251
Mull of Kintyre, 20
Munich, 92, 96
Murdoch, Sir Keith, 108
Murnau, F. W., 38
Murray, W. C., 99
Murrow, Edward S., 160
Museum of Modern Art, New York, 92, 128, 215, 217, 261

Nahanni, 223
Nairobi, 176, 178

291

Index

Index

293

Index

Index

Index

Trevelyan, Julian, 204
Tribune, Winnipeg, 92
Triumph of the Will, The, 236
Trotsky, Leon, 27, 234
Trudeau, Pierre, 119
Truman, Albert, 201, 202, 219
Truman, Harry, 154
Tully, James, 37
Turcotte, Edmond, 99
Turin, Victor, 46, 58
Turkey, 174
Turksib, 46, 58, 62
Turnbull, Walter, 102, 111, 114
Twentieth Century Fund, 159
Tynan, Kenneth, 207

Uganda, 186
Ulanova, 208
Uncharted Waters, 59
Undefeated, The, 172
Un du 22ième, 109
UNESCO, 161, 164–70, 173, 204, 205
Unesco Courier, 165
United Artists, 99, 143, 158
United Nations, 152, 154, 157, 159, 162, 197, 202
United Nations Information Council, 145
United States, 43, 44, 45, 47, 62, 63, 92, 94, 98, 100, 119, 120, 122, 124, 129, 130, 143, 148, 150, 153, 158, 162, 183, 194, 215, 216, 221, 255
United States Consulate, Montreal, 162
United States Embassy, London, 175, 193
United States Information Agency, 221
United States Navy, 159
United States Signal Corps, 120
Universal News, 94
UNRRA, 145, 153
Upstream, 65
Urquhart, Robert, 182
Uruguay, 211

Vaal, Jan de, 197
Vale of Leven, 17
Vancouver, 99, 132, 141, 145, 200, 201
Vancouver Film Festival, 218
Van Dyke, Willard, 98, 217
Variety, 163
Vaughan, Frank Hemming, 212
Vaughan, Olwen, 212, 213
Vechten, Carl Van, 60

Venice Film Festival, 166, 197, 198–9, 218, 219, 239
Venture, 153
Verrall, Robert, 245
Vertov, Dziga, 124, 227
Vicky, 85
Victoria, 106
Victoria, B.C., 132
Victoria Station, London, 48
Vidor, King, 36, 38
Vieux Colombier, 46
View from the Bridge, 260
Vigo, Jean, 116, 124
Viking Bank, 69
Vining, Charles, 129, 130
Visual Education Centre, 223, 240
Voice of the World, The, 68
Volta, Alessandro, 175
Vorticism, 35
Vroom, N. R. A., 174

Wahnerheide, 179
Wales, 59, 195
Wanger, Walter, 36, 41, 99, 124
War Clouds in the Pacific, 120, 121
Wardour Street, London, 58, 63, 72, 90, 183
War for Men's Minds, The, 133
Warsaw, 212
Warwick Hotel, New York, 217
Washington, D.C., 34, 100, 101, 111, 130, 151, 155, 159, 162, 163, 219
Washington Film Council, 215
Waste Land, The, 32
Water, Charles te, 177
Watson (Gordon), Helen, 119
Watson, J. R., 53
Watt, Harry, 58, 68, 75, 76, 82, 84, 86, 88, 91, 123, 197, 200, 256
Wave, The, 98
Waverley Steps, 172, 182
Wealth of a Nation, 87
Weather Forecast, 75, 81, 83
Wedding March, The, 38
Weekly Review, New Zealand, 105
Weir, Molly, 182
Weisenborn, Fritzi, 32, 124
Weisenborn, Gordon, 32, 124, 136, 137, 153, 159
Weisenborn, Rudolph, 32, 35, 124
Weiss, Jiri, 97, 242
We Live in Two Worlds, 81
Wellington, 104, 182
Wells, H. G., 23, 54, 105

Index

Wells, William, 162
Wembley Studios, 53
Wendt, Lionel, 78
Werth, Alexander, 26
Westchester, 160
Western European Union, 174
Wester Ross, 184
West Indies, 68
What Say They ?, 182
Wheatley, John, 24, 29, 60, 229
Whistler, James McNeill, 35
Whistler, Rex, 73
White, William Allen, 32, 34, 35, 42
Whitehall, London, 65, 89, 156, 161, 182
Whitehorse, 142
Wiggin, Maurice, 213
Wilder, Don, 223
Wilhelmshaven, 179
Wilkinson, Ellen, 161
Williams, W. E., 169
Wilson, Donald, 184
Wilson, Sir Harold, 180, 221
Wilson, Norman, 65, 67, 183, 189, 192
Wiltshire, 185, 187, 213, 261
Windmill in Barbados, 69
Winnipeg, 92, 93, 99, 101, 115, 118, 133, 145
Winnipeg Free Press, 93, 110
Winter Kept Us Warm, 220
Withers, Googie, 186
Wolcough, Alexander, 84, 189
Wolfe, Humbert, 60, 73
Wolff, Lothar, 102, 175, 176
Woman of Paris, A, 37, 38
Woman of the Sea, The, 38
Wonder Eye, 158
Wonderfact, 153
Wood, Sir Kingsley, 71, 73
Woolfe, Bruce, 46, 124
Workers and Jobs, 78
World about Us, 259

World Cup, 211
World Film News, 85, 90, 104, 112
World Health Organisation, 197
World in Action, The, 116, 119, 120, 121, 122, 124, 143, 144, 148, 153, 158
World in Action (Granada Television), 258
World is Rich, The, 166, 204
World Today, Inc., The, 152, 153, 158, 159, 160, 162, 201, 227
World Union of Documentary, 175
World War I, 94, 144
World War II, 99, 128, 142
Worldwise, 153
World Without End, 187
Wright, Basil, 57, 58, 59, 64, 65, 68, 74, 75, 76, 77, 78, 79, 84, 85, 87, 89, 96, 105, 110, 111, 112, 122, 124, 127, 135, 136, 152, 161, 167, 175, 189, 239, 256, 263
Wright, Frank Lloyd, 32
Wright, Ham, 128
WR—Mysteries of the Organism, 212
Wyler, William, 38

Yacowar, Maurice, 243
Yorkshire Post, 62
York, University of, 244, 245
Young, Sir Geoffrey, 30
You're Only Young Twice, 182
Youth of Tomorrow, 97
Yugoslav Documentary, Scientific and Short Films, Festival of, 212
Yugoslavia, 144, 175, 189, 212, 242

Zagreb, 212
Zalloni, François, 139
Zanuck, Darryl, 124
Zanzibar, 176
Zavattini, 227, 259
Zéro de Conduite, 116
Zukor, Adolphe, 41